MW00614674

Psychic Development and Empath Abilities

Unlocking the Power of Psychics and Empaths and Developing Mediumship, Clairvoyance, Divination, Telepathy, and Astral Projection

Free limited time bonus

Stop for a moment. I have a free bonus set up for you. The problem is that we forget 90% of everything that we read after 7 days. Crazy fact, right? Here's the solution: we've created a printable, 1-page pdf summary for this book that you're reading now. All you have to do to get your free pdf summary is to go to the following website: **https://livetolearn.lpages.co/silviahill/**
Once you do, it will be intuitive. Enjoy, and thank you!

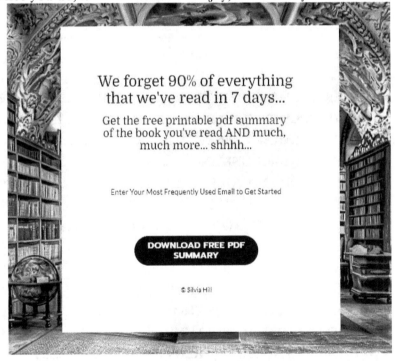

We forget 90% of everything
that we've read in 7 days...

Get the free printable pdf summary
of the book you've read AND much,
much more... shhhh...

Enter Your Most Frequently Used Email to Get Started

**DOWNLOAD FREE PDF
SUMMARY**

© Silvia Hill

Contents

Part 1: Psychic Development

Unlocking Abilities of Psychics and Developing Divination, Mediumship, Astral Projection, Telepathy, and Clairvoyance

Introduction

Whether we like it or not, the world is changing, and what was once hidden is now coming to light. The psychic realm is one such topic that was once put on the back burner but is now coming into full view. We all have psychic abilities; it's just that most of us haven't honed them to their full potential. So, what is psychic development? Psychic development is the process of enhancing and utilizing your natural psychic abilities. This comprehensive guide will help you unleash your psychic abilities and use them to help yourself and others.

The first chapter will explore what a psychic is, signs that you may have psychic abilities, and some well-known psychics. In the second chapter, we will explore your strongest Clair. This includes Clairaudience (hearing), Clairvoyance (seeing), Clairsentience (feeling), and Claircognizance (knowing). In the third chapter, we will discuss Clairaudience in more detail, including tips on how to improve your Clairaudient skills and the different types of Clairaudience.

In the fourth chapter, we will discuss Clairvoyance in more detail. This includes the skill's connection with the third chakra, different types of Clairvoyance, and a list of helpful exercises to enhance your skills. In the fifth chapter, we will discuss

Clairsentience in more detail. This includes the skill's connection with the second chakra, different types of Clairsentience, and a list of helpful exercises to enhance your skills. In the sixth chapter, we will discuss Claircognizance in more detail. This includes how it's connected with the crown chakra, different types of Claircognizance, and a list of helpful exercises to enhance your skills.

In the seventh chapter, we will discuss your astral body and its relation to psychic abilities. Chapter eight will explore Astral Projection and different techniques you can use to achieve an out-of-body experience. Chapter nine will introduce you to your spirit guides and discuss how to connect with them. In chapter ten, we will explore the topic of mediumship and what it means to be a medium.

In chapter eleven, we will explore how to contact the spirit world. This includes different techniques you can use and ways to prepare yourself. In chapter twelve, we will discuss communicating telepathically with loved ones who have passed on. Chapter thirteen will introduce you to the art of divination and different methods you can use to gain insight. In chapter fourteen, we will discuss using a pendulum for divination. In chapter fifteen, we will discuss using Tarot cards for divination. In chapter sixteen, we will discuss psychic protection and defense.

When you're finished reading this book, you'll better understand psychic development and how to get started. So, are you ready to begin your psychic development journey? This book will provide everything you need to know to enhance your natural psychic abilities. Even if you don't consider yourself a particularly strong Clair or if you've never done anything psychic before, this book will provide you with a wealth of knowledge. We're thrilled to guide you on your psychic development journey!

Chapter 1: What Is a Psychic?

We immediately think of hearing, tasting, seeing, smelling, and touching when we think of the human senses. These five senses can help us interact with the world around us, which is a blessing. Many people don't know that there's a 6th sense that enriches our human experience. Clairvoyance, also known as second sight, can deeply enrich our human experience. You can think of it as a way to observe and perceive the different aspects of life without using any of these five senses. Not everyone is ordained with this gift. However, those who are, are at a great advantage.

Psychic individuals have natural skills that aid them in discerning the future and perceiving things beyond the limitations of normal human abilities. This perhaps can make them feel odd and abnormal. However, those who understand the power they hold can learn to harness the benefits of Clairvoyance.

Psychics can predict future events, making them highly sensitive to the surrounding environment. They have heightened senses and awareness, adding depth to their life experiences. Each psychic has its unique way of looking into the future, from tarot and palm readings to sensing auras and vibrations. Many psychics make a living out of their abilities, use their skills to help others, or direct their talents toward looking out for friends and family.

For centuries, people have been studying the zodiac signs, stars, and planetary placements. Psychics are endowed with intrinsic knowledge of the planets and stars, enabling them to orient their readings to your distinct personality. They typically use this skill to guide people through their life journeys by explaining how the movements and changes in the universe impact their lives, thoughts, and feelings.

From time to time, everyone experiences a very vivid dream. Others may have lucid dreams that reveal future events while they sleep. However, for psychics, vivid dreams typically happen as daydreams. This allows them to make more sense of their visions and employ the symbolism from their lucid dreams in their readings.

Psychics are also great at assessing people's behaviors. Since they have an eye for things that other people may overlook, such as each person's aura and energy, psychics can determine which behavior or energy is getting in one's way. They are excellent judges of character and identifiers of personality traits. This is why you'll often find psychics advising people on how to deal with certain situations. They also recommend helpful techniques, such as practicing yoga and mindfulness or using crystals.

This chapter will explore what a psychic is in a deeper sense. You'll also find out how you can become a psychic by learning to tap into your intuition and making sure to practice your skills regularly. This chapter includes interesting facts and information about how Edgar Cayce, a notable psychic figure, discovered and learned to harness his psychic powers. Finally, you'll come across a few telltale signs that you may have psychic abilities.

What Is a Psychic Medium?

You probably have an idea of what a psychic medium is by now. However, there are typically numerous misconceptions about the world of spirituality. This is why it helps to understand what a psychic medium is in-depth. You also need to understand the difference between all the common terminology you may hear.

Crystal balls, incense, tarot decks, Ouija boards, cauldrons, and even potions are among the few things that come to mind upon hearing the word "medium." However, there is much more to mediums and spirituality than most people believe. All stereotypes aside, mediums can link between the dead and the living. To put it another way, mediums are individuals who can communicate with souls. However, this doesn't mean they get to speak to the deceased. Being a medium also involves a transition of the physical to the spiritual realm. The reason behind this communication is that mediums are highly intuitive. As we mentioned above, they are sensitive to their environment, allowing them to feel, view, and hear information from the other side.

Mediums can communicate with the deceased in numerous ways. Some use possession as a tool for the souls that need to communicate with human forms. Other mediums are empathetic, enabling them to partake in the experiences from both realms. Many mediums can interact with souls on the other side as clearly as they can communicate with individuals in the physical realm. Mediums typically sway from one plane to the other.

This all sounds great, but many people don't realize there is a great distinction between mediums and clairvoyants or psychics. The difference between them can be incredibly confusing to the point where there's a common misconception that both terms are synonymous. It helps to remember that while all mediums are psychics, not all psychics are mediums.

As you are probably already aware, everything in the world has energy. This means that your vibration can be influenced by the words you say, the thoughts you think, the emotions you feel, the people you hang out with, the food you eat, the activities you partake in, and more. Mediums have the unique ability to raise their vibrations so high that they can communicate with the other realm. Mediums or psychics that have optimized their supernatural perceptions can connect to the spirit plane. This means that mediums can provide the information they receive from other energies and sources. To deliver a comprehensive message, they can transcend to the spiritual realm and communicate with the divine, spirit guides, and loved ones.

On the other hand, psychics can provide information regarding the past, present, and future. Unlike mediums, they can't deliver information coming from the other side. Clairs or psychics generally receive more potent messages. Clairs can be divided into clairsentients, who can feel clearly, clairaudients, who can hear clearly, and clairvoyants, who see clearly.

Psychics and mediums are very powerful and valuable individuals who can see space and time. Neither is superior to the other as they can both be quite helpful, depending on the information you're seeking or the reading you need. Each serves a specific purpose.

Psychics typically offer intuitive readings. This means that they use the voice of God, guides, angels, or the divine in general to give you a reading. The term "psychic" can also be defined as a connection between two souls. Conversely, a medium is more of a "middle man" between two realms. The message is received from a spirit, through a spirit, and to a spirit). Intuitive psychic readings can provide valuable information regarding various subjects like money, career, love, and relationships. Intuitive responses to your questions can help you make informed insights and decisions regarding your ideal outcome. This allows you to receive conscious and proper guidance on your journey and life experience. Psychic readings can help you understand your purpose and life's path.

Mediums typically connect with your loved ones who have transcended to the spiritual plane. They use their clairvoyant abilities to see the person coming forward to communicate with you. They can describe their features and clothing, which offers evidence regarding the person or soul they see. They then use their Clairaudience to hear the words of your loved ones, which they deliver through a reading. The message you receive is the core purpose of the reading. Many people like to think of this as a healing session. Many people don't believe that your loved ones are aware of what you're doing ever since they've passed away.

There's another type of reading known as a spiritual soul assessment. The chances are that you've thought about the talents that you may possess but have never gotten the chance to discover. It's sad how many people have passed before they've followed their spiritual path and, therefore, never got to know what they're capable of. A spiritual soul assessment is another type of reading based on readings between two souls. It's aimed at helping you discover where you need to be and where your journey desires to take you. This reading allows you to determine all the blocks that come between you and your potential, what your next moves should be, and the path you need to set out on. This reading can help you grow and develop and reach your ultimate potential. These readings are designed to heal.

Becoming Psychic

It doesn't matter where you lie on the psychic spectrum. Whether you have your psychic on speed dial or prefer not to get any readings, the chances are that you have your own psychic tendencies or intuitive capacity. We all have an extra-mundane sense of some sort, but we need guidance in learning how to enhance and unlock psychic abilities.

The terms "psychic" and "intuitive" can often be interchanged. Knowing how to tap into your abilities indicates your capacity to clearly hear, feel, and/or see the things that lie beyond the physical realm. You may be surprised to learn that this happens all the time, regardless of whether we are conscious of it or not.

Perhaps you aren't convinced yet. Have you ever felt that someone was staring at you, causing you to turn around? Have you ever thought of someone or something and just happened to walk into it or them later? Have you ever felt like something bad was going to happen or felt uneasy for no apparent reason when entering a room? Well, this is your intuition, which is considered a psychic gift, in the works.

When you learn to reactivate and unleash your psychic abilities, you give yourself the chance to become stronger, more vivacious, brighter, and more engaged. Your psychic abilities can help you navigate your life experience and its different aspects. It's a tool you can use to make better career choices, improve your relationships, enhance your artistic expression, or ameliorate whichever aspects of the path that you were meant to walk. Did you know that by embarrassing your intuitive abilities, you can influence the intuitive levels of those around you? Developing your psychic gifts can't be done overnight. It's something that takes plenty of practice and determination. We understand that you may feel at a loss for where to start. This is why we are here to walk you through no more than four steps that will help you develop your intuition.

Be Open

The first step to developing your intuitive skills is maintaining openness to the idea. There is nothing worse than being afraid to tap into your intuitive and psychic capacities. Nothing will hinder your efforts faster. We understand that you may feel scared to harness your supernatural powers at first. However, you need to understand that these abilities aren't scary. They are rather there to aid us in navigating through our journey and walking our highest path: express readiness, willingness, and openness to explore your extrasensory abilities. Let the universe know that you are ready to tap into your gifts and not let fear get in your way.

Read Energy

When you feel uneasy around someone or just sense a bad vibe, know that this is your psychic intuition in action. There doesn't always have to be a clear reason for why you feel this way. The most important thing is that you realize that reading people's energies is a skill you can actively work on and improve. You can challenge yourself to read into the vibes and energy that the people you meet for the first time exude. Try to extend your vision beyond their physical appearance or how they speak and interact. Align with their energy to receive information instead. You can do this by being around them and realizing that your thoughts and feelings about them cast back on them. You can do that without even catching a glimpse of that person. Let's say you are paying for something at a store. If someone is standing in line behind you, try tapping into their energy without looking at them first. After you come up with something, you can converse with them to determine whether you picked up on any correct pieces of information.

Predict Ambiances and Environments

As you know, psychic abilities aren't limited to clairsentients and reading energy. Practice your clairvoyance by doing simple exercises. For instance, if you're planning to visit a new place, close your eyes before you go and make it clear that you want to see that place. You can draw what you come up with on a piece of paper and compare it with what you see when you arrive. You probably won't visualize the exact location. However, you may discover that you drew shapes similar to those actually there.

Reach Out to Your Spirit Guides

Everyone has a spirit guide that they can reach out to for guidance and support. They are there to help teach us and navigate through life. Keep in mind that you are also still connected to all the loved ones you've lost and have transcended to the other realm. If you want to reach out to your spirit guides, you may want to ask for a particular sign. For instance, if you want to verify whether you're walking the right path, you can ask your universe to show you a green butterfly. Make sure that your requests are very specific. This way, you'll not question its validity when you receive it.

Here's a bonus tip: keeping your energy centers or chakras balanced can also help you harness your psychic abilities. You can achieve this by engaging in meditation, yoga, and breathwork, as well as using essential oils and crystals.

Edgar Cayce

Cayce made over 14000 psychic readings during his life, many of which came true. This granted him the nickname the "Sleeping Prophet." He believed that his powers were God-given gifts meant to reflect God's and man's love. Cayce first discovered his abilities in 1900. At that time, he was trying out hypnosis to help him recover from a year of speech loss due to laryngitis. When he could finally speak once again, he knew he could make predictions and discover holistic cures for other illnesses.

More and more people started to seek his help, and despite his growing popularity, Cayce never charged others for his services. He worked as a photographer and did psychic readings whenever he received a request. Cayce later set out to Virginia Beach to find the Association for Research and Enlightenment, which is a non-profit corporation.

In February 1925, Cayce accurately predicted the 1929 stock market crash. He also predicted World War II in 1935.

Signs You Might Be Psychic

According to the world's best psychics, we are all a little bit psychic on the inside. Many people are blessed with notable intuitive abilities. However, they choose to pay little attention to them, thinking that it's mere coincidence or just the "norm." Many people display psychic tendencies early on in their childhood. For example, Tiffany Wardle, a Royal & Celebrity TV Intuitive

Guidance Coach, exhibited signs when she was only three years old. Tiffany explains that she could easily manifest whatever she desired, had dreams that turned out to be warnings, and had the feeling that people she couldn't see were always keeping her company. She had bad feelings about certain people and could see her grandmother, whom she had never met before. Many people are inherently psychic but don't realize that they are intuitively gifted. Here are some telltale signs you may be psychic:

You Sense Bad Vibes

You can easily read people. For example, you can see right through people's lies.

Bad Feelings

You may feel unsettled upon entering certain places.

Unprecedented Emotions

Have you ever felt uneasy right before you received bad news? That's you tuning into your awareness of the bad news that was coming.

Strong Gut Feelings

You often rely on your gut feelings to make decisions. Do you "just know," even if there isn't a logical explanation?

Intense Dreamer

Do you often receive intense, meaningful, and vivid dreams? This may be how you receive your information.

Several Deja Vus

You may experience numerous Deja Vus. They may even happen recurrently in a short period.

It's Inherited

If you have a psychic in your family, then the chances are that you are one too. Psychic gifts are typically passed down from one generation to the other.

Childhood Fears

Do you remember specific childhood fears, like a fear of the dark? Psychic children often experience visitations. While you may not necessarily remember all of them, those that leave a mark can leave you with intense fear.

Overstimulation and Feeling Overwhelmed

As you know, psychics are highly sensitive to their surroundings. This is why they easily get overstimulated or overwhelmed in stressful, loud, or crowded environments.

That Feeling

Have you ever felt like there was something more to life? Perhaps you've always wondered whether you have a bigger life purpose. You just constantly have "that feeling" that you can't quite put the finger on.

Psychics can see the root of life events without being influenced by any factors that may be clouding the clarity of the situation. They are incredible at visualizing, which enhances their clarity and ability to see through the surface of situations. They understand that everything in the world has its own unique energy and that there is always a reason for any occurrence. They can easily catch a glimpse of the bigger, objective picture of life. They don't let their opinions and emotions influence their view and understanding.

Chapter 2: What's Your Strongest Clair?

The typical person has a variety of psychic abilities. Someone is rarely a "full" medium or clairvoyant, but it's not uncommon for someone to have more than one ability. Sometimes, two abilities can blend. For example, many people who are good at clairaudience also have clairsentience. But let's look at each ability individually so you can see where your strongest skills lie.

Clairvoyance: The ability to see things that are not there with your physical eyes.

Clairsentience: The ability to feel or experience things that are not there with your physical body.

Clairaudience: The ability to hear things that are not spoken through normal human means.

You can use these skills in several ways. They can give you insight into situations that are going on around you, they can help you make decisions in your life, and they're just flat-out fun. If you want to develop your psychic gifts, start by looking within yourself and asking questions. What do you feel when something happens? How does it make you feel? What do you see when you close your eyes? This chapter will help you identify which psychic ability is most active in you and give you some tips on developing it.

Understanding Your Psychic Approach

To get a good idea of which psychic ability is most developed in you, start by looking at your life. What abilities do you use most often? Do you rely more on your intuition or your logic? Are you someone who is very in tune with your emotions, or do you understand them better through your intellect? Do you answer questions with what you know or how it makes you feel to get the maximum understanding of a situation?

People who rely more on their intuition and emotions generally have clairvoyant abilities. People who rely more on their logic and intellect usually have clairaudient abilities. Clairsentient people are not in tune with their emotions but rather tend to focus on the facts. Of course, there are always exceptions to this rule, but it's a good place to start.

Clairvoyance: Doing What You Do Best

Where do you feel the most confident in your life? Where do you make decisions and trust in your ability to make them? Are you someone who makes decisions based on logic and intellect, or do you tend to follow your intuition and "gut feelings"?

People who are confident in their clairvoyant abilities usually make decisions based on what they see. They take in the facts and then let their intuition lead them to an answer or conclusion. We all have hunches, but clairvoyant people rely on those hunches and trust them the most.

Do you use your clairvoyance in school, work, or home life? Are you someone who enjoys solving puzzles and figuring things out? Do you like playing video games, watching mystery shows on television, or reading books with many twists and turns?

Clairvoyance is probably your strongest psychic ability if you answered yes to these questions.

Clairsentience: Doing What Comes Easily to You

People who rely more on clairsentience usually find it difficult to make decisions. They know how they feel and what they want to do, but explaining those feelings can be difficult. Maybe you're good at speaking in front of people. Maybe you're the person who comes up with all of the best ideas when everyone else is at a loss.

Clairsentient people usually know what they want to do or how they feel about something but need to use their intellect to explain it to someone else. They often work in caring professions such as doctors, nurses, or counselors because they can feel and understand other people's emotions very well. They may also be good at art, fashion, or any type of creative expression because they can see and feel what they want to create.

Are you a big daydreamer? Do you love listening to other people's stories about their lives because you can feel what they're feeling? Do you often cry or get angry when watching sad movies? Clairsentience might be your strongest psychic ability if you answered yes to any of these questions.

Clairaudience: We Hear What You're Thinking

People who rely more on clairaudience usually find it easy to make decisions. They know what they want, and they know how to get it. They use their logic and intellect to make decisions based on what they know. Often, these people are very successful in life because they know how to get what they want and how to go after their goals.

Clairsentient people often need to process on their own before coming up with a decision. They may take time to think about things and understand all of the different aspects of a situation before coming up with an answer. Clairaudient people are often very successful in business because they can solve any problem they encounter and know how to go about it.

Are you good at making decisions? Do you like to take charge and be in control of the situation? Do you have a lot of goals and are always working on achieving them? Clairaudience might be your strongest psychic ability if you answered yes to these questions.

Claircognizance: We Know What You're Thinking

People who rely more on claircognizance usually find it difficult to make decisions. They know what they want, but they don't always know how to get it. They may not understand why they want something or the consequences of getting it.

Claircognizant people often have a lot of knowledge but may not always know where it comes from. They often have a "gut feeling" about things and know when something is right or wrong for them, even if they can't explain why. They may have a lot of knowledge about different topics because they pick up on subtle things that others may not notice. They can also sometimes be very good at solving problems because they know that there is an answer, even if they don't know what it is. Claircognizant people often have a hard time explaining how they feel about something. They just know that it's right or it isn't.

Are you the person who has a difficult time making decisions? Do you often lose track of time because you're thinking about the different possibilities and outcomes your decisions might have? Do you frequently talk to yourself because you're trying to figure things out? If you answered yes to these questions, you might be more claircognizant than another type of psychic.

Quiz: What's Your Strongest Clair?

Now that you've read about the different types of clairs, it's time to find out which one might be your strongest. Answer yes or no to the questions below and see which clair you are most similar to!

1. Would it be easy for you to pick up on the subtle details in a work of art?

2. Do you need to think about something for a long time before deciding how you feel about it?

3. Do you connect emotionally with what you read and watch?

4. Do you often get a feeling about what will happen in the future before it occurs?

5. Do you often predict what will happen to others before they tell you about it?

6. Do you find that other people ask your opinion about things a lot?

7. Do you know a lot of random facts that you can't explain?

8. Do you know what others are thinking even when they're not saying anything?

9. Do you often come up with solutions to difficult problems?

10. Are you very good at solving puzzles?

11. Is it easy for you to explain why you feel the way you do about things?

If you answered yes to six or more of the questions, then clairaudience might be your strongest clair. If you answered yes to four or five of the questions, then you might be more claircognizant than other types of psychics. If you answered yes to three or fewer questions, then you might be more clairvoyant than other types of psychics. Regardless of which clair is your strongest, all types of psychics can develop additional clairs with practice!

Why Are Clairs a Fundamental Gift?

The clairs are a fundamental gift because they are how we connect with the spiritual realm. They allow us to see, hear, know, and feel things that we wouldn't be able to otherwise. All clairs can be developed over time and with consistent practice, but it is also helpful to know which clair one is predisposed to. Developing your clairs can help you connect with the spiritual realm, and it can also help you understand the true nature of the world around you. Knowing how to use your claircognizance, clairsentience, clairaudience, and clairvoyance can help you become a more powerful psychic.

How you connect with the spiritual realm might be different from how someone else connects with it. That's okay, though; there is no wrong way to connect with the spiritual realm as long as you use an effective method. There is no single correct way to be psychic, and each psychic has its unique abilities and skills. So, don't worry if you don't fit perfectly into one of the categories we wrote about. All clairs can be developed and used to benefit you and the people around you.

With practice and effort, anyone can develop their clairs to connect with the spiritual realm. Don't forget to focus on your unique abilities as you continue to learn about the various ways people connect with the spiritual realm. You can be a psychic who works with all of the clairs, but you can also focus on developing your strongest clair and your secondary clairs after that. No matter what, remember to hone in on how you connect with the spiritual realm and use that connection to help you in your life.

Why Is the Strongest Clair Important?

So which type of psychic are you? Like all types of psychic abilities, claircognizance and clairvoyance have their own set of strengths and weaknesses. Clairaudience is great for predictions, clairsentience is perfect for readings, and claircognizance is great for seeing connections. All clairs work together as a team, but some clairs are stronger than others.

Knowing which clair is the strongest for you is important because it can help you focus your energy and practice in the right direction. If you like to use clairvoyance and psychic predictions to help people, you should also try to strengthen your clairsentience and clairaudience. If you like to try and connect with spirit and read other people's energies, you should focus on developing your clairvoyance and claircognizance.

Strengthening your weaker clairs can be helpful, but it is also important to focus on your strongest clair. The stronger clair is the one you'll be using more often, so it is important to make sure that it is as strong as possible. If your claircognizance is the strongest clair, then you should focus on using it in everyday life and practice using it to make predictions. If your clairvoyance is the strongest clair, then you should focus on using it for readings and connect with the spiritual realm in that way. The bottom line is that you should focus solely on using the clair that is strongest for you.

How to Develop Different Clairs

Developing your clairs can be helpful, allowing you to do more than casual psychic work. Psychic abilities are only limited by the extent that you let yourself develop your abilities. All clairs can be developed with practice, but some clairs are more difficult to develop. It is important to remember that you need to focus on your strongest clair if you want to be the most effective psychic.

Developing your clairs is a lifelong journey, and it will not happen overnight. But if you continue to practice, focus, and develop your abilities, you'll eventually be able to do more than just simple psychic readings. You'll connect with the spiritual realm more deeply and use your abilities to help yourself and the people around you.

So, how do you develop your different clairs? The best way to develop your clairs is to identify the clair you would like to focus on. Then, you can begin doing some simple exercises to help you strengthen that clair in your mind. Some clairs are easier to practice than others, so it is important to remember the level of difficulty that you are dealing with when trying to develop a clair.

Exercises to Develop Each Clair

Clairvoyance

- Watch the clouds in the sky and try to guess what shape they make.

- Use all of your senses to practice clairvoyance. Try touching things and guessing what they are, or smelling different things and trying to guess their scent.

- Close your eyes and try to picture a scene in your mind.

- Practice scrying. This is a method of divination that uses a crystal ball or other reflective surface to see images in the future or the past.

- Try using a Tarot deck to do readings.

Clairaudience

- Listen to different sounds and try to identify what they are.

- Practice dictation. This is a method of writing down what you hear, even if you don't understand it.

- Try using an Ouija board to communicate with spirits.

Clairsentience

- This is the ability to feel the emotions and energies of other people.

- Practice meditation. This will help you focus on your energy and other people's energy.

- Try to connect with people that you don't know well. This will help you to read their energies better.

Claircognizance

- To strengthen your claircognizance, you need to try and identify when you are getting psychic insights.

- Practice paying attention to your thoughts and how they connect with the world around you.

- Try journaling. This will strengthen how your thoughts connect with the rest of your life.

- Try using a pendulum to make predictions about events in your life.

Which Clair Is Most Active?

The most active clair for you'll be the one you use the most in your everyday life. If you are using your clairvoyance to do readings, then that clair is more active for you than any of the other clairs. The same is true for clairaudience, clairsentience, and claircognizance. If you are using a clair more often, it will be the one that you have the most intuitive messages from.

You can use this knowledge to help guide you on your journey to developing your psychic abilities. It is important to know which one will be easiest to develop if you are trying to focus on a certain clair. Once you understand which clair will be easiest, it will come down to practice and dedication.

How Practice Makes Perfect

Even if you have a natural connection with one of your clairs, you should never stop practicing. There will be times when it is difficult to use your clair, and you'll need to practice getting back in touch with it. The clairs can be strengthened and sharpened with regular practice and dedication. If you keep up this practice, your clairs will eventually become sharper and more reliable than ever before.

The key to developing your clairs is patience and dedication. There will be days when you want to give up, and it will seem impossible, but this doesn't mean that you should give up. It just means that you need to keep going and never give up on your dreams. With practice, you can develop your psychic abilities to their fullest potential.

Where Do I Start?

If you are just starting on your journey to developing your psychic abilities, then it is best to start with one of the clairs. Since there is no way of knowing which one you'll easily connect with, you should start with the clair that seems easiest. Then just branch out into the clairs that interest you the most after that. Once you have developed your initial clair, it will be much easier to connect with the other clairs. The key is to start small and never give up.

What If I Don't Have Any Clair Abilities?

Don't worry if you don't have any clair abilities. This just means that you'll need to focus on cultivating your ability to connect with the clairs. It doesn't matter how much you believe that you are psychic or whether or not you have had past experiences with the clairs. All of that is in your head, and you'll need to let the mind quiet down to allow the energies to rise. It is very stressful to your brain if you try to force the clairs. So just let them come naturally, and you should be fine.

What Do You Do When You Get a Clair Feeling?

When you get a clair feeling, the most important thing to do is write down whatever the thought was. Write it down in as much detail as possible. This will strengthen the connection between your thoughts and your physical reality. After you have written down the thought, it is time to start working on it. Try to come up with a prediction about what could happen if the thought comes true. This will help you understand the clair better to put it to use.

Clair is a very powerful gift and should be taken seriously. It is important to remember that all clairs can be developed with regular practice. It is also important to remember that not everyone will be able to use all of the clairs. If you are just starting to improve your clairs, it is best to start with the one that seems easiest for you. The clairs are developed in the same way: with regular practice and dedication. So never give up on your dreams and continue working towards psychic development.

Chapter 3: Clairaudience

Clairaudience is the ability to hear messages coming from the spiritual realm, whether they are spoken directly to you or not. In other words, clairaudience is the "psychic hearing" ability. It's a very common talent that most people possess in some way or another. Many people with this ability will experience spontaneous episodes of hearing voices, music, or other sounds that are not related to present-day physical stimuli. This can be quite startling for someone who has no idea what is going on and may even elicit concern from family members. Therefore, it's important to differentiate between clairaudient experiences and auditory hallucinations.

So how do you develop clairaudience? It's not something that just happens overnight. Like with any other psychic ability, you have to put in the necessary work and practice to control it. Patience is required because there isn't an official rule book or guide that will work for everyone. Just like with everything else, you have to find the approach that works best for you. This chapter will explain what clairaudience is and how to unlock it. It will also provide some exercises or guided meditations for activating clairaudience.

What Is Clairaudience?

Clairaudience is the ability to hear beyond the physical world. This includes hearing messages and guidance from spirits, angels, or other higher beings. It can also include hearing the thoughts and feelings of others, even if they are not in your physical presence. It's important to note that clairaudience is the psychic sense of sound, whereas claircognizance is a psychic sense of knowing. They are two different abilities that often work together.

The Throat Chakra

Clairaudience is connected to the throat chakra, which is the chakra of communication. When this chakra is open and balanced, it allows you to hear the guidance and messages from your intuition and other higher levels of consciousness. It also allows you to communicate your thoughts and feelings clearly and effectively. The throat chakra is the center of self-expression, so when it is open and balanced, you'll be able to express yourself authentically in all areas of your life. When this chakra is closed or blocked, you may find that your voice sounds "hoarse," and you may struggle with the words to express your thoughts and feelings.

Hearing Voices vs. Clairaudient Experiences

Auditory hallucinations are not connected to anything in our physical world. They exist without any external stimulus and cannot be perceived by anyone but the person having them. Examples of auditory hallucinations include hearing voices that are insulting, commanding, or threatening, music that only you can hear, or phantom noises such as ringing, buzzing, or clicking. Sometimes these phenomena come together in a phenomenon called "voice-hearers." These people hear actual words of dialogue coming from an unknown source, often resulting in confusion and concern on behalf of those around them.

Clairaudient experiences, on the other hand, are usually related to some kind of external stimulus. However, it's important to note that external sources don't cause all clairaudient experiences. They often come through as messages or guidance from the spiritual realm. The messages can be received in various ways, such as through channeling or automatic writing.

Most of the time, you'll know when your senses pick up on clairaudient information instead of auditory hallucinations because the messages will have a specific meaning or purpose. They are not just there for your entertainment or to scare you. It is still important to be skeptical of the source of these messages and verify that they are coming from a deserving source. It's easy to assume that it's coming from your Inner Wisdom when in fact, it might be coming from a demonic being or negative entity. This is something that you'll have to figure out on your own. Just keep in mind that if the messages are important, they will keep coming back to you until you figure out what they mean.

Clairaudient experiences are typically dependent on external stimuli. Consequently, activating your clairaudience requires you to focus intently on a specific sound. This can be any type of meaningful sound to you, such as the sound of your voice, a particular word or phrase, a mantra, or the name of a loved one. Once you have connected with that sound, you can begin to receive messages from your intuition or higher levels of consciousness.

Real Life Clairaudience Stories

A woman's husband was killed in a car accident before having children. One night, she had a dream of him standing on the other side of a door, telling her that he had been waiting for her and that she needed to come and join him. She found out she was pregnant a few weeks later, and their child had his father's deep brown eyes.

A man was dealing with the recent passing of his mother. He was having a hard time moving on and dealing with his grief. One night, he had a dream in which she came to him and said, "It's okay, I'm okay. I love you." A few weeks later, he found a note from her that had been hidden in his closet. It said, "It's okay, I'm okay. I love you."

A woman was meditating and focusing on the sound of her breath when she heard the words "You are loved" come into her mind. She took this to be a message from her Higher Self, and it helped shift her out of a feeling of isolation and into one of connectedness.

A woman came out of hypnosis after being regressed to a past life. She started talking about her death in that lifetime, saying, "I'm walking around the corner, and something goes off in my chest. I know I'm going to die." A few weeks later, she watched the news and saw a story about a bomb that had gone off in a public square in Baghdad. She knew that she had been killed in that explosion in her past life.

There is another story of a woman who had been through some very difficult times and made the conscious decision that she would commit suicide. As she was getting ready to overdose on pills, she heard a voice in her head that said, "Don't do this. I have a better plan and a better life for you. I'll be back." The woman was completely startled and dropped the bottle of pills as she heard those words. She knew that they couldn't be coming from her and was confused about where the voice could be coming from since she was all alone. As she sat there, wondering why she heard this voice, a man walked in the door. He explained that he had recently died and was now looking over her life. He told her that he spoke to angels and knew that she had a plan for the life she was living, but it wouldn't be this way. The angels had a better plan for her, and he was there to help her see it. He led her to go back to school and start an organization that would allow her to help others.

As you can see, this woman wasn't merely getting random voices in her head. She heard a message from a higher being who had her best interests at heart. This is an example of how clairaudience can be used as a tool to help you find your Alpha state.

Inner Guidance from Twin Flames

A Twin Flame connection means that two beings are joined together as one, and their souls are working together to complete a spiritual mission. When a Twin Flame connection has been made on a soul level, it is often possible to hear their thoughts and feelings in your mind. This can be a powerful way to receive guidance and support from your Twin Flame. If you have established a connection with your Twin Flame, you may find that you can hear their voice in your head, even if they are not in your physical presence. You may be able to hear their thoughts, feelings, and emotions. You may also be able to communicate with them telepathically.

If you have not yet established a Twin Flame connection, you can still begin to hear your inner guidance by working on activating your psychic sense of hearing. This is the ability to hear the guidance and messages from your intuition and other higher levels of consciousness. It is also a way to connect with the voice of your Higher Self.

As you begin to work on hearing your inner guidance with your clairaudience, it will help if you are already in an Alpha state. This means that you are in a state of relaxed concentration, and you have cleared your mind of all thoughts. It is much easier to receive intuitive messages when you're in this state. You can trigger this state by listening to binaural beats. You may need to experiment with different frequencies until you find the one that works for you.

Your intuition is always trying to get your attention, but it can be difficult to hear the messages if you are not in an Alpha state.

Exercises and Guided Meditation for Clairaudience

There are a few exercises that you can do to help activate your clairaudience. While some people may be born with a natural ability to hear intuition, most people need to develop it. The following exercises can help you fine-tune your clairaudience and learn to listen to the inner guidance that is always available for you.

1. Meditation

The first step is to learn how to meditate. When you meditate, you allow yourself to quiet the mind and access your inner guidance. You can use any type of meditation that works for you, but it is helpful to focus on your breath. As you breathe in and out, allow all thoughts and distractions to dissolve away. Focus on the silence that lies behind all of the thoughts. You'll find that you can hear the messages sent your way as you do this.

2. Visualization

As you focus on your breath during meditation, you may also begin to see images and symbols in your mind. These images are often the way that your intuition communicates with you. As you become more attuned to these images, you'll begin to understand the messages that they are sending you. You may see images of nature, such as mountains or the ocean. You may see symbols like stars or heart shapes. These are all ways that your intuition is trying to get your attention.

3. Journaling

When you begin to pay attention to the images and symbols you see during meditation, you can journal about them. This is a way to expand on the messages that you receive and help you understand what they mean for your life. As you journal, be sure to ask for guidance in understanding the images and symbols. The more you do this, the more you'll learn to hone in on your intuition and understand how it guides you.

4. Binaural Beats

As you continue to access your intuition, you can keep it in an Alpha state by listening to binaural beats. These sounds are played separately in each ear, and they help create a deep state of relaxation. As you listen to the beats, you'll find that you can access your intuition more easily and hear the messages sent your way. Each kind of binaural beat will create a different state, such as creativity or concentration. The more you experiment with these beats, the more attuned you'll become to your intuition.

5. Affirmations

You can use affirmations to access your clairaudience. These are simple phrases that you say to yourself repeatedly to influence your subconscious mind. As you repeat these affirmations, you'll find that you can access your intuition more easily and hear the messages sent your way. Some affirmations that can help you access your clairaudience include:

"I hear my intuition speaking to me at all times."

"It is safe for me to listen to my intuition."

"My intuition gives me the answers that I seek."

These affirmations will help you recognize that your clairaudience is a safe and natural ability. They will also help you feel more open to the messages sent your way, so you can hear them and understand them.

6. Earthing

Earthing is the process of connecting with the electromagnetic fields of the Earth. It is easier to access your intuition when you are grounded because you are more open to new information coming in. You can connect with the Earth by walking barefoot outside, sitting on the ground, or lying down in nature. As you do this, allow yourself to be open to what comes in. You may hear your intuition speaking to you or receive images and symbols. As you continue to clear your mind, this will become easier and easier.

7. Tarot Cards

Tarot cards are a great way to access your intuition, and they can also help you understand the messages you receive. When you use tarot cards, you ask for guidance from a higher power. This can be a helpful way to understand the messages that your intuition is sending your way. As you work with tarot cards, allow yourself to be open and do not try to force a specific outcome. You'll receive the messages you need to hear, and your intuition will tell you what they mean for you.

8. Chakra Cleaning

The throat chakra is the chakra that is most associated with clairaudience. When this chakra is balanced and clear, it is much easier to hear your intuition speaking to you. To clear this chakra, take a moment each day to stop and breathe deeply. Imagine that the breath flows in and out of your throat chakra as you do this. You can also use crystals to help clear this chakra. Amethyst, blue lace agate, and sodalite are all stones that can help to clear and balance the throat chakra. As you continue to do this, you'll find that it is easier to listen to your intuition at all times.

9. Dream Time

As you go about your day, pay attention to the images that come into your mind. These images may be pictures, symbols, or sounds. As you pay attention to them, write them down in a journal. This will help you understand the messages your intuition is sending you. You may find that the messages are clearer when you pay attention to them in this way. In addition, pay attention to your dreams at night. You may find that your intuition is speaking to you in these dreams, which can help you understand the messages being sent your way.

People have sought to hear their intuition and access psychic guidance throughout history. This is a natural part of the human experience, and all people are intuitive. However, some people have greater natural abilities than others. Those who are naturally clairaudient can hear their intuition speaking to them at all times. This can be a great asset in life, as it allows you to receive guidance from a higher power.

If you would like to develop your clairaudience, there are many things that you can do. First, let go of any fears or doubts holding you back. Your intuition is a natural part of you, and it is trying to speak with you at all times. Allowing yourself to hear its messages can be a great gift. Next, affirm that you are open and willing to hear your intuition. Let go of any doubts or fears that may be in the way.

Take some time to meditate. Meditation helps you clear your mind and access information on a higher level. You can even ask for guidance from your intuition during meditation if you would like. The exercises and activities outlined above can help you hear your intuition and receive guidance from a higher power. However, it is important to remember that each person is different. What works for one person may not work for another. Trust your intuition and allow it to speak to you spontaneously.

Chapter 4: Clairvoyance

Clairvoyance is the ability to obtain information about an object, person, or location hidden from the normal senses. Clairvoyance may be present in any human being, but it is not developed and refined in most people. The degree of clairvoyance varies from person to person. Some people have developed this quality to a greater degree than others.

Developing your natural clairvoyant abilities will help you see things more clearly in your life. It will also give you the power to see beyond the physical and material world into what is invisible and unknown. When you can tap into this power and use it effectively, you'll be amazed at what you can accomplish with it.

Clairvoyance has many uses. It can help you find lost objects and people, diagnose illnesses and predict future events. The possibilities for exploration are endless once you can tap into this power. This chapter will help you develop your clairvoyant abilities and increase your power to see the unseen. With regular practice, you can achieve great things with clairvoyance.

The Most Famous of Psychic Gifts

Clairvoyance is the most famous and well-known of the clears. Other terms for this type of psychic power include psychic vision, second sight, and remote viewing. Clairvoyance is a French word that means clear seeing. This gift involves using your consciousness to tap into another person's mind, the spirits of the dead, or an object hidden from physical sight. The clairvoyant can gather information and discover things by using this power.

As soon as you open your mind and develop your psychic abilities, you'll begin to notice that clairvoyant abilities are becoming more and more active. Because this is the most well-known psychic gift, clairvoyance is usually the first power that a person develops. For this reason, it is important to be familiar with the ins and outs of this ability before you begin to work on other psychic gifts.

Clairvoyance is the psychic gift of being able to see. It can also involve smelling, hearing, feeling, tasting, or touching something hidden from the physical senses. Clairvoyants can use their psychic power to see things that are not visible to the naked eye. They can see into the future, past, and the present. Clairvoyants can also see things happening in other parts of the world or even in other dimensions.

Clairvoyance and the Third Eye Chakra

The third eye chakra is the gateway to clairvoyance. Your clairvoyant abilities will be enhanced when this chakra is opened or activated. The third eye chakra is located in the center of the forehead, just above and between the eyebrows. This chakra is associated with intuition, psychic abilities, and higher consciousness. When this chakra is balanced, you'll be able to see the higher realms of existence and the spiritual world more clearly.

It is important to realize that clairvoyance does not always involve the third eye chakra. This psychic gift can be activated with any of the chakras. The third eye may be the most common place where clairvoyant visions appear, but it is not the only one that can be used. When you learn to open your chakras, you'll discover that clairvoyance is possible from any of the seven main energy centers.

The third eye chakra is linked to the pineal gland, which is the part of the brain that controls sleep patterns and your experience of reality. When this chakra is activated, your consciousness will become more active, and you'll feel as if you are becoming one with the universe. This allows you to see everything on the planet, not just what happens in your life or surroundings. You can also use this type of clairvoyance to see things happening in other parts of the world.

Clairvoyance is considered a higher sensory ability. People who have developed their psychic abilities to this level will need to open their third eye and activate the clairvoyant pathway. You'll learn to use your clairvoyant abilities more effectively as you progress. The more you use them, the easier it will become to see hidden things from the physical senses.

The Benefits of Clairvoyance

When you develop your clairvoyant abilities, you can see beyond the limitations of the physical world. You'll be able to connect with the spiritual realm and learn more about yourself. This type of clairvoyance can also help you to see what is hidden from others, such as the future, past, and other people's thoughts. Clairvoyance can also help you to connect with your intuition. This is the part of you that knows what is best for you, even if you do not have any logical explanation for it. Intuition is a very powerful psychic ability, and most people do not realize that they have this gift until their clairvoyant abilities are activated.

Clairvoyance can also help you to connect with your Higher Self. This part of you is always in harmony with the universe and knows the truth about everything. When you connect with your Higher Self, you'll have access to all of the knowledge and wisdom that is available to you. You'll also be able to receive guidance and support from your Higher Self whenever you need it.

Real-Life Stories of Clairvoyance

Many real-life stories exist of people who have used their clairvoyant gifts to connect with the spiritual realm. For example, one woman could use her clairvoyance to help her recover from a traumatic experience. After she was raped, she began to have visions of the attacker. She described him in such detail that the police could identify and arrest him.

Another famous case involves a woman who saw an image of her sister in the trunk of a car. She did not give the police much information, but they could recover the sister's body from the car. They had been searching for her for weeks. The kidnapper had killed her and was about to dispose of her body when he was caught.

Another man used his clairvoyance to save his sister's life. She was in the hospital after she had a heart attack, and he began to have visions of her recovery. He gave the doctors specific instructions on how to treat her, and she made a full recovery. The doctors were stunned because they had not been able to find anything wrong with her.

There are also many cases of clairvoyance that have been used to solve crimes. Clairvoyants are often able to describe crime scenes with great accuracy. This is because they can see things that physical eyes cannot access. They can sometimes even connect with the victims and perpetrators of crimes. In addition, there are many stories involving people who have seen what is going on elsewhere in the world during a time of crisis.

There are countless stories of people who have used their clairvoyant abilities to help others. Many people have been able to connect with their spiritual side through this type of clairvoyance. The spiritual realm is a vast psychic realm that you'll be able to tap into when your third eye chakra opens. When you can tap into this realm, it will help you connect with your intuition and Higher Self.

Gift or Ability?

Some people believe that clairvoyance is a gift, while others believe it is an ability. People who believe that it is a gift may be more inclined to view clairvoyance as one of their special psychic abilities. People who believe that it is an ability may be more inclined to view clairvoyance as something to be learned and developed. Regardless of what you believe, it is important to remember that clairvoyance is a skill that can be developed and improved. The more you practice, the better you'll get at seeing things from your higher perspective. The better you are at seeing things from this perspective, the easier it will be to make decisions based on your intuition.

When you use your clairvoyant abilities, you connect with the spiritual realm. This is a place that is filled with knowledge and wisdom. It is also a place to find support and guidance from your Higher Self. In addition, the spiritual realm can provide you with insights into your life path and the lives of others. It can also help you connect with your intuition and make better decisions based on the information you are receiving.

Activating Your Clairvoyant Abilities

There are many ways to activate your clairvoyance and heighten your third eye chakra. The more you practice and work to improve your skills, the easier it will be to tap into these abilities. It may take time for you to see things with your third eye, but you'll be able to do this more and more easily. Here are some of the most effective ways to activate your clairvoyant abilities with practice.

1. Third Eye Meditation Method

There are many meditation techniques that you can use to activate your clairvoyant abilities. One of the most effective techniques is known as third eye meditation. To perform this technique, you'll need to find a comfortable place to sit or recline. Once you are comfortable, close your eyes and take a few deep breaths. As you breathe in, imagine that you are inhaling light and as you breathe out, imagine that you are releasing all of your stress and worries.

When you feel relaxed, focus on your third eye. Imagine that this area is glowing with a bright light, and you can see the color of this light. Keep focusing on this area, and you can activate your clairvoyant abilities. Try to do this meditation for at least five minutes each day. As you continue to practice, you'll find that it becomes easier to see things with your third eye.

2. Chakra Balancing Method

Another effective way to activate your clairvoyant abilities is to balance your chakras. Chakra balancing is a type of energy healing that can help you relax and activate your third eye chakra. This technique can be done with or without crystals. If you are using crystals, you'll need to hold them in your hand while performing the exercise.

To perform this exercise, you'll need to find a quiet place to sit or recline. Once you are comfortable, ground yourself by imagining that you are sending roots into the ground. Then, pick a crystal to use and hold it in your dominant hand. Focus on the chakra you want to balance and imagine that the crystal absorbs all negative energy. As you do this, visualize the chakra's color becoming brighter and more balanced.

After you have balanced the chakra, move on to the next one. Continue doing this until you have balanced all of your chakras. You can also use this technique to balance the chakras of others. This is a great way to help your friends and family members to activate their clairvoyant abilities.

3. Visionary Intuitive Painting Method

One of the most creative ways to activate your clairvoyant abilities is to try visionary, intuitive painting. You'll need to find a quiet place to sit or recline to do this. Once you are comfortable, pick up a canvas and some paint. Begin to paint whatever comes to mind. Don't worry about whether the painting is good or not; just let your intuition guide you.

As you paint, focus on your third eye. Imagine that you see the images and colors with your third eye. As you continue to paint, you may begin to see images from your subconscious. These images will likely make no sense, and they may seem random, but as you finish the painting, you may be able to use it as a form of divination.

4. Pendulum Dowsing Method

Another way to activate your clairvoyant abilities is to use pendulum dowsing. Pendulum dowsing is a technique that uses a pendulum to help you find information about a person, place, or thing. To use this technique, you'll need to hold the pendulum in your hand and focus on your third eye. Imagine that you are seeing the answer to your question with your third eye.

Then, ask a question and wait for the pendulum to swing. The direction of the swing will indicate the answer. If the pendulum swings clockwise, the answer is yes, and if the pendulum swings counterclockwise, the answer is no. You can also use this technique to find lost objects or give yourself a yes or no answer to any question.

5. Crystal Gazing Method

Perhaps one of the most well-known clairvoyant activation methods is crystal gazing. To activate your clairvoyance with this technique, you'll need to hold a crystal in front of your third eye. Start by finding a comfortable seated position, then hold the crystal in front of your face. Focus on the crystal and imagine it glowing with light.

As you stare at the crystal, you may begin to see images and colors. These images will likely make no sense, but you may begin to understand what they mean as you practice with the crystal. Sometimes these images will be literal and easy to interpret. At other times, the image may be symbolic, and you'll need some practice to understand it.

6. Psychic Shield Method

A great way to develop your clairvoyant abilities is to create a psychic shield. This is a technique that will help you to protect yourself from negative energy and psychic attacks. To create your psychic shield, you'll need to ground yourself by imagining that you root yourself into the earth. Then, visualize a radiant golden light surrounding your body. This light will act as a shield, protecting you from negative energy. As you strengthen your psychic shield, you'll find that it becomes easier to maintain your clairvoyant abilities.

7. Chakra Meditation

One of the best ways to open your third eye and activate your clairvoyance is to practice chakra meditation. One of the most important aspects of your clairvoyant abilities is balancing your chakras. You'll need to find a quiet place to sit or recline to do this. Once you are comfortable, focus on your breath and begin to visualize each of your chakras in turn.

Visualize the color and energy of each chakra and spend some time focusing on the third eye chakra. When you feel ready, begin to practice some of the exercises and guided meditations that you have learned in this book. This will help you activate your clairvoyant abilities and start using them daily!

8. Clairvoyant Dreams

One of the easiest ways to develop your clairvoyant abilities is to pay attention to your dreams. Many people begin to develop their clairvoyance through dreams. Simply keep a journal by your bed and write down everything you remember about your dreams every morning to use this method. Then, try to analyze the symbolism of each dream and see how it relates to your life. As you do this, you'll begin to understand the language of dreams better and how to interpret their messages.

One of the most interesting things about this chapter is that it provides clairvoyance exercises. One of the most important things to remember is that clairvoyance is not always easy to understand. Images and colors that you see may be symbolic, and you may need some time to understand them. You'll also need to practice your clairvoyant abilities if you want to activate them and use them daily. With practice, you'll find that clairvoyance becomes easier to access, and you'll be able to use it to gain valuable insights into your own life and the lives of others.

Remember that you can always access your clairvoyant abilities through meditation. By practicing chakra meditation, you'll help to open your third eye and activate your clairvoyant abilities. To get the most out of your clairvoyant abilities, you must be patient and practice regularly. With enough practice and dedication, you'll soon be accessing your clairvoyant abilities.

Chapter 5: Clairsentience

Clairsentience is the ability to know or sense things beyond the range of one's physical senses. You can use ESP (Extrasensory Perception) to gain information about an object, event, person, or location. You may be able to perceive the history of an object without physically handling it. For example, you might be able to sense an object's previous owners and the events associated with it.

This chapter will dive into the basics of psychic development and clairsentience, including its connection with intuition. Information about why an empath might be a highly-developed clairsentient will also be explored. Lastly, tips for controlling and developing your clairsentience will be given.

The Basics of Clairsentience

Clairsentience is one of the most commonly-used psychic abilities. It's the ability to feel or sense things beyond the range of normal physical senses. A clairsentient may be able to perceive the history of an object without physically handling it. For example, they might sense if a gun has been used for murder, or they might sense if a person is holding some grief. A clairsentient may be able to feel the emotions of others, or they may be able to feel the energy in a room.

Clairsentience is the psychic ability to "tune in" to things going on around you or far away from you without using your normal five senses. For example, if someone is talking about you or an event happening in a faraway place, you may suddenly become aware of it. By and large, clairsentience is regarded as one of the more difficult psychic abilities to develop and is also one of the most useful for everyone to have. It can be used for many different reasons such as:

- Helping you make better life choices by tuning into your gut feelings.

- Helping you connect with your spiritual side and connect with your higher self.

- Helping you tune into the thoughts and feelings of others.

- Helping you gain insight into the past, present, and future.

- Helping you heal yourself and others.

Some clairsentients are so sensitive that they can even pick up on physical ailments. They might be able to feel when someone has a headache, or they might be able to feel the tension in someone's muscles. While this may be helpful for some people, it can also be overwhelming. It can be difficult to process if you're not prepared for the energy. The best thing to do is take a deep breath and center yourself. Grounding can also be helpful, as it will even out your energy, so you aren't so overwhelmed.

Clairsentience can manifest in many different ways, including:

- A tingling sensation on the skin that foretells danger

- Physical sensations like nausea or a feeling of unease

- Visions, either during meditation or while you're awake

- Hearing voices

- Smells that no one else can detect, like the presence of gasoline or burning rubber

- Physical sensations related to another person, like a headache when they're upset

- Intuitive knowledge about an event, person, or object

Tapping into your clairsentience requires a quiet setting where you won't be disturbed. It's also best to set aside preconceived notions about what you're trying to perceive and keep a completely open mind. For example, if you want to know more about a particular item, don't focus on just that item. Instead, relax and focus on whatever comes into your mind as you concentrate. You may even see images or "visions" while clearing your mind. Don't worry if they make no sense at first; this is normal.

Over time, the images you see will begin to make more sense. You may also become more aware of smells, sounds, and feelings associated with clairsentience. This is a sign that you're developing the ability. The more you use your clairsentience, the more accurate information you receive. With practice, you may even have the ability to control the amount and type of information you receive.

Clairsentience and Intuition

Intuition and clairsentience are psychic abilities that allow you to know things without necessarily knowing how or why. In other words, you just "know" something. Tuning into intuition is a form of clairsentience and involves your basic instinct, gut feeling, or hunch. Your subconscious mind can sense things and pick up on subtle clues that you're not even aware of consciously.

Clairsentience and intuition work together because all information comes from the same source. Within this collective consciousness is infinite knowledge, which we, as humans, access only when we tune in. As you develop your intuition, keep it open to all possibilities. Avoid getting attached to just one explanation or theory. This will allow the information to flow more freely and increase the accuracy of your readings.

When you're tuned into your intuition, you'll feel like you have a sixth sense that tells you what's right or wrong, depending on the situation. It might be a gut feeling telling you that something feels "off," for example, or it could be an inner voice or sound nudging you to try something new. Intuition can help guide your decisions and help with problem-solving. It's been described as a "flash of insight" where you suddenly know something intuitively that eludes you intellectually.

In addition to developing your intuition, it's important to develop your clairsentience. This will help you learn to trust the information you're receiving and increase the accuracy of your readings. Most people have a mix of intuitive and clairsentient abilities, so it's normal to feel overwhelmed at first as you learn what you're capable of. With practice, you'll be able to discern which type of psychic ability you're using in any given situation.

Clairsentience and Empathy

Many people confuse clairsentience with empathy, but there is a difference. Empathy refers to tuning into someone else's emotions or sensing their feelings. Someone who is empathic might be able to tell when someone else is upset and why just by looking at them. Clairsentient people receive psychic information in images, sounds, tastes, smells, and feelings.

Empaths are naturally in tune with their intuition, but they have to learn to trust the psychic information they receive. This can be difficult because empaths are so sensitive to the emotions and feelings of others. They may feel overwhelmed by the emotions they pick up, but it's important not to shut out the information you receive. Learning to control your abilities and understand how they work will help you avoid being overwhelmed and will help you remain objective during readings.

At first, you may find it difficult to distinguish between empathy and clairsentience. As intuitive empaths, you can tune into the emotions and feelings of others, but you may also receive psychic information in the form of images, sounds, tastes, smells, and feelings. If you're able to tune into other people's emotions and pick up on the "vibes" that you receive, then it's likely that you're an empath.

Tips for Intuitive Empaths

Being an empath can be overwhelming, especially if you're not used to tuning into your intuition. It's important to develop a healthy coping mechanism to deal with the emotions you're picking up. If you're an empath, there are a few things you can do to help control your abilities and remain clairsentient.

1. Avoid getting overwhelmed by the emotions you pick up from others.

2. Learn to control your emotions.

3. Practice shielding.

4. Keep your emotions in check when you're giving psychic readings.

5. Develop your intuition and clairsentience through meditation and psychic development exercises.

6. Practice meditation, yoga, and energy work regularly to build your psychic abilities.

7. Practice grounding techniques.

8. Meditate regularly to clear your energy and keep yourself grounded.

9. Stay positive and remain open to the messages you receive.

10. Trust your intuition and learn to listen to your inner voice.

It's important to remember that all of these tips are just suggestions. You may find that some work better for you than others. It's important to find what works best for you and to develop a routine that you can stick to.

Clairsentience and the Chakras

Your chakras are energy centers that exist in your aura. They are the psychic tools you use to receive information, so it's important to know what each chakra represents and how to activate it. The clairsentient chakra is located at the center of your forehead and governs clairsentience. In fact, it's the location where most clairvoyants "see" their visions. There are other kinds of clairsentience, like receiving messages through dreams, but they all stem from the third eye.

The third eye chakra is sometimes confused with the sixth chakra, associated with intuition and prophecy. Most clairvoyants have intuitive abilities, as well. They tend to get psychic flashes about future events or things that haven't happened yet but will.

They may not understand these flashes at first, but after some practice and experience, they can predict what will happen in their own lives and those of others.

The clairsentient chakra is activated when you feel courageous, self-confident, and brave. When it's open and balanced, you'll be able to trust your intuition and receive clear psychic information. Also, when this chakra is open and balanced, you'll be less affected by the emotions and feelings of others. You may still feel empathy for others, but you'll be able to distance yourself emotionally and remain objective. Activating your clairsentient chakra can be done through meditation and visualization exercises. You can also work on opening this chakra by wearing the color yellow, eating yellow foods, and using yellow crystals such as citrine or tiger's eye.

Clairsentience Exercises

Now that you know what clairsentience is, where your third eye chakra is located, and how to open it up, you may be wondering how you can start developing your intuition and clairsentience. If you're looking to develop your intuition and psychic abilities and become clairsentient, you'll need to learn how to control your energy and emotions. Meditation is a great way to do this. You can quiet the mind and connect with your intuition when you meditate. This is when you'll receive the messages and information you need to develop your psychic abilities.

There are many different types of meditation that you can try, so find one that works for you and stick to it. Regular meditation will help keep your chakras balanced and your energy strong, as well as keep your psychic abilities in full swing. The following exercises and meditation ideas will help you activate your clairsentient chakra and develop your intuition and clairsentience.

1. Visualization

When you practice visualization exercises, you're teaching your mind to focus on one thing and block out all other distractions.

This is a great way to activate your third eye chakra and become clairsentient. When visualizing, you should focus on the images and sensations you see in your mind. See the images as clearly as possible and feel your body react to your surroundings.

2. Candle Meditation

Candle meditation is a great way to relax, calm the mind, and focus on seeing and feeling energies around you. Light a candle and sit in front of it, but don't stare directly into the flame. Relax and meditate, letting your mind wander. After a few minutes, focus on the candle and the energy around it. See the flame as clearly as possible and feel the heat it emits. Now, focus on the energy around the candle. See it as a bright light and feel its warmth. This is the energy of the universe that surrounds everything.

3. Energy Balancing

When you want to activate your clairsentient chakra and become more aware of your energy and intuition, energy balancing is a great way to do it. This exercise can be done with or without crystals. If you're using crystals, find three that work for you. Hold a stone in each hand and close your eyes. Imagine a bright white light filling up your body and cleansing it. When you're feeling balanced and centered, open your eyes.

4. Energy Reading

When you're trying to activate your clairsentience, doing an energy reading can be a great way to start. This exercise involves reading the energy of another person or object. To do this: Visualize what you want to read, whether it's a person or an object. See their energy and feel it. You can also try doing this with a photograph. When you're ready, open your eyes and take in all the information you received.

5. Distance Healing

Try distance healing if you want to become clairsentient and develop your psychic abilities. This can be done with or without crystals, but make sure you have clear quartz if you're using them.

Hold the crystal in your hand and close your eyes. Relax and focus on the person or object you're sending the healing to. Visualize a beam of light coming from your crystal and entering the person or object. See it healing and cleansing them, and when you're finished, release the crystal.

6. Chakra Meditation

When you're trying to activate your clairsentience, chakra meditation can be a great way to start. To do this: Find a quiet and peaceful place and sit down with your legs crossed. Relax and take some deep breaths, then focus on your chakra. Visualize each one as a different color and feel the energy flowing through them. When you're finished, sit for a few seconds, and appreciate the energy around you.

7. Intention Setting

When you want to become clairsentient, it's important to set your intentions. Before you begin: Read through this intention-setting list and find one that speaks to you. Once you've chosen an intention, write it down on a piece of paper. Carry the paper with you or place it somewhere where you'll see it often, like in your mirror or refrigerator. As you go about your day, focus on your intention, and allow it to guide you.

"I am open to the guidance of my intuition and clairsentience. I am willing to receive the messages and information that is meant for me."

"I am a clear and open channel for the messages from the Universe. I am open to receiving guidance and wisdom from higher sources."

"I am in touch with my feelings and thoughts. I am open to receiving guidance and inspiration from the Universe."

"My intuition is strong, and I can receive intuitive messages easily and effortlessly. I am open to the guidance and information that is meant for me."

"I can tap into my clairsentience at will. I can focus on my intuition and receive messages with ease."

"I recognize the connection between mind, body, and spirit. My intuition is strong, and I can easily receive information through my clairsentience."

8. Psychic Smell

The following exercise will help you hone your clairsentience. To do this, visualize your nose as a psychic receptor of smell. Try to pick up on inconspicuous odors that you wouldn't normally smell. For example, smell the perfume of the person sitting next to you or the aroma of a flower. When you start, you probably won't be able to pick up on these odors immediately, but as you practice this exercise often, your psychic smell will become more and more accurate.

When you're ready to give this a try, close your eyes and relax. Take some deep breaths and practice your visualization skills. Imagine your nose as a channel for psychic smell and that you're using it to pick up on the scents around you. Relax and breathe deeply, and when you're ready, open your eyes.

Clairsentience is the psychic ability to receive messages, information, and guidance through one's sense of touch. It's associated with the third eye chakra and is often related to intuition. Clairsentience can be used to receive guidance in all areas of one's life, from relationships to career, and is especially helpful when we're searching for answers. If you want to develop your clairsentience, try using chakra meditation to become more in tune with your intuition. Keep a piece of paper and pen on you throughout the day and make notes of your thoughts and feelings. When you're ready, try practicing psychic smell to improve your clairsentience. With practice, you'll be able to receive guidance and messages through your sense of touch.

Chapter 6: Claircognizance

To be claircognizant is to have a psychic ability that allows you to know things before they happen. Claircognizance works like any other psychic ability, but it tends to be a bit more practical and useful than other types of psychic sense. The term claircognizance is derived from the French word "Clair," meaning "clear," and the Latin word "cognizant," meaning "knowledge." So claircognizance translates as "clear knowledge," which is exactly what this type of psychic intuition provides.

Claircognizance is not just one sense or type of awareness, but it's a combination of several different senses, including precognitive abilities and others that can support clairvoyance. The primary quality that defines claircognizance is the clear sensation or perception of knowing something with certainty before it happens or even before it is known by anyone else.

Claircognizant people can pick up on things they might not understand while they're happening but will make sense later. This chapter will cover the basics of claircognizance, including what it is, how to develop it, and some exercises you can do to increase your ability.

What Is Claircognizance?

Claircognizance is used to perceive unknown information in a variety of forms. It involves an awareness of the present, past, and future events, people, and places outside the range of normal perception. For claircognizance to occur, one must have a psychic ability called precognition. Precognition is the ability to see into the future. However, this ability may be limited to only certain times in the future or certain events that are to come about. It may also be possible for someone with this ability to see into the future and past at will or under specific circumstances.

The information obtained through claircognizance can be visual or auditory (heard in your "mind's ear"). It can be tactile (felt within your body), olfactory (smell), or even gustatory (taste). Claircognizance is also highly prevalent during dreams, especially lucid dreams, which some people regard to be more of a claircognitive experience than a simply psychic one because the dreamer may influence it consciously. Claircognizance is often confused with clairvoyance, but this is a different psychic ability. Clairvoyance is the ability to see things that are not normally visible to the naked eye. Clairvoyance is often used to describe the ability to see spirits, deceased loved ones, and other entities.

Claircognizance is often called the "gift of knowing." It is said to be one of the most common psychic abilities, second only to clairvoyance. Most people use this ability without realizing it or without calling what they are doing by its correct name. This psychic ability is often used to acquire information that is not readily available or to find solutions to problems. It is said to be a very practical ability and is often used in the workplace.

Claircognizance and the Related Chakra

The claircognizant psychic ability is associated with the sixth chakra, also known as the third eye chakra. The sixth chakra is located in the center of the forehead. It is commonly associated with clairvoyance, precognition, and claircognizance, but it can also be associated with other psychic abilities. The third eye chakra is known to be the seat of intuition in psychic development.

When this chakra is open and functioning properly, it allows an individual to see the bigger picture and to have a clear understanding of the spiritual nature of life. It also allows for the development of intuition and psychic abilities. The third eye chakra is also associated with creativity, imagination, and problem-solving. When this chakra is blocked or not functioning properly, it can lead to confusion, anxiety, and difficulty making decisions.

Tuning into claircognizance allows you to see auras, which is your ability to see or feel emotional energy. You can also sense a spiritual and physical presence. The colors you see in auras often give you information about a person's emotional state. Your third eye chakra gives you the ability to develop claircognizance so that you can see into the future and know what is going on around you. The more you work on your third eye chakra, the more easily you'll be able to tune into claircognizance.

Real-Life Stories

One real-life story of someone who used claircognizance to obtain information is that of a woman who could use this psychic ability to help the police solve a murder. She awoke one morning with an image of a dead woman in her head who was not immediately identified. However, she had a strong feeling that she should call the police to provide information about this woman. When she called the police station, they told her that they were investigating a murder and that the victim's description matched the woman she had seen in her vision. After providing more information to the police, they could solve the case.

Another example of claircognizance in action is that of a family who determined that their child's life was in danger. They involved the police, determined that the child had been kidnapped, and could use their claircognizant abilities to get a sense of where the child was being held. They saw a sign that they recognized beyond where the child was being held. They told the police about their vision, and together, they were able to go to the correct spot and find the child.

Another real-life story is of a woman who could use claircognizance to help her find her lost dog. She had a strong feeling that her dog was lost and that she should go to a specific park to look for him. When she got there, she found her dog tied to a tree in the park. The dog had been lost for two days and was about to be taken to the animal shelter.

There are also many examples of people using this psychic ability to help them find lost items. One example is that of a woman who kept losing her car keys. She would always find them in the last place she looked, but she was getting tired of having to search for them. One day, she had a vision of her car keys and where she would find them. She followed the vision and found her keys in the spot that she had seen in her vision. She dropped them in the same spot, which set off the vision again. Over time she was able to see her keys to find them.

Exercises, Tips, and Meditation Exercises

There are many exercises, tips, and meditation exercises that can be used to develop claircognizance. This section divides these into two categories: exercises and tips. The first set of exercises works on opening up your third eye chakra, and the second set works with developing your claircognizance skills.

Exercises for Opening up Your Third Eye Chakra:

1. Color Breathing Meditation

To do this chakra meditation, follow these steps:

Step 1. Begin by finding a quiet place where you'll not be disturbed.

Step 2. Take a few deep breaths to help you relax.

Step 3. Look up at the sky and take one more deep breath.

Step 4. Take a mental look at the third-eye chakra and then visualize a small, white light in that area.

Step 5. Breathe in the light and allow it to fill your entire body.

Step 6. Hold the light for a few seconds and then release it, visualizing it spilling out of your body and back into the universe.

Step 7. Repeat this exercise for five to ten minutes or as long as you want.

2. Chakra Mudra Meditation

To do the mudra: Bend your first and second fingers to touch your thumb. Now, hold your hand in front of you with your palm facing up and focus your attention on the third-eye chakra. Imagine that your entire forehead is glowing with light. You can also try placing a purple gemstone, such as amethyst, on your forehead to help with this visualization.

3. The Third Eye Relaxation Technique

This relaxation technique can help open the third eye by focusing on that chakra. To do this technique, follow these steps:

Step 1. Find a quiet place where you'll not be disturbed so that you can focus on your third-eye chakra.

Step 2. Take a few deep breaths to help you relax.

Step 3. Close your eyes and focus on the third-eye chakra located in the middle of your forehead.

Step 4. Visualize a bright light in that area.

Step 5. Allow the light to grow until it fills your entire forehead.

Step 6. Hold the light for a few seconds and then release it, visualizing it spilling out of your body and back into the universe.

Step 7. Repeat this exercise for five to ten minutes or as long as you want.

4. Auto Writing

Auto writing is a form of automatic writing that allows you to receive messages from your subconscious mind, the collective unconscious, and spirit guides and angels. To do this exercise, follow these steps:

Step 1. Start a blank document in your word processing program and save it as a .txt file so that you can convert it to a .doc file later.

Step 2. Type the following: "Dear (your name), please enter your name here."

Step 3. Now, sit back and relax. Allow your hand to move across the keyboard at its own pace. Do not try to control it.

Step 4. When you are finished, save the document, and convert it to a .doc file.

Step 5. Open the document and read what you have written. You may see messages from your subconscious, the collective unconscious, and your spirit guides and angels.

5. The Mirror Meditation

The technique involves staring into a mirror and looking deep into your own eyes. This meditation is very challenging, but it can help you get in touch with parts of yourself that you may not know to exist. To do it, follow these steps:

Step 1. Find a large mirror for you to see your entire body.

Step 2. Sit in front of the mirror and stare into your own eyes.

Step 3. Do not blink, and do not look away.

Step 4. Hold this position for as long as you can. It is okay to start by holding this position for one minute and then increase the time by one minute every day until you can hold the position for 15 minutes.

Step 5. When you can no longer hold the position, blink, and look away, you'll probably experience a shift in consciousness.

Tips for Developing Claircognizance

1. Practice Meditation

Meditation is a great way to develop claircognizance because it allows you to still your mind, relax your body, and open up your third eye. If you want to develop the skill of claircognizance, make sure that you are dedicating at least 20 minutes a day to meditation. The best time to meditate is in the morning before starting your day. If you find it difficult to meditate for that long, you can break it up into two 10-minute sessions.

2. Use Affirmations

Affirmations are positive statements that you can use to program your subconscious mind. When you use affirmations, you tell yourself that you can develop claircognizance. This can help you gain the confidence you need to develop this skill and build up the motivation to continue practicing. Here are some affirmations that you can use:

"I can develop claircognizance."

"Claircognizance is one of my natural abilities."

"I am using all of my senses to perceive the world around me."

3. Pay Attention to Your Thoughts

When going about your day-to-day activities, pay attention to the thoughts that come into your head. Do not try to control them; just observe them. This will help you get in touch with your intuition and develop claircognizance. You can also ask the universal consciousness for signs. This is a great way to form psychic connections and receive messages from your subconscious mind, spirit guides, angels, and the collective unconscious.

4. Keep a Dream Journal

Keeping a dream journal is another great way to practice claircognizance, especially if you are trying to develop the ability to interpret your dreams. Dreams are a great way to connect with your subconscious mind and the collective unconscious. When you write your dreams down in a dream journal, you'll be able to revisit them easily and look for messages from your higher self.

5. Listen to Your Intuition

Sometimes it is easy to dismiss the thoughts that flow through our minds, but you should listen to them when you are developing claircognizance. While some may be meaningless ramblings, or your subconscious mind attempting to solve problems while you are awake, others could give you valuable information about your life or the world around you. Pay attention to the thoughts that come into your head and see if you can develop a relationship with your intuition.

6. Attentional Control

This is the ability to focus your attention on a particular object or task for a prolonged period without becoming distracted by other thoughts or sensory stimuli. This skill creates the internal conditions for intuition to occur. When you can focus your attention for a long period, you can successfully practice claircognizance. It is also helpful to have an environment free of distractions when trying to develop this skill.

7. Automatic Writing

Automatic writing is a great way to connect your intuition and the subconscious mind. When you practice automatic writing, you allow yourself to flow and write whatever comes into your mind. Automatic writing is a great way to develop claircognizance because it allows you to still your mind, relax your body, and open up your third eye. Moreover, it is a great way to receive messages from spirit guides, angels, and the collective unconscious.

8. Keep a Journal of Your Psychic Development

When you keep a journal of your psychic development, you'll be able to track your progress and look back at your notes to see how far you have grown. Writing down information that you receive from your psychic senses is a great way to practice claircognizance and expand your awareness. You can also write down your thoughts and feelings about your psychic development and any exercises you are practicing. This will help you to stay motivated and on track.

9. Visualization

Visualize yourself in a situation where you need to use your intuition. See yourself using your intuition to make a decision or solve a problem. When you practice visualization, you train your mind to use your intuition. The more you practice, the better you'll become at using your psychic senses. It is also helpful to visualize yourself receiving psychic information clearly and concisely.

10. Health and Rest

When well-rested and healthy, you can better access your psychic mind and intuition. Get plenty of rest and exercise, and eat a healthy diet. Also, try to avoid stress as much as possible. When you are stressed, your intuition will be harder to access. The better your health is, the better you can develop psychic abilities.

Claircognizance is the ability to know things without being told or explained. It is a type of psychic ability that allows you to receive information clearly and concisely in the form of thoughts, feelings, images, or hunches. Claircognizance is associated with the third eye chakra, located in the center of your forehead. When you use your claircognizance, you may feel a tingling sensation in your third eye chakra and your forehead.

There are a few exercises that you can do to help develop claircognizance. One of the exercises is to practice focusing your attention on your thoughts. When you focus your attention on your thoughts, the act of focusing will activate your third eye chakra and increase awareness of your intuition. Another exercise is to practice automatic writing. This will help you to get in touch with your intuition and the subconscious mind. Additionally, you can practice visualization by seeing yourself using your intuition in a real-world situation. When you do this, you train your mind to use your intuition practically. Finally, it is important to keep your health and well-being in mind. When you are healthy and rested, you can access your intuition and psychic abilities.

Chapter 7: You and Your Astral Body

It is a well-known fact that the human mind is an electrical and chemical organ. Its physical structure and properties are similar to those of any other organ. The human body and mind are made up of over 60% water. The brain consists of about 90% water, and the rest is composed of minerals and vitamins. Therefore, it is logical to conclude that the astral body, together with the physical body, forms a duality called the "human being."

The human brain is a computer that receives and transmits to the body nervous impulses to control its functions. However, the astral body transmits information that the brain cannot receive. It receives signals from other dimensions. The astral body is an energy field around the physical body that keeps the body alive and emits bioelectrical impulses that keep its components healthy. When viewed under a microscope, this energy field looks like a web of smoke that is constantly in motion.

The astral body has the duty of protecting the physical body against negative thoughts and feelings that could negatively affect its components. It can absorb, store, magnify, and transmit all types of waves of energy received from many different sources. It is the vehicle of consciousness, and when we sleep, our consciousness travels through it. This is known as astral projection.

This chapter will explain all aspects of the astral body, including its purpose, influence on the aura and the chakras, how it relates to psychic development, and how to determine an individual's own astral body.

What Is the Astral Body?

The astral body is a great reservoir of knowledge. It is the subtle vehicle in which our consciousness travels when we are in between incarnations or during sleep. It is composed of several layers. The astral body is the vehicle for abstract thought and feeling, which cannot be expressed in words. The astral plane is the plane of existence composed of four levels. These levels are the highest, intermediate, and lowest astral planes. The fourth level of the lowest astral plane is where we find the energy from which our physical body is formed. This energy then ascends through the higher planes until it reaches its origin in the Soul, which is on the highest astral plane.

The astral body is the vehicle that allows us to fly and move from one point to another instantaneously and be the vehicle that will enable us to dream when we sleep. Once we become familiar with how it works, we can use it in our daily lives for many beneficial purposes.

The astral body is an energy field that constantly emits bioplasma particles. It also absorbs many different types of waves of energy transmitted to it by its surrounding environment. The astral body is the vehicle that enables us to be connected with all different planes of existence and receive information from other dimensions.

The Importance of the Astral Body

The astral body is responsible for transmitting bioelectrical impulses to the brain to maintain its health. The astral body is the vehicle that allows us to communicate with other dimensions and receive information from them. It is also responsible for the following:

- Sending and receiving of all types of waves of energy

- The absorption and storage of vital energy from the environment sustain life

- Developing paranormal abilities such as telepathy, telekinesis, and teleportation

- The capacity to enter into higher planes of existence

The astral body holds the memory of everything we have lived, as well as the mistakes we have made. It stores all of this information in the so-called Akashic Records, which are in another dimension. Our consciousness travels to the astral plane when we sleep, accessing the Akashic Records. Protecting this information is one of the tasks that the astral body assumes to prevent negative consequences from the information we access.

Astral Projection and the Astral Body

When we sleep, our consciousness leaves the physical body and travels to other planes of existence. We need to learn how to control this process of astral projection because it gives us the capacity to travel to higher planes of existence and communicate with other spirits and beings of light. Astral projection also permits us to receive the information we need to solve the problems we confront in our daily lives.

The first step is to move our consciousness at will, which means that we can send it away from the body while we are awake. The second step is to leave the physical body at will, which means we can project our astral body when we are in the dream state. The third step is to develop our ability to travel outside of our body, which permits us to explore other planes of existence. The fourth step is the capacity to communicate with other people in different dimensions. This allows us to communicate with our deceased loved ones and obtain all of the information that we need.

If someone can leave their body consciously while they are awake, they will be able to see and hear everything happening around them without the limitations of their physical body. They will also be able to access all the knowledge in their memory and other dimensions.

The Aura and Its Connection to the Astral Body

We have different types of chakras throughout our body, and the astral body has a total of 7 major energy centers, each with its type of chakra. These can be found at:

- The tips of our fingers
- The palms of our hands
- The soles of our feet

- The crown of our heads
- The lower part of our abdomen
- The middle of our back
- The center of our forehead.

The chakras in our palms allow us to read other people's minds and feel their emotions, while the ones at the end of our fingers allow us to read other people's auras. The chakra in the soles of our feet allows us to send out waves of energy that can heal other people without having to touch them physically. The chakra in the crown of our heads allows us to send positive energy into other people's minds and our environment.

The chakra in the lower part of our abdomen allows us to send out energy waves from our body to heal other people. The chakra in the center of our back allows us to access information from the Akashic Records. The chakra in the center of our forehead allows us to communicate with people on other dimensions.

Your aura is an egg-shaped energy field that surrounds your physical body. It is created by the chakras in your astral body, connected to your physical body. Your aura is connected to the astral plane and the Akashic Records and contains all the information your consciousness has access to.

The color of this energy field changes depending on the thoughts, feelings, words, and actions you experience, and it can be used as a guide to know if you are using your full potential. If your aura's color is vibrant, that means that you are using your full potential. If the color is dull, then that means that you are not using your full potential.

The connection between the astral body and the aura is very important because when we know how to read the colors of our aura, we will know what types of energies we are sending to other people. Once we can do this, it will be much easier for us to read the colors of other people's auras and know how to send them the type of energy that they need.

It is important to know what our aura looks like before we attempt to read other people's auras because the aura of other people might be interfering with ours. Our own emotions can also interfere with our ability to read other people's auras, which means we must always feel good about ourselves and the people around us. Otherwise, we might end up seeing colors that are not there or reading into other people's emotions and thoughts, which can cause us to make the wrong assumptions about their intentions. They might be having a bad day, and we might misread it as them being mean or dishonest.

How to Detect Your Aura

The best way to detect your aura is by looking in the mirror with your eyes closed. There are seven major colors that you can see when looking at your aura: red, orange, yellow, green, blue, indigo, and violet. If you can see all of these colors, then it means that you are using all of your chakras, and the colors will be brighter than usual. However, if you can only see one or two colors, then it means that you are only using a few chakras, and the colors will be darker than usual.

The colors at the top of your aura are the ones that you'll be able to see the easiest because they are directly related to what is happening in our physical reality. The colors at the bottom of your aura are the ones that we cannot see as easily, which means they represent things happening in other dimensions.

It is important to note that some people can see their aura with their physical eyes, which is called clairvoyance. This means that they were born seeing auras, and they do not need to use any psychic abilities to see them. Other people can only see their aura with the help of a spiritual guide or teacher, which is called clairaudience. This means that they were not born with the ability to see auras, and they need guidance to learn how to see them. It is possible for both clairvoyant and clairaudient people to also read other people's auras, which means they are using their psychic abilities to do this.

How to Read Auras

The aura can be read by looking at specific parts of a person's body. Each chakra is represented by a color, which can be read to know the energy that person is sending to the world. This is why people with clairvoyant abilities need to learn how to read more than just their aura.

The chakras are located throughout the body, so we need to know where each chakra is located to read their aura and identify which colors they are showing us. The first chakra is located at the base of the spine, and this one deals with our physical reality, which means that the color red represents it. The second chakra is located in the lower abdomen, and this one deals with our emotional reality, which means that the color orange represents it. The third chakra is located in the solar plexus, and this one deals with our mental reality, which means that the color yellow represents it.

The fourth chakra is located in the center of the chest and deals with our spiritual reality, which means that the color green represents it. The fifth chakra is located in the throat and deals with our soul, which means that the color blue represents it. The sixth chakra is located in the middle of the forehead and deals with our spirit, which means that the color indigo represents it. Lastly, the seventh chakra is located at the crown of the head and deals with our connection to God, which means that the color violet represents it.

Why Is the Astral Body Important?

The astral body is one of the most important parts of any psychic because it represents our desires and emotions. It is connected to the aura, which means that it can change with its color when experiencing different emotions. For example, if a person is experiencing strong feelings of love, their aura will begin to fill with the color pink. If a person is experiencing strong feelings of fear, then their aura will begin to fill with the color gray. And if a person is experiencing strong feelings of anger, their aura will begin to fill with the color red.

In addition, a psychic needs to know their own astral body and aura before trying to read another person's aura. If a psychic cannot see their own astral body or aura, it won't be easy to read another person's astral body or aura. It is also important to note that every person has a unique aura, and this means that no two auras are the same.

Tips to Detect Your Aura

To detect your aura, there are several different things that you can do. Here are some tips to help you with the process:

1. Meditate

Meditating will help anyone during this process because it allows them to focus their energy on seeing the aura. This is important for any psychic, especially for those just learning how to detect their aura or another person's aura. Once you meditate, you can pick up on the energy more easily, making it easier to see the changes in your aura.

2. Examine Your Hands

If you want to detect your aura, one of the best things that you can do is examine your hands in a dimly lit room. This allows you to see the aura around your body by using your hands as a frame of reference. Then place each of your hands around your body and look at the differences between them. It's recommended that you place your hands against a black background and use white light, such as a flashlight or candlelight, to see the aura surrounding them.

3. Practice Yoga

Another way to detect your aura is through yoga. It helps open up your chakras, which will allow you to detect your aura better. In addition, yoga enables you to see the changes in your aura, and it helps you learn how to control those changes. The more you practice yoga, the easier it will be to detect your aura.

4. Pick Out Colors

Lastly, you can also try picking out colors. Every color in the aura has a different meaning. For example, pink is always associated with love, gray with fear, red with anger, and blue with the soul. So, if you see a specific color emanating from your aura, you know the meaning of this color concerning your energy. The more you practice, the easier it will be to see specific colors in your aura.

5. Practice Everywhere You Go

It is important to remember that you must be patient when practicing. It takes time for anyone, especially beginners, to see their aura. It is important to try this process everywhere you go because no matter where you are, the opportunity will present itself if you're patient enough. All you need to do is keep practicing and searching for auras around you. It becomes easier the more you practice, so don't get discouraged if it doesn't happen right away.

This chapter has taught you what the astral body is and why it's important to any psychic. The astral body is representative of our desires and emotions, but it's also connected to the aura. Every person has a unique aura, so no two auras are the same. When trying to detect someone else's aura, one must first know their aura before they can get a good feel for the energy around them.

The next step that anyone should take when learning how to use their psychic abilities is to learn about their subtle bodies: the mental, emotional, and desired bodies. These are also connected to your astral body, and they will tell you a lot about yourself, which is why it's important to learn about your subtle bodies before learning how to use your psychic abilities.

Chapter 8: Astral Projection 101

Have you ever had a dream that you were so sure was real, but when you woke up, it evaporated from your memory? What if you could remember those dreams in full detail? Astral projection is the art of projecting your astral body out of your physical body at will. Astral projection is similar to lucid dreaming, although the goal is not to control the dream but rather to project yourself outside your physical body.

Astral projection involves separating the astral body from the physical body. It is referred to as "astral" because it is believed that the soul moves through a non-physical plane (the astral plane) while retaining its spiritual essence during astral projection. The astral plane can be an extension of consciousness or be used to contact other planes of existence and even parallel universes. Astral projection is often accompanied by lucid dreaming and out-of-body experiences (OBE). This chapter will explore the types of projections, how to perform astral projection, and the benefits of traveling in the astral plane. It will also provide instructions on achieving this altered state of consciousness.

What Is Astral Projection?

Astral projection is the act of separating your consciousness from your body and traveling into another dimension. Astral projection is one way to access the astral plane, which is believed to be a non-physical realm inhabited by life. It enables you to access higher knowledge, learn about parallel universes, and experience the supernatural. When you have an astral projection, you are conscious but also unconscious at the same time because your body will still be in bed while your consciousness is exploring other planes of existence. Some astral projections are so vivid that you may believe you have been physically gone from your body. Others can be difficult to distinguish from normal dreams. The duration and memory of different projections vary depending on the individual and their level of experience.

The term "out-of-body experience" has been used to describe both "astral projection" and "lucid dreaming." An out-of-body experience (OBE) occurs when you feel that your spirit has left your body and you are observing the world from an outside perspective. While having an out-of-body experience, it is difficult to move your physical body because you are still connected to it by the silver cord. These experiences can be induced using lucid dreaming or deep meditation.

You have probably experienced astral projection already without being aware that you were doing so. The most common form of astral projection is when an individual has a dream that could be categorized as a nightmare. In these types of dreams, you experience distress and emotional upheaval from the horrible events occurring in your dream. However, when you wake up, the memory of the distress is gone, and you don't feel the same emotional vulnerability as before. This is because you are disconnected from your physical body, which is no longer feeling the pain of the nightmare. You are now in an astral state where you can experience anything without being attached to the physical body.

Types of Astral Projection

There are three types of astral projections: conscious, semi-conscious, and subconscious. During a conscious projection, you are aware that you are projecting your astral body from your physical body. You probably have experienced this when you have been in a dream and suddenly realized that you are dreaming. A semi-conscious projection is one where you feel as if your spirit is floating above your body while you are still conscious of the real world.

During a subconscious projection, you don't realize that you have separated from your body until you wake up. This type of projection is also called sleep paralysis. This occurs when your mind wakes up before the rest of your body. You feel like you cannot move or open your eyes because they are still closed. To break this paralysis, you must either force yourself to wake up or ask your spirit to return to the physical body.

How to Perform Astral Projections

Astral projection can be achieved through several different techniques. These range from using a technique that takes a long time to master, like lucid dreaming, to more simple methods that can be performed in a short time, like mantra chanting. Here are some general techniques.

Meditation

Meditation is a simple way to access the astral plane. It requires patience and practice because it takes time for your mind to learn how to relax enough for you to leave your body. Any time you are meditating, focus on achieving a mind that is free of thoughts. Mentally tell yourself that you are leaving your physical body. If thoughts do arise, ignore them and focus on achieving an alert mind free of thoughts.

Mantra Chanting

This technique uses sounds, words, or phrases to induce astral projection. This technique uses repetition of a word or sound to assist in calming the mind and achieving an alert mind. When you are ready, imagine your body leaving your physical body. You can also use a physical technique by sitting cross-legged and walking your fingers up your body. The most common mantra is "om," although any word or sound that creates positive vibrations can be used.

Lucid Dreaming

This is a technique where you become aware that you are dreaming while in the dream state. This technique sometimes causes people to have an out-of-body experience since they are still aware of being in their astral body. To do this, you must be able to control your dreams and remain conscious throughout the dream. You can do this by taking control of your dream at key points, finding and recognizing signs that indicate you are dreaming, and becoming aware of the false nature of your surroundings.

Near-Death Experience

Astral projection can also be achieved through near-death experiences (NDE). People who have experienced an NDE sometimes report that they could see and hear everything that was going on around them, even when they were declared clinically dead. This is because most NDEs occur in a state where the mind and body are in a state where it is easier for the person to project their astral body.

Self-Induced Projection for Astral Travel

The simplest method of achieving an out-of-body experience is to separate yourself from your physical body. You can do this by lying down and relaxing your muscles, then visualizing a cord that attaches your head to the ceiling above you. While visualizing this cord, repeat a mantra or chant that will take you out of your body. The cord will pull you up into a vertical position, and once you are fully out of the body, relax your muscles and enjoy the experience. This is not quite as effective as a full astral projection since your life force is still attached to the body. However, it can still induce out-of-body experiences that are powerful enough to travel into the astral plane.

Tibetan and Egyptian Mystery School Initiations

The final method to enter the astral plane is through initiation. This means you must be accepted into a group, school, or organization that teaches astral projection and techniques for using it. This may take some time to achieve, but the experience is truly remarkable. You'll not only learn how to enter the astral plane, but you'll also experience an attunement with the earth and with yourself that enables you to use your psychic abilities more effectively and with greater strength.

Benefits of Astral Projection

Astral projection has several benefits. From a spiritual perspective, astral projection allows you to gain a different or higher level of consciousness. You can develop your psychic abilities and your ability to heal both yourself and others. It also enhances your connection with the earth and the spiritual realm, which can be a great aid in allowing you to discover more about life and yourself. Here are just some of the benefits of astral projection:

1. Increase in Psychic Abilities

Astral projection is considered to be one of the most powerful psychic abilities. It can allow you to gain access to information that is not readily available in the physical realm and give you abilities beyond normal limits. Many psychic abilities can be developed through astral projection. These include clairvoyance, the ability to see future events or what is happening in another place; telepathy, the ability to communicate with others through thought alone; psychokinesis, which includes moving objects using psychic power, and more.

2. Strengthening Your Aura and Overcoming Negative Energy

When you are in the astral plane, you can also discover more about the energies that surround you, including your aura. Many people don't realize that everyone has both a physical and an astral body, and the two are connected. To have a healthy physical body, you must also work to strengthen your astral aura. This can help balance the energy within your body, allowing you to overcome physical ailments and diseases. It can also allow you to heal others more effectively through psychic means.

3. Meditation and Spiritual Enlightenment

Getting in tune with the astral plane can also help you clear your mind and achieve a deeper level of spiritual enlightenment. Once you can completely separate yourself from your physical body, it will allow you to move into a deeper level of consciousness that is free from the demands of the physical realm. In this state, you can detach from your ego and truly know yourself on a deep level. This is one of the most important steps to achieve a higher state of consciousness in your life.

4. A Better Connection with the Earth

One of the most important lessons to learn from astral projection is connecting to the earth and the natural world. In this state, you'll be able to better understand yourself as an individual and as a part of the earth. Many people are out of touch with nature instead of focusing on conquering it or using its energy for their gain. Astral projection can help you reestablish this connection, which will help you appreciate the earth and all it has to offer.

5. Creating a Spiritual Aid to Discovering More about Life and Yourself

Finally, astral projection can also help you discover more about life. This is the perfect way to explore different dimensions that you might not otherwise be able to reach. It can also allow you to discover more about the universe and our place in it. Astral projection is not only a psychic ability but also a spiritual one that allows you to attune yourself to the universe around you to learn more about your place in it.

How to Achieve Astral Projection

Several steps can be taken to achieve astral projection. Through deep meditation, you'll need to separate yourself from your physical body. You'll then be able to move into the astral plane, where you can explore different areas of consciousness, learn about your true self, and heal or gain information about the world around you. Here are the steps to achieve astral projection:

1. Relaxation

The first step for astral projection is relaxation. Your physical body must be relaxed, but you also need to relax your mind and detach it from the physical realm. You should try meditating for a few minutes at a time to achieve the required state of relaxation. Once you feel yourself becoming physically relaxed, you can focus on your mind.

2. Focus on the Chakras

Next, focus on the main chakras of your body. The root chakra, sacral chakra, solar plexus chakra, heart chakra, throat chakra, third eye chakra, and crown chakra are considered the seven major chakras. You should get a strong sense of energy from each of these chakras and focus on the root chakra first.

3. Move to the Next Chakra

For each of the major chakras, you can become aware of their corresponding colors and symbols. Once you feel you have a strong sense of the chakras and how they correspond to your physical body, you can move on to the next one. You should repeat this process with all seven of the main chakras until you feel like you have a strong connection with each one.

4. Separating Your Astral Body

Once you have a strong connection with the chakras, it's time to move on to separating your astral body. You'll need to visualize your physical body lying on the bed or the floor where you are meditating. You should focus on each chakra one by one and visualize a strong light filling them until they're glowing. Once you have done this with all seven of the major chakras, you should then be able to separate your astral body from the physical one.

Think about your astral body like a second you. You can visualize it as an identical clone of yourself or just imagine you have a second body independent of your physical one. It doesn't matter how you visualize it, as long as you know that it is a completely separate body that can travel into other areas of consciousness.

5. Moving into the Astral Plane

At this point, you should be able to move into the astral plane. Once you have done this, you can explore different areas of consciousness and take your time getting to know who you are and your place in the world. You can also use astral projection for healing purposes or gain information about the world around you.

6. Reuniting with Your Physical Body

The final step in astral projection is to reunite your physical and astral bodies. Once you have finished exploring the astral plane, you'll need to imagine your physical body lying where it was before you separated from it. You should focus on floating back into your physical body, which will happen naturally. Once you feel you are back in your physical body, you should be able to open your eyes and return to reality.

Fascinating Real-Life Stories of Astral Projection

Many people around the world have reported a near-death experience at some point in their lives. A large majority of these people have also reported being able to astral project during this experience. Many people who have had near-death experiences know that they have been able to astral project, but one woman is particularly fascinating.

Sylvia Browne is a well-known psychic who has written over 40 books and appeared on countless television and radio shows. However, she claims to have made many of her predictions by actually astral projecting to the future. She is famously known for having astral projected to the future on her show and successfully guessed several celebrity deaths and the fact that Prince Charles would marry a previously unknown woman.

Another fascinating real-life story of astral projection comes from a 17th-century Catholic nun named Sister Mary. In 1673, she began to have vivid spiritual visions, and she eventually received a series of messages from Jesus. After these messages, Mary started to astral project during her daily prayers. She would astral project and speak with Jesus regularly until he instructed her to find the Order of the Company of Mary. This order is still around today and is made up of nuns who pray all day long.

A final fascinating story of astral projection comes from Donald Tyson, a world-renowned occultist and high magician. In his autobiography, he tells of how he was meditating in a circle with a group of people when he astral projected for the first time. He then successfully took another woman into his astral realm, and the two of them shared the same feelings and sensations.

Astral projection can be an extremely fun and educational experience if you follow the proper procedures. Astral projection has been practiced for centuries, and people all over the world have used it to explore their consciousness and the astral plane. Once you have learned how to astral project, you can explore the world around you from a whole new perspective. Astral projecting has many benefits, including enhanced creativity and healing abilities. Astral projection can also be used for fun activities like ghost hunting or exploring different worlds.

To learn how to astral project, start with getting into a relaxed state of mind. You can do this through meditation or yoga and then move into imagining your astral body separating from your physical one. From there, you'll want to explore the astral plane in full and eventually learn how to reunite with your body. Many people report having successful astral projections by following this series of steps, so try it out for yourself and experience the world of astral projection. Astral projection is one of the most intense experiences that a person can have, so it truly cannot hurt to try.

Chapter 9: Connect to Your Spirit Guides

If you're interested in psychic development, then you might already know that your guides are always around you. You can tune in to them and receive guidance from them. You don't need to be psychic or spiritual to get this information. All you need is a little bit of knowledge about how the spirit realm works and an open mind. This chapter will look at how one can connect with their spirit guides to receive guidance, insight, and wisdom.

The Importance of Spirit Guides

Why do we need spirit guides? Let's say that you're just starting on your path to psychic development. You might begin with a bit of meditation, then move on to the tarot, and then start projecting into the astral plane. As you go about doing this, you'll start to notice that there are people who come to your aid at times. They're kind of like invisible mentors.

Where do these guides come from? These are your spirit guides. They are entities that have achieved a certain level of consciousness after death, reached the same level in the physical plane, or are currently on the same path as you. They are often people who have died, but they can also be living people. The only difference is that people who die continue to live as spiritual entities. Those projects which keep their physical forms still have a soul even if they're not aware of it yet.

When you hear the word "spiritual," what do you think about? Do you immediately think of churches and priests, or do you think of something deeper, like the divine spirit within all of us? Psychic development is very closely related to spiritual growth. As you work with your mind, you'll reach a point when you open the door to the spirit realm. After that, your guides will make themselves known in one way or another.

The Different Kinds of Spirit Guides

Like humans, spirit guides come in all shapes and sizes with various personalities. Some guides are somber, while others are more light-hearted. There are even jokers among them! Therefore, it's a good idea to get a feel for your spirit guides before you start calling on them. Here are some examples of different kinds of guides:

Angels

These are the most commonly known guides. They're kind of like the parent archetype, looking out for you and offering protection. You can call on them for help if you find yourself in a dangerous situation. The angels will come to your aid, but they won't do all the work for you. That's why it's important to develop your psychic abilities. This will give you the ability to defend yourself and protect yourself from harm.

Angels are the closest things we have to a god on earth. They're the beacons of light in a world shrouded in darkness, and they'll help you stay on your path. You can call on them at any time for help, whether you're just starting to open up your mind or whether you're working on your development as a full-fledged psychic. The angels are always there for you.

Deceased Loved Ones

People often ask, "What happens to loved ones when they die? Do they go to heaven even if they weren't Christian or don't believe in god?" The simple answer is yes. Most people who die go to the spirit world and meet their loved ones, or at least those who have passed on before them. They could help you with advice and guidance during meditation if they were close to you when they were alive. They want to help you, especially if they had psychic or mediumistic abilities when they were still physical beings.

Spirits, Elementals, and Nature Spirits

These guides are more like teachers. They'll help you develop your psychic abilities and guide you to the next level. They've reached a certain height in their psychic development, and they want to pass that knowledge on to you. They can also give you instructions on how to develop your psychic abilities. To connect with them, you'll need to meditate outside so that you can hear and feel them. They're always around, even if we can't always see them.

Animal Guides

Different types of animals have different abilities. Animal guides can help you with different challenges in life. For example, eagles see very far distances and are the perfect animals for helping you when you're trying to see into the future or when you need help discovering something that's far away. Horses are very powerful, and they can help you with your power.

Spirits help you to look at the spiritual side of life, and nature spirits target what it is to be natural and part of the universe. Animal spirits help you get in touch with your instincts and intuition. You can work with all types of animal spirit guides, and it's all right to have more than one. Most people have a few just to ensure that they're covered from all angles.

Invisible Mentors

These are the most unusual spirit guides because they're not visible. They appear in your dreams, but only you can see them. They're like spirit guides, but they work on a different plane. They can visit you at any time and help you develop your psychic abilities, or they can visit you in your dreams. They often appear as people close to you who have passed away, like parents or grandparents.

Spirit Guides Overview

When developing your psychic abilities, one of the first things you'll need to learn is how to connect with your spirit guides. They are always there for you and can help you with anything that's holding you back or just trying to teach you a thing or two about life. Just as a guide at school helps you get through the material, your spirit guides are there to help you navigate life.

The various types of spirit guides that might be with you include your higher self, your guardian angels, or your ancestors. Usually, one of these is more dominant in your life than the others but, at different times of need, you'll all come together to communicate when it's needed. The higher self is your ultimate guide and has infinite knowledge about you, the universe, and everything in between. It's like an encyclopedia, but instead of being human learning about stuff and writing it down, the higher self knows all this information because it is you. You and your higher self are the same. This is why it can guide you through life with such ease and grace because, in a way, it knows you better than you know yourself.

Your guardian angels and your ancestors are always around you as well, working with your higher self to help you. Your ancestors are the souls of your past lives who have come together to help you in this life. They have practical knowledge about every aspect of life and can guide you through it. Your guardian angels are souls that have never lived a human life but have chosen to be with you – waiting to help you when called upon.

Real-Life Example of a Spirit Guide

We'll now look at the spirit guide that helped Psychic Susan, who lives in Washington, discover that she had psychic abilities and how she used her spirit guide to help her develop them. Susan didn't believe in anything like this when she was young, but when she turned 34, her life abruptly changed. It was a Friday night, and she had been out having dinner with friends. It was getting late, around 10:30 pm, and the restaurant served them their last drink. Susan was driving home, and it was raining heavily, so she decided to take a shortcut – a dirt road – that would lead her home. She'd done this before, and it was normally fine, but that night something went wrong. A car lost control on the wet road and slid into Susan's car. She was thrown from the car and knocked unconscious. The airbag in her car saved her from being crushed, but she was seriously injured and needed surgery.

Susan's spirit guide appeared to her in her dreams after the accident. Her spirit guide then told her that it would help her with every step of the recovery process. It would help her get into the right frame of mind for surgery, and it would help in every way possible. Susan agreed and was ready to go back home in no time. She recovered quickly and was soon back at home. Susan kept in contact with her spirit guide after the accident, using it to help her through all kinds of problems she faced. It would guide her in the right direction and help her develop her psychic abilities.

How to Connect to Your Spirit Guides

Now that you understand a little more about spirit guides, it's time to start developing your connection with them. Just like a friendship builds over time, so does your relationship with your spirit guides. The more you hang out with them, the more they will reveal themselves to you and the more they can help you with. If you're just starting, the best thing to do is ask for their presence. They will always be around you, but if you ask for them to come and help, they'll be much more willing. Here are some instructions and tips on contacting your spirit guides.

1. Meditate

Meditation is a great way to connect with your spirit guides. All you have to do is sit quietly and focus on your breathing. Doing this for just five minutes can bring on a deeply relaxed state that will open you up to receive your spirit guides. It's best if you meditate before going to sleep, but if that's not possible, then do it in the morning.

2. Write a Letter

If you want to receive help from your spirit guides but are reluctant to leave yourself open for it, then write a letter. Write down exactly what you want from your spirit guides and give it to them. Your letter doesn't have to be formal, but make sure it's clear what you want. Ask for their help in whatever you need and leave the rest to them. Once you've done it, burn the letter or tear it up. By doing this, you're not only asking your spirit guides to help with the problem but also releasing yourself from worrying about it.

3. Use a Pendulum

If you're stuck, your spirit guides may help you in more subtle ways. One way is to use a pendulum. All you have to do is get a piece of string or thread, tie a ring on one end and put something inside the ring to make it swing. You can use anything you want, but crystal pendulums give off the best energy. Ask your spirit guides to help you, and then hold the ring, letting it pendulum back and forth. Once you feel the energy is ready, ask your question aloud and watch as the pendulum swings to indicate "yes" or "no." If you want to know the spirit guides' name, hold a pendulum above each letter of the alphabet and watch which way it swings for each letter. Repeat this process for each letter until you have the answer.

4. Give It Time

If your spirit guides were around you all of the time, it would make life a little more difficult. Like all friends, your spirit guides will only come around when you need them, and they'll stay as long as you want them to. Try your best not to get frustrated if contact with your spirit guides is slow. Once you've done all of these tips, it's time to wait for your spirit guides to come around. At first, their presence will be slight, and you'll notice that things are just a little easier. Eventually, your spirit guides will become stronger, and you'll be able to communicate with them whenever you want.

5. Practice Makes Perfect

Like anything else you're new to, like playing an instrument or speaking a foreign language, connecting with your spirit guides takes practice. Don't get discouraged if you're not getting the results you want. Like your other psychic abilities, it'll take some time to develop. The more you practice connecting with your spirit guides, the better results you'll get.

6. Don't Be Afraid to Ask for Help

If you're struggling and nothing seems to be working, then don't be afraid to ask for help. If your spirit guides aren't enough, consider consulting a psychic medium. A medium can help you with all kinds of problems, and they might even have a higher connection to your spirit guides than you have. If all else fails, seek professional help through a psychic medium or tarot card reader.

7. Don't Forget to Thank Them

Once you have your answer, thank your spirit guides. They helped you because they love you and are always there for you. Never forget to say thank you, no matter how big of a help they are. Like any good friend, you shouldn't take your spirit guides for granted. They are always watching out for you, and if they didn't want to help you, they wouldn't have in the first place.

8. Get Comfortable

This is the most important part of contacting your spirit guides. If you're not comfortable, your spirit guides won't be, or they won't want to talk to you. Make sure that the room is at a comfortable temperature, no matter what time of the year it is. Turn off any distractions like the television or internet and sit in a chair that you feel comfortable in. Once you're ready, light some candles (which will help with the energy) and burn some incense (to make the area smell nice). Once you think you're ready, ask your spirit guides to come around.

9. Know What You Want

You need to know what you want before getting it, like anything else in life. If your spirit guides come around, but all you want to do is talk, then that's all they'll do. They'll only come around when you want them to and give you the information you ask for. Think about what you want to know before your spirit guides come around and ask them only that question when they do appear. It can be tempting to ask them everything at once, but if you do that, then you'll overwhelm them, and they won't come back for a long time.

10. Visualize Your Spirit Guides

Before your spirit guides come around, visualize them in front of you. Remember that they are made of energy, and you can see them, even though others can't. Once they appear in your mind's eye, greet them like an old friend. Ask them what they are there for and look excited. The more excited you are to see them, the more they'll want to appear when you call. After asking what they are there for, let them know that you are ready to begin.

11. Keep Your Guides Around

Now that your spirit guides have appeared, you need to keep them around. The more you talk to your guides, the stronger their presence will be and the easier it will be to connect to them when you need their help. When your spirit guides appear, ask them to stay and talk. If they're willing, then just chat with them for a little bit before you start getting into more serious matters. With your guides around, you'll never feel alone, and you'll know that they are always there when you need them.

Your spirit guide is your best friend. They are always there to help you, and they will never turn you away, so long as you ask them. But like any friend, you need to build a connection with them. You can learn how to contact your spirit guides and make them a part of your daily life by doing the steps above. You'll always be able to find help when you need it. The only thing you need to do is ask. The more you talk with them, the stronger your connection will be, and soon, contacting them won't feel like work at all.

Chapter 10: Are You a Medium?

We explained the difference between a psychic and a medium throughout the first few chapters. People typically use the word "psychic" to explain to anyone with supernormal activities, which isn't accurate. As you know, intuition is our 6th, and very real, sense. It refers to any feeling that we get and cannot reasonably explain, which is, in essence, a product of psychic capacities. As you know, everyone has psychic tendencies to an extent. However, not everyone is a medium.

Mediumship is a lot more dynamic and intricate than being psychic. This is because mediums open themselves up to discarnate energy. Mediumship can be divided into two recognizable categories. Mental mediumship is the most widespread category. It is how most mediums work with their powers. Mental mediumship allows them to communicate with souls while they are completely conscious. As you can infer from the name, this category relies on and employs the mind. However, keep in mind that this doesn't apply to the logical or rational aspect of the mind. This all happens, as you can guess, using the intuitive mind. There are numerous types of mediumships, as you can recall. They can be explained as clairvoyant, clairsentience, clairaudient, clairempathy, clairtangency, clairscent, and clairgustance.

Aside from her incredible live show performances, Theresa Caputo of Long Island Medium, a hit TLC show, can channel the deceased and connect with them. Caputo explains that she's been able to connect with those who have passed away ever since she was only four years old. She believes that it took up a huge part of her childhood. However, Theresa always thought that everyone else naturally felt and sensed the same things she did. It wasn't until she was older that she realized that she was really communicating with people who had passed. At 28 years old, she understood the gifts and powers she held.

Theresa knows she's receiving information when she starts sensing and experiencing things that don't mean much to her but are significant to those around her. She explains that sometimes she feels the presence of her father's energy or is out of breath. Sometimes, Theresa sees flashes that resemble tiny film strips with symbols and signs on them. She uses what she sees to deliver messages to people.

Mediumship can't be turned off whenever a medium desires. Caputo explains that Spirit never leaves and is always ready to communicate. However, she doesn't acknowledge or answer them when she doesn't want to communicate. Sometimes, they don't deliver enough information or push her to communicate enough, which is why she prefers to leave it in Spirit's hands.

Although mediumship is far more complicated than being psychic, Theresa suggests that anyone can connect with loved ones who have passed over. To be more open to Spirit, you must be very aware of everything that happens around you. You need to pay attention to the little signs that remind you of those who have passed away and that you would usually think are odd or coincidental. Know that it's usually a symbol and be open to it.

In her readings, Theresa doesn't reach out for Spirit. Instead, she meditates and lets Spirit know that she's ready to communicate. Spirit then lets their presence known when Theresa starts talking to her client. She explains that they always have something to communicate, and it would often be their way to let go of guilt and burdens. Others use their communication to confirm that they're still around us.

Theresa only allows the souls she communicates with to bring positive messages to make their loved ones happy. They often come with good memories that show that they're still present around us. Spirit often communicates with certain memories, experiences, and emotions that signal to their loved ones that it really is them.

This chapter explores the meaning of Mediumship in a deeper sense and is intended to help you find out whether you are a medium yourself. Upon reading this chapter, you'll realize that mediums are an intermediary or a bridge that connects the living and the dead. We will touch upon the differences between psychics and mediums. You'll also come across examples of real and renowned mediums, along with the skills and traits they share. Finally, you'll find a quiz that allows you to identify whether you are already set out on the path to mediumship.

Communicating with Spirits

Before we explore the dynamics of communicating with Spirit as a medium, there is something that we need to get out of the way first. Many people believe that mediums can see and hear ghosts. However, this isn't true. In short, ghosts don't exist. Well, according to Erika Gabriel, a spiritual medium, ghosts, or particularly these types of spirits, are often the first things that humans encounter as they're stuck with us on the worldly plane. By encountering, Gabriel means that people sense certain energy when they visit an ancient building or enter a room that exudes weird or strange energy.

Gabriel explains that these "ghosts" are actually spirits that you should never fear. While we grew up watching movies and reading stories about terrifying ghosts, this continuously reinforced image is an incredibly rare or even reflective happening. She says that spirits can never harm or hurt us. All they can do is make us feel unsettled. They will give off weird feelings and vibes, but that's just about it.

Although the phrase is used metaphorically or to try and bridge the gap between the living and the dead, Gabriel explains that spirits don't literally pass to "the other side." They are still present in the worldly element, so communication is possible. Our spirit continues to live even when we die. Something is weighing them down to Earth for some people or spirits, which is why they stay stuck here and can't go elsewhere.

Communicating with spirits seems irrational to those who aren't involved with mediumship. People often wonder why anyone would open themselves up to that energy and risky communication. Gabriel explains that getting in touch with the spirit realm allows you to communicate with guides that can aid you in your life journey, given that you hear their messages. She suggests that the spirit plane is so much more than "ghosts." It can be a beautiful experience for people who learn to set their fear aside.

Elevating your frequency and shutting down the unnecessary voices in your mind allows you to get in touch with the higher vibration of the spirit realm. At that point, all you need to do is pay attention to that vibration and embrace the connection with your loved ones. This is where you receive information, guidance, and energy to help you heal and navigate your life journey. There is no right or specific way to connect with Spirit. The chances are that most people have connected with them in one way or another, even without the help of a medium. Your loved ones are with you no matter where you go, and not with the medium. Gabriel likes to think of the process as if she were tuning into the radio and trying to find the right frequency. Mediums raise their vibrations, while spirits move to lower ones so they can both meet somewhere in between. This is where mediums can feel and sense Spirit.

Best Practices

Gabriel explains that anyone who wishes to communicate with Spirit should avoid using tools like pendulums and Ouija boards if they're not well-trained. Everyone should know what they're doing before using these platforms because doing so allows any spirit to make its way through. This can cause you to pick up on plenty of stuck energy and even "ghosts." The expert medium says that intention is the most important element of communicating with Spirit. You need to set yourself in a very focused and particular zone when you want to reach out.

Keep in mind that opening yourself up to the realm of Spirit can be very overwhelming, especially at first. This is why you need to be mindful of your intention and energy and be clear about who you're aiming to connect with. As you know, mediumship uses the intuitive part of your brain. You can think of your gut feelings as thoughts and emotions triggered by the intuitive area of your brain. If you receive a message from Spirit, you'll feel it in your gut. Do you know how you feel uncomfortable around certain people even if they didn't do anything wrong or feel like you need to take a risk even though all logic points against it? This is your Spirit and intuition prompting you. They are urging you to quiet your brain so you can attentively listen to your gut. The process is unique to everyone, and it will take you time to figure out what works for you. You can try to take a break from technology, take a long walk in nature, and practice mindfulness and deep breathing. You can do activities that help raise your vibration and quit the habits that hinder it.

Some mediums receive messages from their spirits in their sleep. Those who have passed away often show up in our dreams, especially if their passing was recent. They typically do that to reassure their loved ones and let them know they're okay. Many mediums like to communicate with Spirit through a practice commonly known as "automatic writing," or spirit-focused writing meditations. According to Gabriel, you can light down a white candle before sitting down comfortably and closing your eyes. Take a deep breath and declare that you would like to work with " the highest vibrational guides available to you." Afterward, you may ask them a question, take another deep breath, and loosen up your hand. Write down anything they say. Know that it's normal if they start speaking rapidly. The most important thing is that you don't stress if you're unable to connect with Spirit even when you have the best intentions at heart. Mediumship is a long process that takes plenty of practice. If you're keen on connecting with Spirit, the whole procedure can be very frustrating. However, it's good to remember that mediumship can't happen overnight like anything else in the world. The best thing is that you'll keep discovering and learning new things even after you've been practicing for years.

Mediums vs. Psychics

We explained the difference between mediums and psychics in-depth in the very few chapters of the book. However, now that you know what mediums are and how they operate, it helps to touch upon the difference between both types of practitioners.

In a nutshell, psychics are people with extrasensory abilities who can tap into the energy of others. This allows them to know and communicate the past, present, and future of others. Contrary to popular belief, psychics don't read a person's entire life- they don't see it on film. Instead, they provide a handful of very important details that they gather from Spirit. The person receiving the reading should use this information to improve aspects of their life. Most psychics use a cold psychic technique to do their readings. This means that the psychic will conduct their reading without obtaining any previous information about their client. All they need is the client's energy, and some will need to find out the client's traits and observe their behaviors.

On the other hand, a medium is people with a psychic ability to generate mental or physical phenomena found in nature. They basically bridge the gap that exists between the living and the deceased. They can do that by communicating with Spirit or channeling guides from the spiritual realm. While all mediums are psychic, not all psychics are mediums. Some mediums, however, claim that they aren't psychic. This is because either practitioner requires a lot of practice, and it makes sense that mediums would focus more on mediumship. However, they do have a very important psychic trait, which is intuition. We are all intuitive to an extent, which means that we are all psychic (or have psychic tendencies) in one way or another. Since you can practice and grow your intuition, you can become psychic. Mediumship is a lot more complex, making it harder to become a medium. It isn't impossible, though.

Mediumship involves cooperating and communicating with one or more discarnate spirit entities. This happens when mediums go into a trance, opening up a channel through which spirits can communicate. Mediums typically obtain information during the process. They may also channel energies, and paranormal activities may happen. There are two types of mediumship: physical mediumship and mental mediumship. Mental mediumship is also known as telepathic mediumship, which we'll cover in more depth throughout the following chapters.

Types of Mediumship

There are two types of mediumship in modern-day spiritual mediumship. Physical mediums are otherwise known as spirit communicators. They typically manipulate energies and their systems. Mental mediums use telepathic communication and are also known as spirit operators.

Physical Mediumship

This type of mediumship is the opposite of mental mediumship, which involves communication that only the medium can experience. Physical mediumship can be observed by everyone present, not just the medium. This is because it requires mediums to manipulate energy. This often includes automatic writing, levitation, moving things around, and ectoplasmic activities. Some mediums can channel spirits and have them control their physical body. This allows Spirit to communicate with a client. This is different from possession in the sense that the medium welcomes Spirit. The process is voluntary.

Ectoplasm is a substance that the medium takes from its body and mixes with an etheric substance. This enables Spirit to influence physical matter. Ectoplasms are sensitive to light, and therefore the process has to be conducted in complete darkness or low light. Raps are commonly known as percussion and were among the first types of physical mediumship. The medium would hear raps and knocks in answer to yes and no questions in the process. Levitation is the movement of objects without normal human interference by using either telekinesis or ectoplasm. Physical mediumship can often accompany the materialization of Spirit faces, hands, or even entire bodies. Automatic writing, which we discussed previously, is another form of physical mediumship.

Mental Mediumship

Mental mediumship happens inside the medium's consciousness. The five basic human senses aren't involved in the process. It often happens through telepathy, thus the term "telepathic mediumship." The medium associates what they feel, hear or see to their clients. They can attain this information through many states of trance. The three main forms of mental mediumship are clairvoyance, clairaudience, and clairsentience.

Clairvoyance is being able to see things that aren't physically present. This happens through one's intuition and can be seen in the mind's eye. While some mediums may experience clairvoyance in their regular vision state, others need to indulge in practices like meditation beforehand. Mediums can see Spirit in a physical body (human form), or they may appear in the form of a photograph, movie, or film of some sort.

Clairaudience is the ability to hear voices that other people don't hear, particularly those of Spirit. Some mediums hear their voices as if they were talking to them, while others experience clairaudience through thoughts or mind reverberation. Other than spoken thought, clairaudients may hear singing or music.

Clairsentience is the ability to sense the presence of Spirit physically. Mediums can experience clairsentience through smell, touch, or changes in temperature. Some mediums feel the physical pain that the spirits experienced while they were alive.

Renowned Mediums

William Stanton Moses was a medium who communicated with Spirit in the late nineteenth century. Psychic lights appeared as he conducted mediumship. Moses was also reportedly involved with levitation and the emergence of some distinct scents like freshly mown hay and musk. Additionally, musical sounds would be heard in the rooms where he practiced mediumship, even when no musical instruments were around. He also experienced the materialization of pillars of lights and illuminated hands. In his lifetime, Moses generated a multitude of automatic writings. Spirit Identity, which was revealed in 1879, and Spirit Teachings of 1883 were among his most well-known automatic writing scripts.

Francisco Xavier, also known as Chico Xavier, was a renowned Brazilian medium. He was born in 1910 and achieved great fame that he was usually featured on television. His first automatic writing script was made when he was just in grade school. He explained that this was an essay that Spirit gave to him. He produced a collection of automatic writing scripts in a wide array of literary and scientific areas from that point on.

Daniel Dunglas Home was among the most famous mediums of the nineteenth century. The Scottish medium channeled Spirits for royalty and other noble individuals. He was mainly known for experiencing levitations. The most remarkable one occurred just outside a third-story window.

Colin Fry and John Edward are more recent examples of well-known mediums. Both have hosted television programs aimed at helping people communicate with their deceased loved ones. Along with other mediums, Allison DuBois is famous for using their gifts to help catch criminals and aid law enforcement. Jane Roberts and Esther Hicks have described their spiritual experiences in books.

Am I a Medium?

After reading this chapter, then the chances are that you'd be able to tell if you have mediumship tendencies. However, here's a small quiz to help you confirm your speculations.

1. Have you ever encountered a spirit (through a vision, unexpected audio, or even signs?)

- Yes

- No

- I'm unsure

2. Have you ever felt like you were in the presence of a spiritual entity?

- Yes

- No
- I think I have been

3. Do you believe in mediumship?

  - Of course
  - Not really
  - I do, but I have my doubts

4. Were you ever told that you have an inexplicable aura/ that of a medium?

  - Yes
  - No
  - Probably

5. Are you scared of death?

  - No
  - Who isn't?
  - To an extent

6. How would you use your gifts if you really were a medium?

  - Help people communicate with their loved ones.
  - I wouldn't use them
  - I don't know

7. Are you an empath?

  - Yes
  - No
  - I've been told I am

If you checked off:

  - Most of the first boxes, you probably are a medium.

- Most of the second boxes, you aren't a medium. Fortunately, you can develop the skills!

- Most of the third boxes, you probably need to pay attention to more signs. Don't give up!

Mediums are psychics with refined senses and superhuman perceptions, allowing them to communicate with spirits in other realms. Mediums can feel, see, and/or hear thoughts, images, and/or mental impressions from the spirits' plane. Mediums can be entirely receptive to the higher energies and frequencies o which the souls vibrate.

Chapter 11: How to Contact the Spirit World

You've probably heard about contacting the spirit world, but what does it mean? How does it work?

With a little practice, you can contact the spirit world and talk to your loved ones who have passed on. You'll see them and hear them, and they will be able to see you and hear you. It sounds too good to be true, but psychic abilities are not a fantasy; they are real abilities that anyone can learn.

You don't need to be psychic or believe in spiritualism or the occult before you try contacting the spirit world. All you need is an open mind and an interest in how the universe works. It's easy to get caught up in the skepticism of what you don't know, but remember that your life is more than just what you know at this point. There is far more out there that you do not understand yet. We won't pretend to know everything about the universe because we simply don't. However, we do know that people have contacted the spirit world for centuries, yet no one has been able to prove that it's impossible to do so.

This chapter will teach you about contacting the spirit world, what you have to do to prepare yourself for this sort of experience, and how to protect yourself before trying to contact the spirit world.

Preparing Yourself to Contact the Spirit World

Just as you do not get in a car without buckling your seatbelt, you must prepare yourself to contact the spirit world. When you first try contacting a spirit, it won't be easy. It takes effort and practice, but you can do a few things to help. The first thing to remember is that you should not force yourself into this sort of experience. It will happen when the time is right. However, before it happens, you should be prepared so that you'll recognize what's happening and react accordingly.

Your state of mind is important before contacting the spirit world. You should be in a calm, relaxed mood where you're not looking for anything to happen or expecting anything to happen. If you're looking forward to the experience, it will make things more difficult for you and may cause your mind to play tricks on you. You should also get plenty of rest and eat a healthy meal before you begin the process of contacting the spirit world. This helps you achieve a more balanced mental state, allowing your mind to remain clear and focused on what you're trying to do.

Before you attempt to contact a spirit, it's also a good idea to protect yourself in some way. This will allow you to have the experience you're looking for without anything negative interfering with it. If something goes wrong and you encounter a spirit that's not of the purest energy, you should be protected from any harm. This is not a guarantee that nothing bad will happen to you, but it does help to keep your mind and body safe.

Tips for Contacting the Spirit World

Here are a few things you should keep in mind when attempting to contact the spirit world:

1. Practice Makes Perfect

If you're just starting, it's okay to try contacting the spirit world just once every few days. Allow yourself enough time to practice, learn and develop your skills between each session. Some people choose to make it a nightly ritual, but you shouldn't push yourself if you find it's too much for you. Remember that this is something new and different, so you need to give yourself time to adjust to it before trying to contact the spirit world more frequently.

2. You May Encounter a Spirit That Isn't Ready to Communicate

Be patient with spirits because they're still adjusting to the transition from the physical world into the spiritual realm. Don't force the issue if you try to contact a spirit and it isn't ready to communicate. Spirits aren't like people that can be pushed into doing something they're uncomfortable with. They will only appear when they're ready and when they feel like it, so be patient with them.

3. Don't Feel Bad If Nothing Happens on Your First Try

Just like you had to learn how to walk before you could run, it's natural that you'll need to try contacting the spirit world more than once before it works. Don't get discouraged if you feel like you're doing everything right, but nothing happens. Just try again and remember that you may encounter a spirit that isn't ready to communicate.

4. Try Different Things and Use What Works for You

As you try to contact the spirit world, you should try different methods until you find those that work for you. The process of contacting a spirit can be unique for each individual. This means that you may have to try various ways of reaching out to the spirit world until you find something that feels right for you. No two people will contact the spirit world the same way, so it's important to experiment and find out what works best for you. Each person is different and has different needs and desires, so the method of reaching out to a spirit world will vary from person to person. Just try different things and use what works for you.

Methods for Contacting Spirits

You can use several different methods when trying to contact the spirit world. You should try each method until you find one or two that you feel are the most beneficial to your psychic development. Every method will have its own set of pros and cons, so just use the ones that feel the most comfortable.

1. Meditating

One of the best methods for how to contact spirits is through meditation. This method is usually one of the easiest and can help you reach a light trance state in which spirits can make contact with you. To meditate on contacting spirits, you should find a quiet place free of distractions. Set aside enough time in your schedule for this method to work because it can take some time. Once you're ready to start meditating, sit in a comfortable chair or on the floor. Begin by relaxing your muscles and taking slow, deep breaths. Do this for about five minutes to help yourself relax and prepare your mind for contact with the spirit world. Once you're relaxed, focus your attention on the center of your forehead. This is sometimes referred to as the third eye, a focal point for psychic energy. While you're focusing on your third eye, try to clear your thoughts and relax.

Take several deep breaths while you focus all of your attention on the center of your forehead. While you're focusing on the third eye, a spirit may make contact with you and send images to your mind. If this happens, try to make a mental note of them and see if you can interpret the images in any way. Once you feel like your meditation session is complete, slowly count to 10 and then open your eyes. You should feel relaxed and calm, ready to begin using your psychic abilities.

2. Using a Pendulum

A pendulum is a tool that you can use to answer yes or no questions. Mediums typically use this method for contacting spirits to discover information about a spirit. To use a pendulum to contact spirits, you should begin by finding a pendulum that feels right to you. This means that it should be small and lightweight, easy to swing, and not too expensive if something happens to it.

Once you have a pendulum, you should cleanse it to remove any negative energy. To do this, hold the pendulum over a candle flame and say an incantation to cleanse the pendulum. Some people may want to repeat this step several times until they feel like any negative energy has been removed from the pendulum.

After you have cleansed your pendulum, you should begin using it to determine if a spirit is present. To do this, you should make sure you are in a quiet area free of distractions. Hold the pendulum over your wrist and start asking yes or no questions. Keep your arm and hand relaxed and determine if the pendulum moves in a circular motion. This indicates yes, while side-to-side movements indicate no. If the pendulum moves in a circular motion, this means that a spirit is present, and you can begin asking questions.

To help yourself become more familiar with this method, you should use the pendulum to answer simple questions that don't require psychic energy. For example, you can use it to determine if there is anything around you or if a spirit is present. As you practice with the pendulum, you should ask more specific questions for contacting spirits. This method will take some practice, so don't get discouraged if you don't see results immediately.

3. Using a Ouija Board

Another method that some people use for contacting spirits is through an Ouija board. This is typically used in groups to help connect everyone's energy when trying to reach spirits. This method involves placing your hands on the planchette and asking questions to make contact with the spirit world. Before you get started, you should set up your Ouija board in a quiet room free of distractions.

Next, you should determine who will play the part of the spirit. For this game, one person will be chosen to guide everyone through the process. They will place their fingers on the planchette and ask questions of the board to receive answers from spirits. After you have determined who will be the spirit, everyone should place their fingers on the planchette. Make sure you are all touching it and that no one's fingers are blocking the letters on the board. If you were all touching it and a spirit has made contact, the planchette should move to certain letters to spell out the answer.

Before you start asking questions, you should discuss what type of information they are hoping to receive with everyone participating. This means discussing things like who is trying to contact them, what they might want to know about that person, or how the spirit can provide evidence of their existence. This conversation will help you determine the best questions to ask while using the Ouija board.

After discussing what information you are looking for, each person can ask a question and wait to receive an answer. You may want to go around the room clockwise or counterclockwise, so everyone gets a chance to ask a question. If you feel like you aren't receiving any answers, you may want to try again later. If the planchette moves to certain letters, this indicates that a spirit is trying to spell out an answer. For example, if you ask who is with you, the planchette may move to the letter "M." This means that your spirit guide is trying to tell you that the letter "M" represents their name.

After you have received answers to all of your questions, you can end this session by saying thank you to your spirit guide. You should also make sure to thank everyone who participated in the session before cleaning up your board and storing it away safely.

What Is a Séance?

A séance is a ritual intended to make contact with the spirit world. People conducting the séance will gather together and use specific tools to allow spirits to communicate with them. It's important never to attempt a séance alone, as you can't ensure that the spirits in attendance will be benevolent. Furthermore, you'll risk injury to yourself if you do not protect yourself.

Preparation for a Séance

Before conducting your séance, you should create a plan. This includes choosing how many people will be taking part in the process, as well as what tools you'll need to make contact with spirits. You should also choose a time and place for your ritual.

Ideally, no fewer than three people would be participating in the séance. If fewer than three people agree to participate, you should *not* take part. The exception is if the other participants are experienced with séances and can assure you that they will keep your best interests in mind.

Participants should sit around a table and use a medium such as an Ouija board or tarot cards. This allows spirits to communicate with each person more easily. If a table is not available, participants should sit on the floor in a circle. You should not be sitting so close to someone that you are touching them, nor should you be sitting so far away that your messages would have to travel a long distance before reaching the person. Instead, participants should be sitting around the ritual space at about arm's length apart.

Setting Up the Séance

Once you have everyone ready, you should designate someone to perform the séance. They will act as your guide throughout the process and orient you to the ritual. They should also be able to communicate with and dismiss any spirits that come through during the process. The next step in the séance is to bring in a specific type of spirit. You'll want to call upon one who can provide accurate and helpful information. You should ask your spirit guide or guardian angel to come through and answer questions.

At this point, you should be able to begin using your tools to communicate with spirits. If you are using an Ouija board or tarot cards, you can ask questions directly to the spirit. This will work best if you ask a question, wait for an answer to appear on your board or cards, and then proceed around the room. If you are using a medium, you should wait until one of the participants has a direct message from your chosen spirit. Once you indicate that this has happened, you can begin your session.

The séance should end by thanking everyone who participated, asking them to release the spirits that they called upon, and thanking your spirit guide, guardian angel, and any spirits who helped during this process.

Séance Etiquette

Though you'll be the one who designs the ritual, there are some expectations for séance etiquette. When it's your turn to ask a question, you should direct it to your spirit guide or guardian angel. You should only ask the head of the ritual for clarification if you feel lost or confused at any point in the process.

All participants in the séance should be respectful of each other and provide answers only when prompted. If you feel that there is valid information that you wish to offer, you should wait for an opportunity to share it. You should also be able to dismiss any spirits who come through respectfully. Finally, when the séance is complete, you should thank all participants and dismiss any spirits in attendance.

It's recommended that you leave your séance ritual as a group so that you can process what occurred together. If one of the participants feels uncomfortable with this, they should be able to leave without drawing attention. You should also thank the host for maintaining positive feelings about the ritual and reflect on what occurred.

Honing this skill takes time and patience. If you are interested in connecting to spirits, it's recommended that you practice with their guidance. To start, you should ask your ancestors to make contact and see what type of information they can provide. If you feel comfortable, then you may move on to other spirits.

A psychic séance is one of the best ways to connect with spirits outside of your body. It gives you direct access to information on the other side and allows you to better understand the metaphysical world around you. If you're interested in learning more about psychic abilities, this is a great place to start.

Contacting the spirit world can be a very rewarding and transformative process. When done properly, you can gain significant insight into the other side and better understand your abilities. This is a great way to get started with developing your skills and delving into the otherworldly if you're already a psychic. It's recommended to start with ancestral contact and then move on to other types of spirits as you become more comfortable. The séance is also a great way to let go of the physical world for a time and focus on your connection with other entities. By honoring the spirit world and offering up gratitude, you can ensure that everyone will have a rewarding experience.

Chapter 12: Communicating Telepathically

Psychic development is a fascinating subject that anyone can learn. There are books, courses, and tapes available and a few reputable psychic schools with legitimate trainers. The process of developing your psychic abilities takes time and patience, but it's worth the effort. For many people, the desire to communicate telepathically is strong enough to motivate them to enhance their development. Psychics can use their powers for themselves as well as help others. They can also make a living as a professional psychic or start a psychic business.

For all of us, the path to communicating telepathically begins with focusing on a single thing and then becoming completely absorbed in it. This is what we mean when we talk about psychic development, and it's a natural part of the process of personal evolution. You have an advantage if you are already a good meditator or have practiced yoga or some other form of exercise that demands your complete attention. This chapter will discuss some of the basics of telepathic communication. We'll also give you tips that will help you develop your intuitive abilities.

What Is Telepathy?

A person who possesses telepathic abilities is called a telepath. Telepathy is the communication of thoughts or ideas through a type of non-sensory perception that most people refer to as "psychic." It's the ability to communicate with another person without using the traditional five senses. There are many examples of telepathy in everyday life. For instance, have you ever had the experience of thinking about someone and then moments later they telephone you? Or have you ever been in a crowded place and had the feeling that someone was looking at you? These are just a few examples of telepathic communication.

How Does Telepathy Work?

There are many theories about how telepathy works, but no one knows for sure. Some people believe that it involves transmitting some type of energy or vibration from one person to another. Others believe that telepathy is a type of sixth sense that allows us to communicate with others beyond the physical world's limitations.

Telepathic communication doesn't always happen between people familiar with each other. It also doesn't seem to be restricted by time or place, which makes the occurrence of telepathy even more mysterious. The following sections list examples of telepathic experiences that many people have reported over the centuries.

Telepathy in Everyday Life

When a mother is nursing her baby, she often has the experience of knowing what her child needs before they cry out. This is an example of mother and baby communicating telepathically. It has been suggested that parents often have the same kind of understanding with their young children because they are so closely bonded to them.

Many people had had the experience of knowing who was calling them on the telephone before they answered it. Some people even know what the other person is going to say. This is another example of telepathy in everyday life. There are also many cases of people who have dreamed about a family member and then received news that something had happened to them. They may not even have received this information through normal communication channels, making telepathy the most likely explanation.

Telepathic communication can also happen between people who are not physically together. This is common in cases of love at first sight when two people fall in love with each other at first sight. They may not even know who the other person is or what they look like, but they feel a strong connection. This kind of communication can also be seen in cases where people begin to establish relationships with others after only talking to them via the Internet.

Telepathy in the Afterlife

There are many stories of people who have communicated with loved ones who have died. In some cases, the deceased family members have made their presence known by sending a message that had meaning only for the person who received it. In other cases, people have seen the deceased in their dreams or a vision.

There are also many cases of people who have received telepathic messages from animals. For example, a person may dream about a particular animal and then see it in their neighborhood shortly afterward. This type of communication is often called "animal telepathy." The interpretation of these experiences depends on a person's beliefs about what happens when they die.

Telepathic Communication and Twin Flames

The most important kind of telepathic communication is related to our connection with our Twin Flame. After we experience this intense connection, we will begin to receive telepathic messages from our Twin Flame. This communication can be in the form of thoughts, images, or feelings. It is important to learn how to interpret these messages because they will provide important information about our Twin Flame's thoughts, feelings, and intentions.

Every Twin Flame relationship has its unique telepathic communication. Some Twins will respond telepathically to the thoughts and feelings that their partner sends them, while others will respond with thoughts or images of their own. It is important to learn how to trust the information we receive through telepathy because it can be very accurate.

Benefits of Psychic Communication

Psychic communication is more than just a fun party trick. People who can communicate telepathically with their loved ones and friends will be more aware of their thoughts and feelings daily. This will allow them to have better relationships because they will understand one another more clearly.

In addition, people who learn to develop their telepathic skills will be able to understand themselves better. This is because the thoughts and feelings that we send out will be the same ones that are returned to us. When we get accurate information about ourselves, it is easier for us to make the changes necessary to become happier and healthier. There are several other benefits to the development of psychic communication as well. These include:

1. Better Understanding of Others

The first benefit of psychic communication is understanding other people better. This will allow us to have better relationships with them because we will be able to understand their thoughts and feelings. The ability to communicate telepathically with others is a skill that everyone can benefit from.

2. Better Understanding of Ourselves

The second benefit of psychic communication is the ability to understand ourselves better. When we begin receiving thoughts and feelings from our telepathic connections, we learn more about what we think and feel. This will allow us to make the changes necessary to become happier and healthier.

3. Improved Intuition

The third benefit of psychic communication is the development of intuition. When we can understand what other people are thinking and feeling, it becomes easier to intuit their thoughts and feelings. This can be very useful when trying to determine what other people think about a particular situation. We may also use psychic communication to better understand the thoughts and feelings of animals, plants, or even inanimate objects.

4. Improved Mental Health

When we understand ourselves better, it leads to improved mental health and well-being. When we know ourselves better, it is easier for us to make the necessary changes to become happier and healthier. The same is true for our relationships. When we have better relationships, it leads to improved mental health and well-being.

5. Greater Sense of Purpose

The fifth benefit of psychic communication is a greater sense of purpose. When we can communicate better with others, we will feel more needed. This can lead to a greater sense of purpose in our lives because we can help others without being asked for assistance.

6. Improved Physical Health

Another benefit of psychic communication is improved physical health. When we are happy and healthy, our bodies respond better to the environment. Over time, this can lead to greater resistance to disease and a longer lifespan. If we are unhappy or unhealthy, our bodies will respond negatively to the environment. This can lead to various health problems, including diseases and early death.

The Science Behind Telepathic Communication

There have been several scientific studies that have looked at the ability to communicate telepathically. One study that Dr. Gary Schwartz conducted at the University of Arizona found that people could communicate telepathically with others up to 100 miles away. The study also found that the mind can communicate through time, allowing people to communicate with others in the past or present.

Other studies have shown that people can communicate telepathically with others who are in a different room or even a different country. Other studies have shown that some people could communicate telepathically with animals, plants, and even inanimate objects. The ability to communicate telepathically is a skill that we all have the potential to develop.

How to Use Telepathic Abilities

The most important thing to remember is that anything psychic is still very much a part of the natural laws of this universe. This means that you must approach your development in the same way you would develop any other skill by using persistence, patience, and practice.

There are many ways to develop psychic abilities and many different avenues that one may take. Some people believe in channeling, while others simply want an increased awareness of the world around them. Regardless of your reason for developing these skills, the most important thing is to be patient and understand that progress may be slow at first but will increase as you continue to practice your skill. The second most important thing to understand is that there is no such thing as overnight success or a miracle pill for instant results with any skill. You must commit yourself to developing your skill and put forth the effort to do so if you wish to see results.

Some people learn best when in a group setting with others who also practice psychic development. If this is true for you, make sure to find a group that shares your interests and is willing to help you learn. Many online courses and groups can be found with a simple web search. When you are ready to begin your development, it is recommended that you start with learning meditation and the art of focusing your mind.

Many different techniques can be used for telepathic communication. The following are a few exercises that you can use to help you communicate telepathically with others.

1. Sending Information to Someone Else

To begin, find a partner that you would like to send information. This can be someone you are close to or even someone you have never met before. It is important to make sure that your partner is willing to receive information from you. Once you have found your partner, sit or stand in front of them and close your eyes. Take a few deep breaths and relax your body. Once you are relaxed, focus your mind on the person you are sending information to.

Picture them in your mind and send them the information you would like to share with them. It is important to keep your thoughts clear and concise when sending information. You may also want to use visualization to help you send the information. See the information traveling from your mind, through your body, and out to the other person. Once you have sent the information, open your eyes, and allow your partner to ask you questions about what you sent.

2. Channeling Information

It is possible to channel information from a spirit guide or another being by picturing them in your mind. Once the image of the being is clear in your mind, begin to ask them questions. Write the answers down as they come to you. Be sure to ask the questions you want to be answered and not the questions you think someone else wants to be answered. If you are uncomfortable with any of the answers you receive, do not hesitate to ask the being to leave your mind.

3. Automatic Writing

This technique can be used to receive messages from a spirit guide, deceased loved one, or another being. To begin, sit or stand in front of a piece of paper and pencil. Relax your body and allow yourself to be still for a moment. Close your eyes and picture the person or being that you would like to communicate with. Once they are in your mind, ask them the questions you would like answered.

Once you have asked your questions, begin to write down the answers that come to you. Do not try to think about what you are writing; just allow the words to flow. If you do not understand a word or phrase, simply write down what you see and leave it for later if you need to. Continue writing until the words begin to fade or you have written all the answers you have been given.

4. Memorization

To begin, find a friend to practice telepathy with. Stand face to face and begin to pass information back and forth without speaking. This is a great way to learn the skill of telepathy without information being lost in translation. If you are practicing on your own, try using a deck of cards. Shuffle the cards and deal them out face down. Turn over two cards at a time and begin to send the information on the top card to your partner. Once they have received the information, they should turn over the next two cards and send that information back to you. Continue until all of the cards have been turned over.

5. Mirroring

This is a great exercise for developing your intuition. To begin, find a quiet place where you can sit or stand and be alone. Take a few deep breaths and relax your body. Once you are relaxed, focus your mind on the person you are trying to connect with. Now, imagine yourself walking behind them and looking over their shoulder at everything they see. As you do this, begin to send them the information you are seeing. Be sure to keep your thoughts clear and concise when sending the information. If you are practicing this technique with a partner, begin to speak aloud about what you are seeing. This will allow your partner to practice mirroring with you.

6. Trance Mediumship

This is a technique that can be used to communicate with the deceased. To begin, find a quiet place where you can sit or stand and be alone. Take a few deep breaths and relax your body. Once you are relaxed, focus your mind on the person you would like to connect with. Imagine that there is a light inside your chest that glows brighter and brighter as you inhale. Let the light expand until it fills your entire body. Now, imagine that the light is a doorway and step through it. You'll find yourself in a place where you can see the being you are trying to connect with.

Begin to ask them questions and write down what you hear. Do not let your mind doubt the answers that you are receiving. If you practice this technique with a partner, begin to speak aloud about what you hear. This will allow your partner to connect with the same being.

7. Receiving Information from Nature

Begin by sitting in front of a tree and closing your eyes. Imagine the tree sending you the energy that it needs to survive. Now, imagine that the tree is sending you the energy of everything it has seen and experienced. Begin to write down the information that you are receiving. If you are practicing this technique with a partner, have them sit in front of a different tree and repeat the exercise.

8. Receiving Information from the Moon

First, find a window where you can sit and look out at the moon. Take a few deep breaths and relax your body. Once you are relaxed, focus your mind on the moon. Now, imagine that the moon is sending you the energy of everything it has seen and experienced. Begin to write down the information that you are receiving. If you are practicing this technique with a partner, have them sit in front of a different window and repeat the exercise.

9. Receiving Information from a Crystal Ball

Begin by lighting a candle and sitting in front of the crystal ball. Take a few deep breaths and relax your body. Once you are relaxed, focus your mind on the crystal ball. You may want to ask a question before you begin. Now, imagine that the crystal ball is sending you the energy of everything it has seen and experienced. Begin to write down the information that you are receiving. The more you practice, the easier it will become to establish a telepathic connection.

10. Receiving Information from a Dream

Begin by waking yourself up after a dream and writing down any information you can remember from the dream. Dreams are a great way to receive information because they are often full of symbols that can be interpreted. This is a technique that can be used with any type of dream. The only thing that you need to do is write down your dreams as soon as possible after you wake up.

Telepathy is the ability to communicate with someone without using words. Most of us can establish telepathic connections with others. There is no reason that you should not be able to connect with someone regularly. The key is to focus your mind and relax your body. There are many different ways to develop your telepathic skills. The techniques that have been listed in this chapter are just a few of the many that are available. The most important thing that you can do is to practice regularly. The more practice you put in, the easier it will be to establish a telepathic connection. You'll be able to communicate with whomever you choose, given time and patience.

Chapter 13: What Is Divination?

Now that you have delved into spirit guides, distinct types of Clairs, astral bodies, and telepathy, this chapter will shift the attention towards divination. In the past, divination was used as a spiritual guide to learn more about a person's destiny and illustrate their fate. The future has always fascinated humans, so they tried different ways to predict it. From everyday objects to intangible guides, practitioners used distinct types of media to exercise divination. These practices include a set of rituals or standardized procedures to tap into the spiritual realm and peek into one's fate and future.

What Is Divination and How Does It Work?

As mentioned, people have tried several divination practices since the dawn of time. Most practitioners used these practices to predict the future, whereas others simply sought to widen their knowledge and perspective of the spiritual world and the "unseen" dimension. They believed that certain supernatural powers guided the world and every human being, which needed to be decoded to discover concealed knowledge and omens. In certain cultures, divination was directly linked to the divine power or a deity, which gave worshippers power to discern the future and manipulate human phenomena.

In a way, divination is a mixture of philosophy and spirituality, at least at a paradoxical level. At a practical level, it can be deemed a systematic method that delves deep into several facets of reality and existence, which brings forth a social character and helps the practitioner connect the dots between reality and spirituality. Despite being popular, practical thinkers and the scientific community do not really praise divination. It was primarily associated with God's will or the divine energy's calling in the past. However, divination took different forms in several cultures and was mainly perceived as astrology over time.

Types of Divination

With several types of divination in various cultures, the most prominent ones stood out and have been in practice worldwide for a while now. Some of these are still practiced by psychics and spiritual gurus. These include:

- Nordic Runes
- Automatic Writing
- Sand Divination
- Tea Leaf Reading
- Osteomancy
- Full Moon Water Scrying
- Numerology
- The Celtic Ogham
- Clairvoyance
- Tarot Card Reading

- Lithomancy

- Palmistry

- Graphology

- Pendulum Divination, etc.

As previously mentioned, some of these are still in practice but are heavily modified by spiritual gurus over time. This section will discuss some of the most prominent types of divination.

Norse Runes

The Runes are a significant part of Norse mythology as they are believed to have been created by Odin, the main Norse god. Essentially, Runes are holy symbols (or ancient alphabets) carved or transformed into stones. You can still find thousands of runestones scattered around some parts of Scandinavia and Northern Europe. The ancient Germanic runic alphabet, known as the Elder Futhark, comprises 12 sacred symbols.

General Characteristics

Unlike other divination practices, Norse ruins do not tell your future but help navigate you through your life path. It helps you become more self-aware and elucidate your hidden emotions and questions. Even though there are several Rune alphabets (like Gothic Runes, Younger Futhark, Cirth, Anglo-Saxon Futhorc, and Hungarian Runes), the Elder Futhark is the most popular. Your reading method and practice results may vary according to the type of alphabet you want to read.

How to Practice It

You can read Runes using four methods:

> • **Method 1:** Place the Runes in a pouch and close it. Close your eyes, focus on a question, and pick a stone.

> • **Method 2:** Toss or shuffle the stones while placing them on a soft surface. Ask your question and pick a stone.

> • **Method 3:** Make a grid or a pattern using the Runes and hover your non-dominant hand over them while thinking about your question. The one that attracts you is the stone of your choice.

> • **Method 4:** Pick three stones from the bag and place them in a line. The leftmost Rune will depict your past life, the middle stone will tell your present state, and the future stone will describe your future.

Use the instructions and legend card with the Runes set to determine what each symbol represents.

Automatic Writing

As the name suggests, this practice involves writing messages or thoughts beyond your conscious mind. Your spiritual energy or subconscious mind allows you to automatically transfer your hidden thoughts and emotions on paper without thinking about them. This helps unravel the deepest secrets and actual feelings that you are typically unaware of. This practice became popular after the famous 19th century Spiritualist movement.

General Characteristics

You simply hold a pen and put everything on paper or into your journal without validating them with your conscious mind. At a psychic level, automatic writing is associated with the spiritual world, wherein divine forces or spiritual energies act as a channel to help you unravel and write down your subconscious or unconscious emotions. In some cases, psychics claim to talk to spirits and deceased figures and gather information from them, which is put forward through the practice of automatic writing.

How to Practice It

Find a quiet place to practice automatic writing. You can play calming music to relax your mind and avoid any distractions. Get a notebook and a pen and sit comfortably. This is where the actual practice begins- start writing down words without thinking about them. Simply let the words flow on the paper. If you are stuck and don't know where to begin, ask yourself a question. It can be a random question about your everyday life, routine, relationship, or career. Keep writing until you naturally run out of words. For some, this practice can take hours as there is so much they need to unravel, decode, and dump.

Do not worry or judge the words you are writing down. This practice will help you deal with your darkest emotions and acknowledge or enhance your positive feelings. Automatic writing is about becoming more self-aware and combating all negative forces in your life. So, do not worry about writing down any kind of thoughts. When you are done, review your writing. You may come across some patterns and words that are focused or repetitive. These reflect the theme that is currently the most important or problematic for you. Try to find hidden messages and act on them. You can also try meditating before beginning this practice to clear your mind and become more self-aware.

Tea Leaf Reading

This practice involves reading tea leaves left in a cup after drinking. It can be traced back to the 17th century, making this divination practice relatively new. It is believed that the Chinese tea trade within Europe during this era made this practice quite common. Psychics and mystics also refer to this practice as *tasseography* or *tasseomancy*. This word originates from the Arabic word *"tassa"* (cup) and the Greek word *"mancy"* (divination).

General Characteristics

This form of divination also became popular due to its simplicity and flexibility. As tea became more and more common in some parts of the word, tea leaf reading was also encouraged (which was also majorly due to its accuracy). The tea leaves used in a teacup left specific patterns after being consumed, which told a lot about the consumer's fate and personality. Certain symbols and grids are formed by the leftover tea leaves, interpreted by an experienced and knowledgeable psychic.

If some moisture or water is left in the cup, it will either be absorbed using a napkin or swirled around further for the tea leaves to make a definite shape. Typically, the cup should be upturned on the table or the saucer before the psychic starts reading the patterns when the person is done drinking. Some even use specific teacups with special brims and patterns to read more accurately.

How to Practice It

For this practice, you need loose tea leaves (preferably small in size for reading accuracy) and a cup of water. However, if you are just starting, use bigger tea leaves. They make definite shapes and are easy to interpret. Make a cup of tea and drink 95% of the quantity. Swirl the remaining moisture for the tea leaves to make another pattern. Turn it upside down once you are done and leave it on the table or the saucer for 1 or 2 minutes. Hold it up again and look for one of these common signs or shapes:

- **House:** You'll soon be blessed with success or a major change in your life.

- **Spade:** Beware because this shape signifies failure or disappointment.

- **Heart:** You are or may be blessed with abundant joy, new friendships or relationships, happiness, and good luck.

- **Acorn:** You may be blessed with abundant wealth sooner or later.

- **Snake:** You are surrounded by or may encounter falsehood or make new enemies.

- **Mountain:** One mountain signifies blockage or hindrance, whereas two mountains mean success.

- **Line:** You are going to embark on a new journey. Look for the line's shape- if it is straight, you'll not face any hindrance on your way. However, if the line is curved, your journey may be delayed or derailed for some time.

- **Question Mark:** Whatever life path or personal/professional project you are on may be uncertain, and you must find answers to get back on track.

Numerology

Numerology is the practice of telling one's fate using a series of numbers. It is also used to decipher a person's true passion, fears, holistic outlook, and inner workings. Some practitioners use this art to gain wisdom, whereas others explore it for self-development. Letters, ideas, names, concepts, words, etc., are all connected to a numerical value, defining your life path number. Once you successfully decipher your path number, you can find your hidden purpose or help yourself achieve success and self-awareness. Numerology entails deep insights into your daily life and inner emotions.

The effective practice of analyzing and deducing certain numbers in your daily life and using it to find your true self is what makes numerology popular. This art is also associated with your birthday as it reflects who you were when you were born and the active planets at the time of your birth.

General Characteristics

The numbers 1, 2, 3, 4, 5, 6, 7, 8, 9, 11, 22, or 33 are the main blocks of the numerology practice. Numbers 1 to 9 are deemed the main or building numbers of this art, whereas 11, 22, and 33 serve different purposes. However, all 12 numbers are highly regarded in numerology. Your life path number can be any of these 12 blocks. The idea is to decode a set of recurring numbers in your everyday life and acknowledge them.

Some numbers may even show up in the form of key concepts or patterns. You just need to be more aware and intuitive to decipher the pattern to trace your life path number. Here is what each number signifies:

- **Number 1:** This person is blessed with amazing leadership qualities. However, if they let their insecurities get in the way, they may need additional support from friends and family to ward off loneliness.

- **Number 2:** They are the peacemakers and try to bring harmony in all kinds of forces, especially the chaotic ones. At times, they may feel unacknowledged, so they often seek validation from others.

- **Number 3:** They are expressive, creative, and inspiring. They want others around them to be happy. At times, their loved ones may have to deal with their moodiness, which mindfulness practices can mitigate.

- **Number 4:** This person is responsible and hardworking. They think practically and focus on scalable growth. However, if they follow the rules to the extent of inhibiting them, they may become quite stubborn.

- **Number 5:** They enjoy their freedom and are progressive in nature. They want to embark on every adventure thrown towards them, which makes them quite impulsive and restless. At times, they must take a step back and deal with daily responsibilities to stay on track with life.

- **Number 6:** The native is empathic and supportive. They possess a nurturing instinct that helps them resolve issues while being gentle and kind. They care for their loved ones and are aware of their responsibilities. If the protective energy is overused, the native may become dominating.

- **Number 7:** They are detail-oriented and analytical. They can easily pick issues and flaws in any assignment or system- a trait typically possessed by perfectionists. To combat this, they must find harmony between their skeptical thinking patterns and tangible realities.

- **Number 8:** The natives are bound to attract financial success and abundant wealth. They are goal-oriented, ambitious, and responsible. However, since they take their work and tasks too seriously, they can turn into a workaholic or become possessive.

- **Number 9:** This person is the most "experienced" of the lot. Essentially, they have been through every ups-and-downs of life, making them conscious and self-aware. However, this often pushes them into an intangible plane where they fantasize about scenarios, making it difficult to differentiate between reality and fantasy.

- **Master Number 11:** The native shares traits with Number 2, as the sum of 11 (1 + 1) is 2. They can use their healing power to resolve life's circumstances and combat curveballs. Their extrasensory talents help them develop spiritual insights and philosophical enlightenment.

- **Master Number 22:** Commonly known as the "Master Builder," Number 22 shares traits with Number 4. The natives are innovative (mainly due to their experiences and encounters during their childhood) and quite dependable.

- **Master Number 33:** The natives are wise and knowledgeable. They possess strong intuition and vivid dreams. They let their imagination run wild, which makes them lucid.

How to Practice It

To find your root number, start by charting your birth date and turning it into a single digit. For example, if your birthday is January 12, 1971, the first month will bring forward the number 1. Your birth date, number 12, will be $1 + 2 = 3$. The year 1971 will be $1 + 9 + 7 + 1 = 18$. It will further be reduced to $1 + 8 = 9$. Add all these final numbers together. So, $1 + 3 + 9 = 13$, which will further be reduced to $1 + 3 = 4$. This means that food is your root number or life path number. If you get numbers 11 and 22, do not reduce them as they are master numbers in numerology. You can also make a chart using master numbers or associate your name's letters with definite numbers to reveal your true purpose.

Palmistry

The art of reading a person's palm is called palmistry and is also commonly known as chiromancy. This practice can be dated back to 5,000 years ago and is native to India. It slowly spread towards some parts of East Asia, the Middle East, and Europe and is now quite prominent across the world. Since the famous psychiatrist Carl Jung took an interest in this fascinating form of astrology or fortune-telling, it has been widely popular among mystics and psychics. The hand is believed to be a direct gateway to a person's inner soul, making palmistry a persuasive way to tell one's fate.

General Characteristics

The lines and marks on a person's palms are interpreted based on the teaching of Palmistry. The practitioner can thereby read and predict the person's future. It is believed that each line on a person's hand is vaguely connected to their brain, which can help determine their personality. In a way, it also provides a deeper look into their future. The person's non-dominant hand illustrates their core character and personality, whereas the dominant hand describes whether or not the traits are prominently displayed.

Ideally, you should find four main lines on one's palms. These are:

- **Heart Line:** A deep Heart line depicts emotional depth.

- **Head Line:** A curved Head line depicts creativity, and a straight Head line symbolizes rationality.

- **Fate Line:** Every person may not necessarily have a clear Fate line during their childhood. It only appears or becomes apparent when they enter their 20s or 30s. This line indicates a person's fate and their education or career path.

- **Life Line**: It represents how long a person will live and how enthusiastically they will perceive their life. A faint or broken Lifeline may indicate a lack of passion or zest to live life.

Collectively, all these lines represent a person's entire life and fate. From education to their passion for life, you can decipher their core personality through the art of palmistry.

How to Practice It

For beginners, it is important to focus on the larger picture and then delve into the specifics and details to gain more expertise in that area. Start by noting some small or "implicit" observations like the palm's texture and cleanliness. These details can make a difference in your intuitive reading as everything is represented by a meaning. The next step is to familiarize yourself with the four elements: earth, water, air, and fire, as these represent every hand's shape. The plains and mounts of a palm should also be studied and noticed.

Look out for six types of mounts: Mount of Saturn (problems, boundaries, decisiveness), Mount of Mercury (inventiveness, creativity, ideas), Mount of Apollo (sensitivity, creativity, talent), Mount of Luna (psychic abilities, imagination, spiritual interests), Mount of Jupiter (authority, leadership, ambition), and Mount of Venus (passion, love, sentimentality). It is necessary to delve deep into this practice to become a master at it. The more you practice palmistry, the better you can interpret all lines and mounts to tell a person's fate and illustrate their personality.

Two other types of divination (which are also quite common) are Tarot card reading and Pendulum divination. Clairvoyance, which you already learned in one of the previous chapters, is also a type of divination practice that can enhance your psychic ability. As you learned, most of these divination practices can be used to tell one's fate and illustrate their core personality. Some are rising in popularity, whereas some ancient practices are dying with time.

Chapter 14: Using a Pendulum

People have been using pendulums for almost four centuries since Galileo first started studying them in 1602. His experiments piqued scientists' interest for the following years, and many people who were concerned with spiritual practices used swinging crystals to practice divination. In fact, the use of pendulums has been traced back to the ancient Egyptian and Roman civilizations. Nowadays, many people use them for spiritual healing, cleansing auras, and discovering their inner guidance, which helps them to make important decisions in their lives. Let's take a closer look at pendulums, how to use them, and how you can make your own pendulum at home.

What Is a Pendulum?

A pendulum is a tool that is usually made of a gemstone hanging from a string or chain. It could also be made from various materials like wood, metal, or glass. Crystals are commonly used because they possess healing powers and spiritual significance. People use it to establish an open communication channel with their higher self. In a healing session, you would usually ask questions to seek guidance for different concerns in your life. This should help you clear your head and understand more things about yourself. A pendulum is used to access your subconscious and connect with the universal levels of consciousness. It can be moved either back and forth or in a circular motion.

A pendulum is used in the dowsing technique, which helps you access unknown or invisible spiritual realms. During the session, the pendulum's movement guides you through answering your questions. It receives your inquiries and responds to you by transmitting energy from the spiritual realm. The most effective way to use a pendulum is to ask it simple questions that require "yes" or "no" answers. It can also be used to find something you lost or cleanse negative energy in your house. Dowsing techniques are commonly used to find water sources using swinging pendulums.

How to Connect with a Pendulum

Using a pendulum can help you access your intuition to find those hidden answers within, which can be a challenge. You'd have to untangle a lot of layers in your soul to tap into your inner truth. Pendulums facilitate this process by harmoniously combining both sides of your brain, which otherwise work in opposite directions. This merge helps you find your inner balance and reach the level of wisdom you are seeking. They work on the innermost levels of spirituality to connect you with a divine guide.

As previously mentioned, it is best to ask simple questions to your pendulum. Try to reframe any question you have to fit this format. The clearer you are, the more accurate the answer will be. You have to be mindful when asking your question. Visualize the situation that you are concerned with. For the pendulum to work, you need to connect with your deeper self and inner energy. Bear in mind that our energies are in constant motion. The answers you receive from a pendulum can be different depending on the time of day, your mood, and how you can connect with your inner self. With time and practice, you'll be able to focus your energy and intention on your questions, which will result in clearer, more straightforward answers.

You can ask your pendulum for guidance in anything that concerns you. Consider it a meditative or spiritual session similar to religious prayers. Practice it whenever you feel the need to connect with your spirituality. Whether you have a problem in your life or need to find some peace or clarity, using a pendulum can help you get through tough times. Hold it from the string and let it move freely to connect with your pendulum. Let your energy flow through your swinging pendulum. It will absorb your energy and respond to you depending on your vibes at that moment.

When you buy your gemstone from the shop, examine different materials and shapes. You don't have to stick with crystals or the most popular choices. Try a few stones to see which one you connect with. Remember that no choice is right and wrong for you. It all comes down to your intuition and how the gemstone feels to you. If you have a preference, such as amethyst, jade, or quartz crystals, see a selection of them and find out if they speak to you.

If you can't make up your mind, try one of the following options. Amethyst stones help to open your crown chakra. This opens your mind to higher realms of spirituality and helps you to see your life from a different perspective. This precious stone promotes clarity and helps you to make important life-altering decisions.

A clear quartz stone helps augment your energy, which helps you set your intention and increase your personal vibrations. This helps you reach the wisdom you are looking for and find solutions for the obstacles you face in life. It also promotes tranquility and balance in your quest to find your true self. If you seek guidance in matters of the heart, consider getting a rose quartz crystal. It represents love and purity and helps you to understand your emotions by tracking their root causes and accepting them.

How to Cleanse a Pendulum

Before using your pendulum, it must be cleansed from any energy it might have absorbed while sitting in the store. Cleansing helps to reset your stone's energy so that it is ready for your personal vibrations. Just like you cleanse a room before meditating, you can cleanse your pendulum by smudging, washing, placing it under sunlight or a full moon, burying it in the ground, leaving it with your other personal crystals, and gemstones, or sound cleansing, among others.

Smudging

If you decide to cleanse your pendulum by smudging, you'll need a lighter, metal bowl, and an incense stick. You can use a sage bundle, the most common incense used in smudging. You need to set your intentions on cleansing your pendulum. Focus on your breathing and think about channeling away bad energy and allowing good energy to flow through you. Light your sage bundle and watch the smoke go over your crystals. You can recite some prayers if you want at this point, just as you would when you are cleaning the room. The smoke is intended to carry your wishes and desires to your higher self.

Be careful of flying ash from the sage bundle as it may be a fire hazard. A safer option is to place the bundle in the metal bowl or Abalone shell if you have one and then light the bundle. You can walk the bowl around the pendulum or gemstones you want to cleanse or direct the smoke toward the stones with a feather or your hands. Open your windows and doors to allow air circulation and let the smoke take the negative energy away from your house.

Washing

Another way to cleanse your stones is by washing them under running water. You can use running tap water at home or a stream if you are outdoors. Make sure that your stones are completely underwater for a whole minute, and then let them dry. Avoid using this technique for fragile stones like selenite and halite.

You can also use salt water to wash your stones. Salt is believed to remove negative energy from any object. The best option is to use fresh seawater, but you can use a solution of salt and water instead. Dissolve a tablespoon of any type of salt you have in the house in a bowl of water. Leave the stones submerged in the water for a couple of days and then allow them to dry. Avoid using this technique on porous stones or those containing trace metals like malachite and calcite.

Sunlight and Moonlight

You can cleanse your stones by placing them under the natural light of a full moon or the early morning sunlight. Avoid placing them under direct sunlight at noon because it could damage the surface of fragile stones. You can place the stones directly on the soil to allow energy circulation from the earth. Make sure you set it on the ground in a safe spot that is not accessible to kids or animals. You can expose your stones to both night and morning lights by placing them under a full moon for the whole night and picking them up right before noon by 11 am. Afterward, wash the stones under running water and allow them to dry.

Using Other Stones

You can also keep your small stones with a larger stone like quartz or amethyst for a whole day. It is believed that larger stones remove the low frequencies and bad vibrations from stagnant stones. Another technique is to use several small clearing stones. Place them in a bowl as the base, and then leave your gemstone on top for a day. You can use this technique to cleanse any stone and use any type of stone for an energy-clearing effect.

Sound Cleansing

This technique entails using a tool that creates a sound like a tuning fork, bell, drum, or even your hands. You can chant and clap your hands over your pendulum to deflect any bad or stagnant energy left in the gemstone. Singing and chanting help to spread a positive vibe in the whole room, which will be transmitted to your pendulum. Feel free to recite a prayer you use during meditation in this cleansing method.

Burying It in Rice

Rice is used in many cultures as a sign of blessing and prosperity. You can cleanse your pendulum by burying it in a bowl filled with brown rice for a whole day. This method can be used to cleanse any type of stone. The rice must be thrown out of the house right away to dispose of the absorbed energies.

How to Use a Pendulum

After cleansing your pendulum, it is important to plan your questions before starting the session. Prepare multiple questions about your concerns to get the answers you need. Sometimes, the pendulum won't respond to your question at a certain moment by staying still or swinging randomly away from the answers. You need to learn how to read and connect to your pendulum. First, establish which movements mean "yes" and "no" with your pendulum. To do this, place the stone in your palm and close your eyes. Feel the connection between you and the gemstone for a few minutes to establish a spiritual bond.

The next step is to communicate with your pendulum how to move to answer "no" and "yes." For example, hold the string of your pendulum between your thumb and index finger. Make sure that you use your dominant hand and keep it very steady. Move the pendulum right and left and say "no" to instruct the pendulum to use this motion to respond "no." Use another motion to indicate "yes" while saying the word. The motion could be a front and back motion. It also helps to use another motion for "maybe" or "don't know," like moving the pendulum in circles while saying the word.

Next, use simple statements at first to test the process. Before asking the questions you prepared, you can start by mentioning your name and where you live and observe how the pendulum responds to your statement. Make sure to start with the simple questions first. This will help you be more confident in setting your intentions, which triggers the pendulum's movements. After asking the basic questions, you can move on to the more important ones.

You want to be seated comfortably during a session. Take a few minutes or as long as you need to empty your brain from any thoughts. Set the scene for a meditative ritual of your choice. Take a few deep breaths to calm your nerves until you have a steady and calm rhythm. Any agitation at this point will distract you from connecting with your pendulum.

If this is your first time using a pendulum, it is important to keep an open mind. You might not be successful the first couple of times. It takes time and practice to establish a connection and sync your energy with your gemstone before you see some results. Take your time to understand your gemstone better and allow it to absorb your energy. Maintain your focus during a session and remove any distractions that could block your energy flow. Try not to force your mind into thinking about a certain direction. The whole idea is to build a relationship with your stone before it starts to answer you.

Remember that whatever answers the pendulum gives you comes from within you. The truth lies inside you, which is why you need to give yourself the time to relax completely and be ready to receive those answers. Sometimes, you think you want answers to a few problems in your life, but you might be afraid of the outcomes. You must be able to enjoy the whole experience and trust in the process. Consider the pendulum a tool to get in touch with your deeper and higher self. If you feel too agitated to embark on this journey, you can postpone the session for another time. Don't force yourself to meditate or use your crystals unless you feel you need to.

Some people use a pendulum board to answer more complicated questions as an advanced technique. A pendulum board is similar to an Ouija board. It has letters and numbers on it. You would hover the crystal over the board while asking your questions and allow the pendulum to fall on the letters to spell out the answers.

You can use a pendulum board to find a lost object, similarly to a dowsing rod. Many people use a map instead of a board to find lost things. You can also draw a diagram or an outline of a city, area, or your own house and use the pendulum to guide you toward the location of your lost object. Some people use the dowsing technique to find lost pets or a water source. After the pendulum points toward a direction, it is then carried to the specified location and used to point to the exact area where the object is placed. The pendulum would start to vibrate strongly or pull you toward a specific area to indicate the object's location. Some people combine this technique with Tarot cards by using the pendulum to point toward a specific card that holds the answer.

How to Make Your Own Pendulum

If you didn't find a pendulum that you are comfortable with at the store, you could easily create one at home. You'll need to get a crystal or gemstone that catches your eye, a string or wire, and a chain to hang your stone. Ensure that the chain is not too heavy to allow the pendulum to move freely. Here's how you can create your own pendulum at home:

1. Take the wire and wrap it around the gemstone several times.

2. Leave a small loop at the top of the crystal to attach the chain to it.

3. Fix the chain in the loop and make sure it is not too long so that you can swing it comfortably.

4. Make sure the wires are tightly wrapped around the gemstone to avoid scratching your skin.

5. Charge your pendulum by cleansing it using one of the aforementioned methods.

6. Calibrate your pendulum to test if it is working by asking it simple questions as mentioned previously.

This chapter discussed everything you need to know about using a pendulum. When you get started, try to manage your expectations on how the pendulum should work. It is best to keep an open mind about the whole process. It will take time for you to establish a rhythm and bond with your pendulum. After some time and practice, you'll be able to easily access your subconscious and higher self and find the answers you are looking for.

Chapter 15: Using Tarot Cards

Tarot cards were used as playing cards in the 15th century in Europe. Three centuries later, Tarot cards were used for divination practices. There are 78 cards in a Tarot deck: 22 Major Arcana cards and 46 Minor Arcana cards. Each card holds a certain meaning, which could be different depending on the cards drawn for a reading. Tarot cards are used to tell you about events that might happen in the future and how you should act in these situations. This chapter will provide an overview of Tarot cards and discuss how you can do basic reading and create your own deck.

The Major Arcana Cards

The 22 cards of Major Arcana have the most impact in a Tarot deck. Each card reflects a major life-altering event that might happen in the future. When these cards are drawn, they are meant to give you a message to guide you through tough times. The Major Arcana cards are concerned with the bigger picture and journey of life. Each card drawn in a single Tarot reading represents one piece of the puzzle. Let's take a look at what each card of Major Arcana means.

The Fool

This card is the first one in the deck, representing the main character of a Tarot deck. He is considered a naive character who hasn't had much experience in life. He has no idea what to expect in life and cannot imagine the challenges he's about to face. The Fool also lacks self-knowledge about his ability to overcome these obstacles. The Fool card is a sign that you should be more open in your life and leave your worries behind you.

The Magician

This card makes you pay attention to your hidden talents. It is a reminder that you have unique abilities that no one else possesses. These skills or abilities are what sets you apart from everybody else. This card is a sign to continue with a project or plan you've been simmering for a while because you have great potential in seeing it through.

The High Priestess

This card indicates great intuition and connection with the subconscious mind. It is a sign to listen to your guts and do what you feel is right. The card urges you to trust yourself more, stop seeking advice from others, and turn to yourself for guidance.

The Empress

The Empress card is a sign of love, beauty, and femininity. She is strongly connected with nature. If this card is drawn, it is a message for you to get in touch with nature and explore the energy around you.

The Emperor

This card represents an authority figure or a strong leader. Unlike the Fool, the Emperor is an experienced character who has been through a lot of ups and downs in his life. If this card is drawn in your Tarot reading, it is a reminder of your inner strengths and how you can control your own life.

The Hierophant

This card represents a divine messenger who knows the secrets of the universe. His experience lies in the spiritual realm and heavenly wisdom, and he is concerned with communicating his lessons to the people on earth. The Hierophant card is a sign to look for answers on a spiritual level.

The Lovers

This card resembles the most intimate relationships in your life. If this card is drawn in your reading, it is an indication that you need to pay attention to your closest relationships. It may come up when you have an important decision to make in your life and need to look at the situation from all angles.

The Chariot

This card represents moving forward toward your goals. It is a sign of determination, which means you need to push through your current obstacles to achieve success in life. If this card is drawn in your reading, it is a reminder to connect logical thinking with your fiery spirit and passion for reaching your full potential.

Strength

As the name suggests, the Strength card resembles strength but nothing concerning the body. This card reflects your courage and resilience, enabling you to overcome any problems you face in life. This card urges you to have faith in yourself because you possess the strength to face life's challenges.

The Hermit

The Hermit is a loner who likes to isolate himself from the crowd to process his emotions and reflect on his thoughts. He is aware that the only way to make a decision is to stay away from everyone so that he can hear his own voice. This card is a sign that you need some time off to figure out a solution on your own.

Wheel of Fortune

This card is the ultimate sign of the fluctuations in life. It indicates that sometimes you'll face hardships, and other times you'll thrive in life. It is a reminder that nothing stays the same, whether good or bad, and it is a lifelong lesson to remember at that point in your life.

Justice

The Justice card reminds you that what goes around comes around. It is a reminder to face the consequences of your actions. Anything you are experiencing now results from something you did in your past. It could be good or bad, depending on how you've acted before. This card is a reminder to be fair to everyone.

The Hanged Man

The Hanged man is a sign that you are at a crossroads in your life or can't seem to make up your mind. It is a sign that you need to let go of something for the greater good. Search for that thing in your life that brings you down and try to detach yourself from it.

Death

Contrary to popular belief, the Death card resembles the end of things but not literally death itself. The end of things is also marked by the beginning of new things, which is also a reminder that everything passes. Whether it is a job, a relationship, or emotions, sometimes it is better to let go of the past and open your heart to new experiences.

Temperance

This card indicates peace and harmony and avoidance of conflicts. It reminds you to be open to the flow of life and enjoy the ride instead of trying to direct it a certain way. This card is a sign of adapting to the changes that happen in your life.

The Devil

This card represents a certain situation or event that is happening in your life, which is beyond your control. You don't like being in that situation, and you can't seem to pull yourself out of it. This card tells you that you have convinced yourself that there is no way out, which is why you are unable to move on. It is a reminder to take back control of your life.

The Tower

This card is a sign that everything in your life might fall apart. There is no way out of it, and sometimes it is best to let it happen. Sometimes, you need to break things down to build them back up the right way.

The Star

The Star card indicates hope of recovering from some kind of loss in your life. This card resembles the positivity and healing you'll experience in the near future. It is a sign that things are looking up for you and a reminder to have faith in what the universe has in store for you.

The Moon

This card reflects your innermost thoughts, desires, and fear as it is connected to your subconscious mind. You may experience anxiety when this card is drawn, but consider it a reminder not to indulge in those feelings. Try to acknowledge and accept them and then let them go.

The Sun

This card exudes positivity, optimism, and overall happiness. It is a sign to keep moving along the path you choose. Take time to acknowledge the positive events happening around you and the people you have in your life right now.

Judgment

This card represents the intersection of your past and future. It is a sign that you need to review your past actions to plan a way forward and rectify your mistakes. If this card is drawn, it is a reminder that you can do better in the future.

The World

This card is an indication that you have achieved success in your life. It's a reminder that you have come a long way and that it is time for the next stage in your life. The World card means that your life has reached full circle.

The Minor Arcana Suits

There are four suits in the Minor Arcana, with 14 cards included in each suit. These cards are concerned with the day-to-day interactions we have in our lives. When you draw one of these cards, it reflects something happening in your daily life, whether it is a situation, feelings, or emotions. These cards hold the answer to how you should handle this situation right now as opposed to the Major Arcana cards that point toward the bigger picture. If many Minor Arcana cards appeared in your reading, it is an indication that these situations are not long-lasting. Consider them a learning opportunity that will allow you to gain more experience in life. Suppose you are doing the Tarot reading with playing cards. In that case, the suit of Wands is represented by the suit of Clubs, Cups is represented by Hearts, Swords is represented by Spades, and Pentacles is represented by Diamonds.

Suit of Wands

This suit is correlated with the wood element, representing a force to reckon for since it can catch fire that could be difficult to extinguish. Wands is the first suit in Minor Arcana and represents the birth of an idea. If a few cards in this suit were drawn, it is an indication that whatever project or plan you have in mind is still in the early stages. The Wand cards indicate that you are a creative person who has the willpower and determination to see their plan through.

The suit of Wands also stands for the fire element. Fire is a sign of passion and indicates that you are a hard worker who welcomes challenges as a growth opportunity. If the cards are reversed, however, it is a sign that you are an impulsive person who cannot strategize properly and might often make mistakes.

Suit of Cups

The cards in this suit resemble the water element, which is a sign of life and nature. This suit is the second one in the Minor Arcana, and it reflects the emotional turmoil you might experience between the creative stages and the execution. It is a reflection of your innermost fears and desires. If you have a few of these in your reading, it is a sign that you are experiencing a lot of emotions and still haven't decided on the right action. The Cup cards are connected with feelings of love and the close relations you have in your life. It could refer to your personal or professional relationships.

If the cards were inverted, it indicates you are overwhelmed with emotions and going through a lack of passion. The cards tell you that you are detaching from reality and channeling your excessive emotions by creating your own fantasy world.

Suit of Swords

The cards of this suit resemble the air element. The two sides of the sword represent opposite forces. One side could be the solution to all of your problems, while the other could destroy anything in its path. This suit is the third one in the Minor Arcana and represents the execution stage. The Sword is a sign of action and fighting of some sort. If most of your reading contained Sword cards, it is an indication that you are struggling with the execution stage. It is a reflection of your thoughts and actions. The Sword cards refer to intelligence and logical thinking, which are powerful aspects that need to be balanced with your emotions and spirituality to avoid the sword's other edge.

The two edges of the sword represent destruction and construction. This suit is the most powerful of the four suits and may indicate violence. The cards in the suit in a reading indicate you have decisions to make or are struggling to act on your decisions. It is a reminder to be aware of your enemies and to be prepared for what life has in store for you. You can consider this as an advantage as you can use it to make positive decisions. If the cards appear inverted, it refers to anger, violence, guilt, and lack of compassion toward others.

Suit of Pentacles

This suit resembles the earth element, which represents money and career prospects. This is the fourth suit of the Minor Arcana and the only one that resembles materialistic things. These cards represent the stage of completion when all the thoughts, ideas, and strategies have been executed in real life. If many Pentacle cards were drawn in your reading, it means that your plans have succeeded in materializing in the physical world. They resemble financial security, business, and possessions. It also reflects how you deal with the things surrounding and altering the world around you.

If the cards appear inverted, they resemble greed, lack of managing business or finances, and materialism. It could be a reminder to stop focusing too much on your career and make space for other important aspects of your life. Try to get away from work and your possessions and get in touch with nature to try and rediscover yourself.

How to Read a Basic Tarot Spread

You can do a basic Tarot reading by yourself, but there are a few things to keep in mind. First, get acquainted with the meaning of each card in the Major and Minor Arcana. You can check out the meaning of each card on the internet, especially if you are just beginning to practice Tarot reading. The whole idea is to get in touch with your inner guidance and wisdom. Start by asking the cards a simple question about something that is concerning you.

The next step is to shuffle the cards. You can either use the deck in one hand and shuffle with the other, cut the deck and divide it a few times, or lay all the cards in front of you and arrange them back together. Then, you can pull one card for your first reading or several ones to get a more advanced reading. Lay the cards on their faces and then turn them one by one while focusing on each image and symbol on them. The key is to stay relaxed while reading to tune in with your inner wisdom.

You can use a basic spread if you are experiencing a lot of ups and downs in your life. Pull three cards after shuffling the deck and turn them one by one. The first card is what you need to do to accept the changes in your life. The second card represents a self-care practice you need to do for yourself, and the third card guides you to stay true to yourself in the process.

You can create your Tarot cards featuring your own creative designs. Use a chart to cut 78 cards and customize them with the illustration you see fit. You can print pictures online and paste them on the cards or draw the illustrations yourself. You can be creative with your diagrams and as intricate or as simple as you want. Experiment with a few materials or order a set of blank cards to draw on.

This chapter mentioned an overview of Major Arcana cards and Minor Arcana suits and what each of them represents. Bear in mind that Tarot reading is a vast universe of knowledge and practice, and it will take a lot of time to get an accurate reading. The whole concept is meant to allow you to be more aware of yourself, learn how to deal with your daily struggles, and recognize your inner truth.

Chapter 16: Psychic Protection and Defense

The ability to sense and control your psychic abilities is the greatest power you can have. It comes with responsibilities, however. Psychic ability has great potential for harm if it is not controlled. You must learn to protect yourself from the negative energies around you and those that other people send out into the world.

Developing your psychic abilities without learning how to protect yourself and others can lead to serious problems. You may begin to experience physical ailments like headaches, muscle aches, or even nausea. Many times, when a person begins to develop their gifts, other psychic attacks may be brought on by jealous people or entities who don't want this person to keep developing their abilities.

A psychic attack can happen without you knowing it. The negativity associated with these attacks can manifest itself in many ways, such as fatigue, illness, depression, anxiety, nightmares, insomnia, and many more. This chapter will offer advice and techniques on keeping yourself and your psychic space healthy and free from negative energy.

Why Protection Is Important before You Start

When you begin your psychic journey, it's very important to establish a strong defense against outside influence. This is because the first time you start developing your abilities, you are particularly open and vulnerable to attacks from negative energies. When you first get started in the psychic world, you may encounter energy that is not yours and is invading your personal space. This is called a psychic attack, and if it isn't stopped, it can cause lasting damage to your well-being and even cause physical harm.

Many people think that once they begin doing psychic work or develop their abilities, they will see everything. This is not true! You can never see everything or everyone around you, but there are always negative energies lingering around waiting for an opportunity to pounce on unsuspecting people like yourself. You need to protect yourself from these types of attacks. The first step is learning about psychic protection.

You must also protect yourself from your thoughts and projections. When you start working with the psychic world, you'll discover that thoughts have certain energy of their own, and they can even materialize. This means that if you send out negative thoughts, they can be just as harmful to yourself and others around you. This is why you need to learn how to protect yourself, even on the mental plane.

Types of Attacks

As you develop your abilities, you may encounter any one of these types of energy attacks:

1. Sudden Bad Moods

You may experience a sudden and unexplained bad mood that can't be explained by anything in your life. The sudden mood may come with a headache or some other physical ailment. If this happens, you should immediately put up a psychic shield. The mood and accompanying bad feelings shouldn't be ignored as they may very well be a psychic attack on you. This type of attack can be prevented by putting up a psychic shield.

2. Flashes of Anger

You may experience sudden flashes of anger for no reason. These flashes should be taken seriously as they could indicate a psychic attack from someone sending out negative energy into the world or a spirit that is angry at you. Surround yourself in white light at the first sign of anger and put up a psychic shield. When something like this happens, it's important to ground yourself.

3. Bad Luck or Trips/Accidents

When you encounter some type of bad luck or find yourself in accidents without any apparent cause, you may be under psychic attack. Surround yourself in white light and put up a psychic shield if this happens. The bad luck may also come as a string of serendipity where everything seems to go your way. In this case, it's important to know that sometimes negative energies can attempt to send positive things your way. This is done to give you a false sense of security.

4. Personality Changes

You may notice that you just don't feel like yourself. You may feel irritable, or you might experience sudden mood swings. These changes could be the result of a psychic attack. Your personality changes could be attributed to the fact that you're opening up to the psychic world. This is why it's important for you to learn how to protect yourself.

5. Sudden Illness or Injury

When you suddenly become sick or injured, you may be under psychic attack. Illnesses and injuries can be your body's way of protecting you from the negativity coming at you. If you suddenly become ill or injured and you're not under medical supervision, or even if you are, surrounding yourself in white light and putting up a psychic shield is an important step to take.

6. Inexplicable Losses

You may experience a string of unexplained losses, such as your keys or wallet. Losses like these may be the result of a psychic attack. It's important to know that these types of losses can be a warning sign if you're put under a psychic attack. If the unexplained loss was accompanied by a headache or a sudden bad mood, you were most likely under a psychic attack. A common example of this is when you leave your keys somewhere, and they mysteriously disappear.

7. Nightmares or Dream Visits

You might notice that you're having nightmares more often than usual. If this happens, you should put up a psychic shield. You may also notice dream visitations during your sleep. These are not ordinary dreams but rather visits from spirits or other entities. Many people don't realize that these types of dreams are psychic attacks from those on the other side, as opposed to dreams where you're visited by a loved one who has passed over.

8. Voices in Your Mind

You might hear voices in your mind that have a negative message for you. Pay attention to what the voice is saying. If it tells you to do something, the voice is not your own. If you feel like you're under psychic attack, or if you find yourself constantly putting up psychic shields, it's important to seek advice from a psychic. They can tell you if you're under psychic attack and, if so, how to stop it.

9. Attacks of Panic

If you suddenly start to panic for no reason, you could be under psychic attack. It's helpful to know that when you feel like someone is watching you, or you have the feeling that someone is standing right over your shoulder, or if you feel like your home isn't safe when no one else is there, these are all signs that you're being attacked psychically. A psychic attack puts your body and mind into flight, fright, or freeze mode because of the fear you feel. If these feelings become persistent, seek guidance from a psychic.

10. Feeling Trapped or Out of Control

If you feel like you're trapped and can't go anywhere, or if you feel like you're stuck in a never-ending cycle of bad luck, you may be under psychic attack. The same goes for when you feel like no matter how hard you try, you can't get ahead in life. If this happens and it feels like you have no control over your life, you're most likely under psychic attack.

How to Protect Yourself Before You Start

One of the most important steps in communicating with spirits is creating psychic protection and defense. Psychic protection is intended to make sure that you don't bring any negative influences, like evil spirits or psychic attacks, with you when you attempt to contact a spirit. Psychic defense is used to repel any negative energies or entities that may come after you before or after your session. Here are some of the best ways to protect yourself before, during, and after your session:

Before Your Session

Meditate - Meditation creates an energy vacuum within your body, allowing spirits to enter. Meditating before attempting a spirit reading creates a barrier between your body and any outside spirits or entities. You can also do this by sitting quietly and closing your eyes for at least five minutes before attempting to contact a spirit.

Perform a Banishing Ritual - A banishing ritual completely removes all outside influences from around your body. It's especially important to do a banishing ritual if you live near a "haunted location." There are many different rituals for this. For example, you can use sage or sweetgrass to remove negative energies from your home or a room. You can also recite an incantation to remove all outside influences from a particular space. After performing a banishment, you'll be free from spirits or entities that could potentially harm you during your session.

Perform an Affirmation - Affirmations are powerful thoughts that reinforce the intentions of your mind. If you want to keep any negative influences away while contacting spirits, repeat an affirmation every few minutes during your session saying, *"I only want positive spirits to come through right now."* Or *"I am open and receptive only to positive spirits."*

During Your Session

Charging Place - Find an open space or room before you start to contact a spirit. You can either ask your spiritual team to meet you there or use the charging place as a home base for your session. You can illuminate the area with candles or light incense so that you have both light and an aroma to attract spirits. You can also charge your connection with the room by asking for its protection before you start.

Stay Grounded - Staying grounded makes you more protected during your session. Find something to occupy your mind, like playing a game on your phone or listening to music while you contact spirits. If you can, keep one foot on the ground at all times during your reading. This will keep you from floating into the spirit world. If this isn't possible, at least breathe with one foot on the ground for stability.

After Your Session

Clear Your Space - After your session, it's important to clear the area of all negative energies. Fire is a powerful tool for clearing a space, and it's also the most common element for this purpose. You can use sage, palo santo (a type of wood from South America), sweet grass, or any other herb that is burned as incense to rid a space of negative spirits. Here's an example incantation that can be used to clear a space:

"I cleanse and release this space of all entities, beings, or negative energy. May this space be filled with love, joy, and happiness."

"I release all entities from this space who may wish me harm or ill will. I release all entities from this space who wish to interfere with my connection with Spirit." If you're sensitive, it's a good idea to perform this cleansing ritual before, during, AND after every reading.

How to Protect Your Aura

There are many ways to protect the aura and strengthen the psychic energy. One of them is crystals. Ancient shamans and healers used crystals because they have different frequencies that enhance our psychic abilities. They can help to make the shield impenetrable and unbreakable.

One of the most powerful crystals that can strengthen the aura and help to find lost objects is black obsidian. It is a glass-like crystal with a shiny, black surface, and it protects its owner from negative energy. There are no special rituals needed to use black obsidian – you just have to have it with you all the time. The main condition is that it should be placed near a window or door to get direct sunlight during the day.

Place black obsidian on a windowsill or beside your bed at night, so it absorbs all negative energies before they get inside your home. This powerful stone cleans everything around you from negative energies and makes your aura stronger and healthier when you sleep. You can also wear black obsidian as an amulet for protection. You don't need any particular ritual for this – just put it on a neck or underclothes, close to your skin where it can absorb bad energies during the day and protect you at night when you're the most vulnerable.

How To Create Daily Protections

There are several simple yet powerful rituals that you can do to protect yourself against negative energies during the day. Here are examples of the most useful ones:

The Circle of Protection

This ritual comes from Wicca, and it's used to create a protective circle of energy around you. Draw a circle around yourself on the floor with a candle in the middle of it if you're indoors, or simply imagine the energies circling you if you're outside. Once the circle is complete, visualize all kinds of brightly-colored shields and energy barriers surrounding your body to keep you safe. Poke the centers of your palms with your finger and say: "I grant myself psychic protection!" or clap your hands three times and say: aloud or in your mind, "I grant myself psychic protection!"

The Energy Shield

This ritual uses four colors of light to create a protective shield around you. Imagine four balls of different light colors spinning around your body at the same time, or visualize separate balls of different colors rotating around you until they connect at the four corners of your aura. Then, imagine them spinning faster and faster until they form a huge, impassable shield surrounding you at all times.

The Oil Cleansing Ritual

This simple cleansing ritual uses essential oils to protect yourself from negative energies. Simply mix lavender, chamomile, and rosemary essential oils in equal parts. Put the mixture in your palm and visualize your entire aura being cleaned out by the mixture. Then, rub the oil into your skin or put it on your pulse points to protect yourself throughout the day.

How to Protect Your Home

Your home is the place where you spend most of your time, so it's essential to make sure that it's always protected from negative energies. First off, the best way to create complete protection is to clean your home thoroughly and then place crystals around it to purify and cleanse the energy. For daily protection, place the fennel in every corner of your home and all closets and cupboards. This will clear out any negative energies that come in contact with your home and make the energy inside it purer and more beneficial for you and your family.

Vetiver is another great element for protecting your home – place some in every corner of the house and ask it to protect your home from negative energy. Also, remember to keep your windows and doors open so the positive energies can get in and out easily. And, last but not least, don't forget to check the aura of your house at least once a month. The best time for this is right after sunrise or right after sunset since this is when the sun and moon are in perfect balance with each other. If the aura is too damaged, watch it and see what kind of negative energy has attacked your home. Then you can cleanse the damage by placing white candles in each corner of your house and moving them around the aura to heal it.

Psychic protection is an essential part of starting any psychic practice. At first, it might feel like a hassle to do all these rituals daily, but as soon as you experience the positive effects of shielding yourself from negative energies, you'll never want to stop. After all, who wouldn't want to live their lives with complete protection from all the harmful energies of the world?

To protect yourself from psychic attacks, keep your aura and your home shielded at all times. The easiest way to do this is by cleansing your aura and your home regularly. This will also reduce the chances of getting negative thoughts, emotions, and illness into your body. If you ever come under attack from a negative spirit, immediately cleanse yourself and your home by placing saltwater and white candles around your house. Also, remember to meditate every day by keeping your thoughts positive and refusing to think about harmful intentions.

You never know who might want to send negative thoughts and energies into your life, but you can be sure that they won't succeed with psychic protection. Whether you shield yourself or meditate every day, the important thing is to remain positive and stay away from any negative energies.

Appendix of Terms

If you're new to the world of spirituality and psychics, then the chances are that you have come across many unfamiliar terms in the book. This appendix can be your quick go-to guide if you need help understanding or remembering the definition of each term.

Psychic

Psychics are gifted individuals who can provide information about one's past, present, or future. They can't communicate with the deceases nor deliver information coming from them. Their main power comes from their strong intuition. You can become a psychic by developing and strengthening your intuition.

Clair

Being a "Clair" means having heightened senses in one or more areas. The word "Clair" comes from the words "clear" and "clarity." For instance, if someone is a clairvoyant, they can see things clearly (in a spiritual sense, not a literal one). There are four main ways in which someone can physically receive extrasensory information. These are clairvoyance, claircognition, clairsentience, and clairaudience. Some people are naturally born with these abilities. However, they can be developed, grown, sharpened, and tapped into during our lifetimes. These powers are crucial to receiving guidance in our life paths and journeys. Honing and making use of them can help us raise our consciousness. There are several types of supernatural sensations and intuition, such as:

Clairvoyance - "Clear seeing."

Clairvoyance is extrasensory seeing. People with this type of gift can see things with the mind's eye that anyone else can't see. These can be people, objects, spirits, symbols, colors, scenes, etc.

Claircognition - "Clear cognition"

Claircognition refers to having very strong gut feelings. Claircognizant individuals trust these feelings enough to use that information for guidance. They also use this ability to interpret messages that they receive during readings.

Clairsentience - "Clear feeling."

Clairsentience is getting a certain feeling or vibe that you just can't explain. For instance, clairsentients can walk into a room and feel like something doesn't sit right or shake hands with someone and feel instant comfort. This particular feeling can help them infer important information.

Clairaudience - "Clear hearing."

Clairaudience is the ability to hear messages that aren't audible to the normal human ear. These often sound like reverberations or loud thoughts.

Clairempathy - "Clear emotion."

Clairempathy refers to the supernatural ability to strongly sense or feel, within oneself, the emotions or attitudes of others.

Clairscent - "Clear smelling"

People with clairscent abilities can smell odors and scents that others can't pick up on. These often carry significant meanings or messages delivered by Spirit.

Clairgustance - "Clear tasting."

Clairs can often taste a certain substance brought by the Spirit in order to convey a certain meaning or essence. This ability is known as clairgustance.

Clairtangency - "Clear touching."

Some psychics or mediums can tell who an object belongs to just by touching it, known as clairtangency.

Chakras

The word "chakra" refers to a body's energy centers. In Sanskrit, the word literally translates into "wheel" or "disk." This symbolizes the wheels of the spinning energy in the body. Each wheel corresponds to a major organ or specific nerve bundles. Our chakras need to stay balanced or open to maintain their optimum function. When one falls out of tune, one may experience emotional or physical symptoms associated with this particular chakra. We have seven main chakras running along our spines. These are:

The Crown Chakra

The crown chakra can be found at the top of the head. It represents our spiritual connection to the universe, people, and ourselves. The crown chakra also plays a great role in a person's life's purpose.

The Third Eye Chakra

The third eye chakra can be found between one's eyes. This chakra is responsible for our gut instincts, making it responsible for a person's intuition. This is why it's very significant in the world of mediumship and psychics. The third eye chakra is also associated with imagination.

The Throat Chakra

The throat chakra is found in one's throat. It is responsible for our ability to communicate and express ourselves verbally.

Someone with a blocked throat chakra may face problems with self-expression.

The Heart Chakra

The heart chakra is found near one's heart in the chest's center. The heart chakra is responsible for our ability to love and express compassion. We need to open our heart chakras to give and accept love.

The Solar Plexus Chakra

The solar plexus chakra is found in the stomach area. It is representative of one's self-esteem and confidence. We need to balance our heart chakras to feel in control of our lives.

The Sacral Chakra

The sacral chakra is found right below the belly button. It is associated with one's creative and sexual energy. The sacral chakra is also responsible for your ability to relate to your and other people's emotions.

The Root Chakra

The root chakra can be found at the base of one's spine. It offers a foundation or a "root" for life. It allows us to feel grounded and provides us with the ability to hold out against challenges. It is also responsible for our sense of security and stability.

Twin Flames

There's a common misconception that twin flames are synonymous with soulmates. Twin flames can be described as a soul connection or a mirror soul. There's a theory that suggests that our souls can split into two halves after they reach a high frequency. In that case, your twin flame is your soul's other half. Think of it as a soul split into two bodies. Soulmates, however, are people who match the same energy as you. You can meet several soulmates, but you'll never have more than one twin flame. While the strong connection of twin flame is often found among romantic partners or leads up to a romance, your twin flame can be a friend or even a mentor. Twin flames feel strong, intuitive soul connections, share the same interests, thoughts, and feelings, are naturally drawn to each other, share an effortless understanding of one another, can be their authentic selves around each other, and may even have the same dreams.

Binaural Beats

When you listen to two tones with slightly different frequencies, your brain creates an illusion known as a binaural beat. Binaural beats can boost creativity, help with cognitive enhancement, allow you to enter a meditative state, reduce anxiety, improve your sleeping habits, enhance your mood, and help with attention, memory retention, and focus.

Astral Body

Your astral body is your physical body's counterpart. It accompanies your physical human body during its lifetime and doesn't separate from it. However, a person's astral body would survive their death.

Astral Projection

An astral projection is a voluntary out-of-body experience. When this happens, your "brain's body schema," or the way that your brain perceives your physical body or form, gets altered. In an out-of-body experience, nothing literally leaves your body when you're in astral projection. It's that your brain no longer perceives your physical form the way it's used to. This makes you feel detached from your consciousness for a short while. However, in spirituality, astral projections are perceived as the soul exiting its body and entering a new consciousness plane.

Aura

An aura is a spiritual energy field around living things that can't be seen. Any living thing has an aura. Auras have different colors, each of which offers insight into the person's (or any other living object's) spiritual and emotional energy. While aura colors aren't visible to the naked eye, auras can be felt. You can tell if someone is negative or is extremely friendly and outgoing. There are 7 Auratic layers:

Physical Aura Plane

This layer is representative of physical health and is the closest auratic layer to the skin.

Emotional Aura Plane

This Auratic layer corresponds to one's emotions. This layer will tell if you're feeling emotional or under the weather.

Mental Aura Plane

This plane is associated with reasoning, logic, and thoughts. It is the third layer away from our skin.

Astral Body Aura Plane

This plane is associated with our spiritual health and our ability to love.

Etheric Aura Plane

This plane is where our psychic abilities lie, allowing us to tap into the energies of others and connect with people who are on the same wavelength.

Celestial Aura Plane

This is the plane where you can find your intuition and dreams. It is associated with enlightenment and creativity.

Causal Aura Plane

This is the last and 7th plane and is responsible for harmonizing all the other Auratic layers and guiding you on your life's path.

There are 9 Auratic colors, most of which correspond to a certain chakra. White auras are rare and related to the crown chakra, while violet is related to the third eye chakra. Blue corresponds to the throat chakra, green and pink are the heart chakra colors, and yellow relates to the solar plexus chakra. Orange is related to the sacral chakra, and the root chakra is red. A black chakra represents a block in the flow of chakras.

Mediumship

Mediumship reflects being a spiritual medium. Mediums are middlemen or individuals who can bridge between the world of the living and the realm of the dead. Mediums can communicate with souls who have passed away. They use various methods to interact with Spirit and deliver their messages to loved ones. Mediums can typically hear, see, or feel the information that Spirit provides.

Physical Mediumship

Physical mediumship happens in the medium's environment, making it visible, audible, and felt by everyone present. This type of mediumship involves the manipulation of energies and includes various techniques like:

Levitation

Levitation is the movement of things without human interaction or interference. This usually happens through telekinesis or ectoplasmic activities. Telekinesis is the movement of objects using one's mental power.

Ectoplasm

It is a substance extracted from a medium's body and mixed with an etheric substance.

Raps/Percussion

Spirit raps and knocks in response to yes and no questions.

Materialization

It is the turning of Spirit into a physical entity.

Automatic Writing

It is a means of interacting with spirit. Mediums empty their brain and "automatically" write down messages from Spirit.

Mental Mediumship

Mental mediumship occurs inside of a medium's consciousness. It utilizes the five physical senses and often occurs through telepathy. This is why it's often called telepathic mediumship. The medium relates the messages they see, hear, or feel to their client. They can obtain this information by using several states of trans like clairvoyance, clairaudients, and clairsentience.

Séance

A séance is an attempt to communicate with the deceased. The word is French for the words "session" and "seat," and later became used in English to describe a meeting of individuals who are attempting to receive spiritualistic messages. A séance is typically conducted by a medium who is trying to go into a trance, creating a channel for communication with Spirit.

Divination

Divination is the act of determining or interpreting the hidden cause, meaning, or significance of events. Sometimes it involves the foretelling of the future. Divination is done by numerous psychological, natural, and other methods. It is most commonly conducted using horoscopes, crystal balls, astrology, tarot cards, and Ouija boards.

Numerology

Numerology is often used as a divination tool. It refers to the study of numbers and interpreting them through a spiritual lens. It is based on the idea that everything in the universe is related to a master number: 1, 2, 3, 4, 5, 6, 7, 8, or 9, each of which has a certain theme. People use spirituality to make deeper sense of various areas of their lives. While a person's life path number is calculated using their birth date, their expression, soul urge, and personality number are calculated using their birth name. These core numbers can tell a lot about a person and their journey.

Palmistry

Palmistry is a divination tool that is also known as chiromancy or chirosophy. It involves the interpretation of undulations and lines that are found on a person's palm. It helps read character, how a person makes decisions, and how they approach actions.

Conclusion

There are many misconceptions and stereotypes about psychics and mediums. Many people believe that psychic mediums are scammers. While many people take advantage of the industry, many psychic mediums are blessed with intuitive gifts. Taking the time to read about a psychic medium's abilities, what you should expect during a reading, and the type of questions you should ask will allow you to spot scammers easily. Psychics can't magically make you rich or rid you of bad luck. Fortunately, there are very few scammers in the market as they tend to get exposed for their bad reputation. Each psychic is gifted with unique abilities in different degrees. The best ones always have the client's best interests at heart.

Most people also believe that psychics can read minds, which isn't true at all. Psychic mediums can tune into a person's energy field, allowing them to obtain information about that person. However, they're not capable of exploring a person's thoughts. Psychics have heightened senses and states of trance, like clairvoyance, clairaudience, and clairsentience. These allow them to obtain messages and conduct relatable readings. While the information can be related to a person's past, present, or future, psychic mediums don't know everything that happens in the individual's lifetime.

Finally, mediums and psychics can't predict the future. Instead, they help people by tuning into their energies and using their gifts to provide insights into possible outcomes. They often do that by using tools like numerology, palmistry, astrology, tarot cards, and their pre-eminent extrasensory abilities. This allows them to deliver and interpret information as accurately as possible.

Now that you have read this book, you are qualified enough to tell between genuine and fraudulent psychic mediums. You also have extensive information about the abilities of psychics and mediums and the difference between each. This book explores the different states of trance and supernatural abilities that psychic mediums possess and comprehensive details into psychic development. This means that you are now equipped with all the information you need to unlock the abilities of psychics and develop divination, mediumship, astral projection, telepathy, and clairvoyance.

This book is perfect for beginners and experienced individuals alike. This is because it offers detailed definitions, backgrounds, and step-by-step procedures on spiritual and psychic terms and various psychic, mediumship, and divination-related activities. This would come in handy for people looking to discover and develop their abilities and those who wish to practice and enhance their gifts. It is also suitable for people who would like to expand their knowledge of the spiritual and psychic world and anyone interested in the matter, even if they don't intend to put the information into practice.

Reading this book, you should be able to determine your strongest Clair, detect your own aura, achieve astral projection, connect with your spirit guides, contact the spirit world, communicate telepathically, and use various tools of divination. This indispensable information, along with persistence and practice, can help you become an incredible psychic medium.

Part 2: Empath

How Empaths and Highly Sensitive People Can Thrive by Harnessing Their Powers and Psychic Abilities

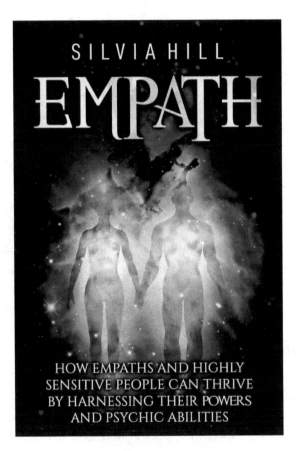

Introduction

Empathy is a feature of the human personality that manifests itself in varying degrees and can impact a person's life in more than one way. Simply feeling someone else's position and being able to place yourself in their shoes is empathy, but the accuracy with which you can do this and the impact of this empathy on your own life is something that needs your attention. This book will explore all the ideas, concepts, pros, and cons of being an empath and even living with one. We all have some degree of empathy. On one end of the spectrum is a person who feels empathy so strongly that it can often override their own emotions, becoming a hindrance in their lives. At the other extreme are people classified as psychopaths who live in their own shell, and even if they want to, they are unable to feel anything for another person. The average person lies somewhere in the middle of this spectrum. We will look at why and how empathy is developed in a person and how it can influence their life.

Similarly, understanding the level of empathy in people around you is also a vital tool. We all have different emotional needs, and those with a higher level of empathy are different from those with a lower level of empathy. To communicate and co-exist with these people appropriately, we need to know how we can connect with them at a deeper emotional level. When you have a spouse, a child, a parent, or a coworker who has a different place on the empathy spectrum than you, it can be challenging to get along with them and develop a meaningful relationship.

In this book, we will look at various tools, techniques, and strategies that you can use to more effectively communicate and connect with individuals who are different kinds of empaths. We will look at the key things that make an empath different from other emotional conditions, such as a highly sensitive person. Based on the latest research, we will also look at how an empath can even be physically different. They are literally wired differently, and we will look at how this influences their lives and the people around them.

If you fall into the empathy category, this will impact your entire life, it's part of your personality, your mind, and it's something that cannot be looked at in isolation. This book will look at all the different aspects of life from the lens of an empath and how you can make the most of each situation that you come across. Whether facing challenges at work or dealing with intimate relationships, this book is a complete roadmap of how you can navigate life as an empath.

If you are looking for an easy-to-follow guide, one that's filled with helpful advice from people who have actually been there and done that, this is the resource you need. If you are ready to improve your life today, let's get started with the empath's journey.

Chapter 1: Empathy: An Introduction

"I know how you feel." This is a sentence that so many people say when we're sad or crying. We just assume that they are trying to be nice because how can anyone really know or understand what we are going through? Well, an empath can.

An empath is very sensitive and is unusually attuned to other people's emotions and feelings. In other words, they don't only sympathize, but they can feel what everyone around them is feeling as well. They are the last people you ask to put themselves in your shoes because they are already there. For instance, when at a funeral, an empath can take on other people's feelings and sense their loss, pain, and sadness. If they are at a wedding, they can feel everyone else's happiness and excitement as well. Depending on the situation, it can feel like either a gift or a curse. It's a gift when it helps the empath establish healthy professional and personal relationships. They can emphasize more than most people and tell what someone is feeling by looking at their face. When someone is upset or going through something, but they smile and pretend to be ok, they can fool anyone in the room except an empath, who can see through anyone's mask.

Empaths can feel other people's feelings because their brains function differently from most people. An empath's brain contains highly-responsive mirror neurons that trigger feelings like compassion and allow empaths to mirror the emotions of the people around them. An empath can be very sensitive to the electromagnetic waves emitted by other people's hearts or brains, allowing the empath to feel their emotions on a deeper level. Simply put, an empath is like a walking sponge that absorbs other people's emotions, whether negative or positive, which can be overwhelming at times. For this reason, empaths need to set healthy boundaries to protect themselves from the overwhelming emotions they feel when they are around others. In the coming chapters, we will discuss in detail how to set healthy boundaries.

Being an empath has many advantages. If you are an empath, you'll find making new friends and maintaining those friendships quite easy. This is because empaths are great listeners, are always there for their friends whenever needed, are generous, and have big hearts, all of which are qualities that make a person a great friend. But being an empath can be a curse as well. All of these qualities that make them such great friends can take a toll on their mental health. Since empaths can feel what everyone is feeling, they will be attuned to their friends' emotions. So, when your friend comes to you with a problem, and they are feeling anxious, sad, or angry, you will find yourself taking on these emotions as well and thus feeling extremely overwhelmed. The problem that empaths face is that they tend to adopt other people's issues as if they are their own. So, when someone comes to them with a problem or asks them a huge favor, they just can't say no even if it's inconvenient. Empaths find it hard to set proper boundaries, which is why they cannot say no, no matter how big the ask is.

Spending time with other people can drain an empath. Think of an empath like a battery that's constantly working when surrounded by people – eventually – it will drain and require recharging. For this reason, you'll find that most empaths are actually introverts. Introverts, by nature, like to spend some time alone to recharge after spending time around other people. If introverts don't recharge, they can feel anxious or even depressed. Additionally, empaths can also suffer from social anxiety because of how overwhelmed they get in a crowd. Other people's chatter and noises can affect the empath's sensitive nature. An empath will feel more relaxed and in their element when they are in a quiet place like nature.

In addition to panic attacks, an empath can also feel tired, depressed, and anxious when they are overwhelmed by other people's emotions or in a stressful situation. They may also exhibit physical symptoms like headaches, exhaustion, and fast heart rate. When an empath takes on other people's emotions, they usually have trouble differentiating these feelings from their own, which is why they exhibit these mental and physical symptoms. To avoid feeling overwhelmed, an empath needs to be able to recognize their own feelings and separate them from other people's feelings.

What Is Empathy?

To better understand what it feels like to be an empath, you'll first need to have a better understanding of what empathy is. Empathy is the ability to put yourself in someone else's place so you can understand their thoughts and feelings and see things from their perspective. Not to be confused with sympathy, which is being moved or touched by someone else's feelings while keeping an emotional distance. For instance, if an empath sees a person mourning the loss of a pet, they may be able to understand their pain by easily putting themselves in this person's shoes and feel their loss, even though they have never lost a pet themselves – or even have one. However, a regular person may simply sympathize by feeling sorry but without a deep understanding or feeling the person's emotions. Feeling empathy doesn't require you to go through the same experiences or live in the same circumstances to understand other people's feelings. Your brain will simply mirror their emotions, and you will feel them as if they are your own.

It's easy for most people to understand their own emotions and see things from their own perspectives. However, stepping into someone else's shoes may not be as easy. You need empathy to understand and feel exactly other people's emotions. That said, just as there are people in the world who aren't honest or caring, you will also encounter people who aren't empathetic. You will find people who are dismissive towards other people's feelings or get aggressive or angry when they see someone suffering or crying. For instance, we hear in the news people committing the most horrendous acts, and we wonder how they can do this without feeling any remorse? Notorious serial killer Ted Bundy didn't have interpersonal empathy and didn't feel any pity for his victims or guilt for any of the crimes he committed. Empathy isn't universal, so don't expect people to feel the same way you do or respond to other people's pain and suffering like you do.

That said, it isn't just serial killers or criminals who cannot feel empathy. If you take a look around you, you'll probably notice a few people who are unable to feel or even sympathize with other people's pain and suffering. Some managers refuse to give an employee a day off to attend a family member's funeral, husbands who can't seem to relate or understand their wives' struggles with raising a new baby alone at home.

As we have mentioned, not everyone can feel empathy. One of the main things that influence a person's ability to feel empathy is genetics. As a matter of fact, women are more likely to feel empathy and understand other people's emotions than men. So, does that mean that empaths are born, not created? Well, there is no denying that genetics play a huge role, but your environment and social interactions can help you develop empathy, among other things.

For instance, a child raised by one or two empath parents will more than likely develop empathy as well. This is because they grew up watching and observing their parents' emphasis on their needs. They were taught the importance of emotions and how to build relationships and connections with others. When a parent creates a connection with their child and establishes a shared experience, this will enable the child to connect with other people's emotions and develop empathy.

Different Types of Empathy

Renowned psychologists Paul Ekman and Daniel Goleman have broken down empathy into three categories.

- **Emotional Empathy**

    Emotional empathy allows you to feel other people's emotions as if they are your own and put yourself in their position. You may even feel their physical pain as well. For instance, if you are sitting with a friend and they get a paper cut, you may cringe or even yell "Ouch" as if you are the one who cut their finger. You are basically feeling whatever the people around you are feeling, whether physical or emotional, on some level. These emotions cause you to feel worried or distressed when someone you care about is going through something.

You will find that great friends, supportive parents, compassionate leaders, and caregivers have all developed emotional empathy. But this type of empathy can overwhelm you and impact your emotional well-being because you'll be so concerned with other people's problems you'll start ignoring your own.

• **Cognitive Empathy**

Cognitive empathy gives you the ability to understand people's mental states. Simply put, you can understand what they are thinking in any given situation. Cognitive empathy is different from emotional empathy because you will find that you can put yourself in another person's shoes without taking on or feeling their emotions. Therefore, you will respond to other people's emotions using logic rather than feelings. In other words, you won't be clouded by your emotions, which can make a person seem cold in some situations.

Cognitive empathy can help you in your personal and professional life. Since it gives you the chance to understand what another person is thinking and get inside their head, negotiate business deals, resolve conflicts, and motivate your team.

• **Compassionate Empathy**

Compassionate empathy is the balance between emotional and cognitive empathy. It connects your heart with your brain to create a middle ground to understand both a person's emotions and thoughts in any given situation. In addition to feeling and understanding what a person is going through, compassionate empathy will also move you to act to solve other people's problems. This type is considered the best and most helpful of the three types we have mentioned because it allows you to consider the intellectual and emotional side of a person so you can respond properly.

What Does an Empath Feel?

Empathy is about feeling other people's feelings but is that it? An empath has various emotions and thoughts when they are around other people. They may not be able to recognize these feelings since they are usually overwhelmed and can't distinguish their feelings from those of others. Understanding an empath's feelings will give you a deeper understanding of your abilities.

- **Art Can Affect You**

    Do you cry when you listen to a sad song? Do you get emotional when love conquers all at the end of a movie? Are you able to feel the emotions behind a painting or a picture? If you answer yes to any of these, then this means that you are easily affected by different types of arts like paintings, movies, or songs because, most certainly, you are an empath.

In addition to art, tragic news and violent scenes can also negatively impact an empath. If you are watching news happening on the other side of the world or a violent scene in a movie, you will feel the pain as if it's happening to you. This can be extremely overwhelming and affect your mental health. For this reason, try to avoid the news and violent media content as much as you can.

- **You Identify as an Introvert**

Unlike extroverts who feel more energetic when surrounded by crowds, an empath will probably identify more with introversion. They feel overwhelmed in crowds, so they choose to be around one or two people to avoid feelings of being overwhelmed. As mentioned, after spending time with people, an empath prefers to spend time alone to recharge. You can recharge by taking a walk in nature, sitting by yourself in a quiet room, or practicing your favorite hobby. One of the most famous introverts in history is the late famous painter Vincent Van Gogh who found refuge and escape from the loud world in his paintings.

- **Intimate Relationships Can Be Difficult**

There is no denying that every relationship has its struggles. However, for someone who can feel every little thing their partner is feeling and can tell when they are lying, being intimate in a close relationship can be overwhelming; having someone sharing your space can be challenging for an empath like you. Your home is where you spend some time alone to recharge, so having someone with you at all times and their emotions just waiting for you to absorb can be challenging. For this reason, you may find that many empaths prefer to be single. On the other hand, others manage to have successful relationships by learning to set boundaries and finding a person that respects these boundaries.

- **You Feel People's Physical Pain**

As mentioned earlier, being an empath doesn't mean only feeling other people's emotions, but you can also feel their physical pain as well. If you are in a hospital or around a friend who is injured or sick, you may feel their pain as if it's your own. We don't mean here that you will feel worried about them or sympathize with their pain; we mean that you will feel the exact pain they are feeling. For instance, if a friend of yours was in a car accident and they broke their left arm, you may feel pain in your left arm as well. The neurons in your brain will mirror what the other person is experiencing physically in your body. It's as if you are the one who was in the accident and broke your arm.

- **Experiencing Sudden Emotions**

You are out with a friend having lunch at a restaurant, you are joking and laughing, and suddenly, you feel sad. You don't understand why or how you are feeling this emotion. When an empath is around people, they can take on anyone's emotion at any time. It can be the waiter serving your food who got upset about something at work or a person at the next table who just received terrible news. As an empath, when you are in a public place, you can take on anyone's feelings without even trying to.

- **You Seek Peace and Quiet**

The vibe or a feeling of a room can have a massive effect on an empath. They prefer peaceful and quiet environments where they can recharge and calm themselves. This is why you will find yourself gravitating towards beautiful and quiet places like outside in nature, a garden, a museum, or a beautifully decorated room. You will be able to flourish in these places. On the other hand, loud and chaotic environments can drain your energy.

- **You Always Care**

Empaths always care about other people. When they pick up on what others are feeling, they have the urge to want to help them, and they act accordingly. If you can't find a way to help someone in distress, you will feel very disappointed. It's always great to lend a hand and help others, but you should also pay attention to your needs and energy, or you will burn out and won't be able to help others or yourself.

- **You Avoid Conflict**

Empaths hate conflicts and will do anything to avoid them. Since they are infinitely more sensitive, they may not be able to handle conflicts. They can't help feeling hurt and take comments personally. When an empath is arguing with someone, they aren't only dealing with their emotions but also with the other person's emotions and absorbing them. This can be very overwhelming.

- **You Feel Different**

Although you can feel what others are feeling, you will struggle with relating to other people. Absorbing people's emotions and feeling them as your own may make you feel you don't fit in because you constantly struggle to understand all these emotions you are absorbing. You could start to feel alone and that no one understands you, and possibly, you will keep your emotions and sensitivities to yourself to avoid feeling judged for being different. However, empathy is a unique gift that you should never hide or be ashamed of.

- **You Can't Set Boundaries**

Learning to set boundaries is essential for any empath. However, many empaths struggle with doing it because empaths can't simply press a button that will stop them from absorbing others' emotions or wanting to help them.

The sensitive empath may think that they don't care about helping other people if they set boundaries. On the contrary, setting boundaries allows you to protect your mental health and energy from feeling overwhelmed by your and others' emotions. When you take care of yourself, you will be able to take care of the people in your life.

Being an empath is a beautiful gift that many people have used to help themselves and others create something beautiful. You will find many sensitive artists to be empaths – Ed Sheeran uses his gift to create beautiful, authentic, and relatable lyrics. You will feel that he is describing your emotions. Nelson Mandela was another excellent example of an empath who felt others' pain, so he sacrificed his own needs to help them. Mother Teresa and Mahatma Gandhi are also empaths who lived their lives in the service of others. The world can use more empathy, and it's a good thing that there are more empaths like you around.

We need more empaths in our lives. People who care, love, and heal. This is a unique gift that will allow you to make a difference in the world. We know that being an empath can be a struggle sometimes, but hopefully, in the coming chapters, we will be able to help you to understand your gift better and to learn to use your abilities while setting healthy boundaries.

Chapter 2: The Abilities of an Empath

Most empaths believe that having heightened sensitivity and awareness is burdensome. The thing is that they don't take the time to learn more about their abilities and understand how gifted they are, which is why they try to shut their empathy off. You must learn how valuable your abilities as an empath are. Learning more about your unique traits and how they set you apart from the rest of the world will help you appreciate your gift and come to see that your high sensitivity puts you at an advantage. There will be times when you feel no one understands you or reciprocates your ability to cater to others' physical and emotional needs. However, embarking on the journey to self-discovery and learning about the fantastic upsides of being highly empathetic can help you shift your view.

Being highly sensitive in the world we live in is tough. You may have been called an introvert or a buzz kill when you just needed some alone time. You may have had people take advantage of your compassion or inability to just say "no," or constantly struggle to identify which feelings are yours. Being an empath comes with endless emotional fatigue and intense waves of emotions. Your tendency to care about the most minor details, which also causes you to feel upset over those small details, may have thrown others off. It's hard to communicate with others when their feelings deeply influence yours or when they don't understand why you can't just "let things go." It comes as no surprise that you've always thought that something was wrong with you.

It's about time that you let go of the false belief about yourself and realize that you're not an alien. You can do that by delving deep into your authentic nature as an empath. It also helps to see that you aren't alone and work toward accepting your heightened awareness and sensitivities. Fortunately, this book will teach you many helpful methods that will allow you to use your abilities in ways to benefit you rather than drain you.

In this chapter, you will discover that everything you believed was wrong with you is actually your key to making the world a better place. You'll learn all about your abilities as an empath and why you are gifted. This chapter also covers the different types of empaths and the differences between introverted and extroverted. Finally, you'll come across a list of common careers adopted by empaths.

The Abilities of an Empath

So many online resources focus on the downsides of being an empath and the things that highly aware and sensitive people should take care of. This is perhaps why you, and numerous other individuals who possess this incredible ability, underestimate the powers you have. It's why countless empaths try to get rid of their abilities to "fit in" and just experience life like the rest of humanity. The fact is that there are numerous reasons why it's incredible to be an empath. Perhaps another reason you forget to give yourself enough credit's that you're more concerned about the well-being of everyone else. Once you verse yourself in your abilities, you will become a compelling force in your community. The most significant proof is that some of the most influential historical figures, such as Mother Theresa, Nelson Mandela, and Mahatma Gandhi, were empaths. The following are some of the abilities that empaths possess.

- **Highly Analytical**

Empaths are excellent at viewing and analyzing situations deeply, from all sides. A non-empath is likely to see a situation from only their own perspective or at least have certain biases. However, empaths can look into situations from the points of view of everyone involved. Empaths are likely to pick up on symbols and themes, making them the center of pivotal interactions. Their insights and ability to see right through things and straight to the point allow them to disengage from events to analyze the root of the issue. This means that they're likely to develop ideal solutions and compromises for any type of problem or disagreement. They are very helpful at fixing the problems or offering advice to the people they care about. This ability makes empaths prominent visionary leaders.

• Very Intuitive

Empaths are very compassionate and may find it hard to say no to any requests for their help, even when it costs them mentally or emotionally. Fortunately, empaths are blessed with highly intuitive abilities that can help them protect themselves from energy vampires and self-absorbed individuals. Empaths are very in tune with their own feelings and emotions and those of others, which helps them keep negative situations at arm's length. You probably often have this inexplicable and robust gut feeling if you're an empath. This is your intuition trying to communicate with you, so be sure to listen.

• Empathy Over Long-Distance

We've all experienced that sensation when someone we haven't spoken to for ages pops into our minds, and we get that feeling we should contact them. In empaths, this ability is particularly strong, and they can tell when people, no matter where on Earth they are or how long it's been since they spoke to them, need them. Empaths can just feel it whenever someone they care about is having a bad day, even when they aren't around. Some may even experience similar symptoms to that of the person they're "sensing." For instance, an empath may get headaches despite not getting them frequently if someone they're deeply connected to has a migraine.

• Having an Impactful Presence

When empaths are around, their presence can be felt. Empaths can use their energy in incredibly positive ways, such as healing others, when they learn to put their fears behind them. Loosening up emotionally and avoiding using their gifts wherever they feel drained and overwhelmed can be quite beneficial. Empaths are blessed with natural caretaking abilities. Remember how we mentioned that Mother Theresa was an empath? They are gifted with the ability to heal by just being present. This is perhaps because they can see right through facades and determine the uncommunicated feeling of those around them. Empaths can tune into the needs of others and adapt themselves and their attitude in a way that they could be of help. However, many empaths may not feel comfortable putting themselves out there, so they reveal this ability to those closest to them.

- **Heightened Creativity**

Empaths are very creative, which is why many of them, like Nicole Kidman and Oprah Winfrey, excel in artistic and inspirational fields. Empaths have the unique ability to delve deep into abstract concepts, like emotions, and come up with corresponding concrete ideas and solutions. Once empaths realize and unleash their creativity, they'll be able to make great things happen. Even those who end up working in analytical fields approach their careers with more innovative mindsets. Empaths may end up feeling unfulfilled if they find themselves trapped in environments where they have to conform to traditional ways of doing things.

- **Refining Your Powers**

Many empaths are born with potent abilities. This is especially the case for those destined to achieve greatness, just like the aforementioned influential figures. However, in most cases, empaths will need to develop and grow their abilities. They need to enhance and nourish their skills to turn into fully-fledged powers. While growth in an empaths' skills happens naturally, considering they'll learn more about the world and find their place within it, active development can allow them to use their skills to help themselves and those around them.

If you're hoping to refine your skills, the first thing you need to do is accept that you're an empath. If there's something you've learned while growing up, it's that you can't just turn your abilities and emotions off. Reading this book means that you've finally decided to embrace your nature and stop fighting it. Now that you've acknowledged your gifts, you can start channeling them for the good of the world.

Listening to your gut and following your instincts are also essential aspects of refining your empathetic abilities. As an empath, your instincts are almost always accurate. However, they're only worth something if you decide to listen to them. Spend time refining your intuition. You can practice meditation and use tools like crystals and essential oils to open your third eye chakra if you're into spirituality. You can also simply practice listening to your gut instinct even in the smallest situations throughout your day.

A lot of empaths struggle with their self-esteem. Besides growing up feeling insecure about their abilities, many empaths are easily drained and used by energy vampires. Changing how you think about yourself and knowing that you're worth it can help you realize and build your strength. There is nothing more powerful than a confident empath.

Since you're probably easily influenced by the energies of those around you, you need to protect yourself from negative individuals. Everyone has their bad days, and your ability to cater to the needs of those around you is what makes you special. However, some people constantly exude negative energy, hindering your equilibrium and peace of mind. This is why you need to set strong boundaries with harmful individuals and prioritize preserving your energy.

Part of being an empath is being a natural caretaker. Another huge trait's the dire need for some alone time. If you want to stay mentally, physically, and emotionally healthy, you need to be able to determine when you've had your fair share of giving for the day. You should make sure you have sufficient time to unwind and recharge from the day., whether this means indulging in self-care, sleeping, or participating in an activity that you like. Remember that you can't practice your abilities or help others out when you're drained.

Since changes in energy easily influence you, you need to practice seeing the silver lining. Negative things happen all the time. If your energy levels take a dive every time an unfortunate event takes place, you'll get exhausted. Since your empathy can't be turned off, you need to train yourself to see the glass half full of each situation. Changing your mindset takes a lot of time and effort. You also won't be able to maintain it all the time. However, working on it can help maintain your well-being.

Last but not least, you need to love yourself to nourish your skills. Compassion makes up a massive part of being an empath. So, here's food for thought: why do you show everyone compassion but yourself?

Why Being an Empath Is a Gift

Being an empath means that you're a natural healer. You are gifted with healing energy; you can communicate to others through your voice, hands, or even through a form of art. In fact, many empaths practice energy healing techniques because they believe they were destined to heal themselves and other people. Your heightened sensitivity isn't just internal; it extends to your other senses, allowing you to enjoy the aromas of beverages, flowers, food, and essential oils more than the average person. Empaths who further refine their sense of smell may smell diseases and deaths in people and animals. This is an ability that could save lives.

Empaths also have an enhanced intuition, or sixth sense, allowing them to sense potential dangers before they occur. While heightened senses and feelings mean you feel negative situations more intensely than others, you also get to experience greater highs. Many people would think that an empath's ability to feel so profoundly would make them somewhat prone to depression and anxiety. Although this is true in some cases, most empaths are highly enthusiastic. They approach life and its experiences with great joy and an inclination to be more caring, tolerant, compassionate, and understanding. These are precisely the traits that the world needs more of to be a better place.

Everyone in the world needs some alone time to unwind and relax from the pressures of the world. However, empaths particularly find comfort in being alone or spending time with themselves. Their heightened awareness and sensitivity make alone time crucial for regaining balance and de-stressing. If you're an empath, you may need your fair share of alone time to recover and re-energize, which as counter-intuitive as it sounds, is actually a good thing. Spending time alone allows them to be more self-aware, introspective, and reflective.

Empaths have a very creative approach to life, in general. Not only are they usually artistically gifted, but they can also think out of the box regarding scenarios, possibilities, solutions, and experiences. They have a different way of viewing things, which allows them to conceptualize things far higher than the average person.

Aside from being emotional themselves, empaths are great at reading emotional cues, making them sensitive to other people's feelings. They're great at sensing other people's emotional and physical needs without any form of verbal communication. This skill is beneficial for handling infants, animals, and plants.

Being extremely sensitive to the emotions and feelings of others makes them especially aware when they're being lied to. Do you know how people tend to say that they're fine when they really aren't? Empaths can see right through that. They can tell what's going on beneath the facade that people may put up.

Types of Empaths

There are numerous types of empaths, each of which links to the world in a unique way. While some traits are found in all empaths, each different type has heightened sensitivity and emotional reactions toward specific types of beings and situations. Many believe that there are six to eight types of empaths, at max. You may be surprised to learn that there's a total of 11 types. Some empaths are typically more powerful than other types. The Heyoka empath, for instance, is considered the most forceful. This is because they are highly spiritual, serve as emotional mirrors, and are thought to be able to read minds. If you're an empath, you may possess traits that trace you back to more than one type. However, the chances are that you'll display dominance in just one type.

The following are the 11 types of empaths:

1. Claircognizant Empath

Claircognizant empaths are also known as intuitive empaths. These individuals know what they need to do or how they need to act in certain situations, even when there is no solid reason or rationale behind these gut instincts. Besides being able to tell what they should or shouldn't do, these empaths can sense the energetic fields of others and can read people easily.

2. Psychometric Empath

These individuals can obtain information from the energy that photographs, places, or significant objects r significant emit.

3. Flora Empath

Flora empaths can communicate with plants. They use their energy to cater to their needs, allowing them to live and thrive.

4. Fauna Empath

Fauna empaths can communicate with animals and send them messages. This type of communication is typically initiated by the individual and not the animal.

5. Geomantic Empath

These empaths can receive signals and respond to signs from the earth or soil, which makes them particularly sensitive to natural disasters. They can tell that they will happen beforehand.

6. Telepathic Empath

These empaths use all their senses to determine other people's thoughts and feelings, even when they aren't verbally expressed.

7. Precognitive Empath

These individuals can feel certain events or situations before they occur. They may feel a wave of nervousness or anxiety as their intuition heightens.

8. Emotional Empath

These empaths can sense the emotions of others without obtaining background knowledge of the person's situation.

9. Physical Empath

Physical empaths can feel the pain and symptoms of others as if they were their own.

10. Medium/Psychic Empath

These types of empaths can see, hear, and communicate with spirits who have crossed over.

11. Heyoka Empath

As you know, this is the most powerful type of empath. They have an unconventional way of thinking and tend to mirror the emotions of others. They can foster emotional healing, among others.

Introverted vs. Extroverted Empaths

There are a lot of prevalent misconceptions about empaths. Most people believe that all empaths are introverts. While some empaths are introverted, many of them are extroverts. Like other people, each empath has their way of interacting and socializing with people. Introverted empaths have very low levels of tolerance when it comes to socializing. They typically despise small talk. Introverted empaths are also relatively quiet during social gatherings and may want to leave as early as possible. This is why they may prefer to show up with their own car. This way, they will not depend on others to get home. Introverted empaths prefer sticking to their small and close circle of friends, as this is where they feel most safe and comfortable. They shy away from parties and large gatherings. They often get overstimulated if they spend long periods surrounded by groups.

Extroverted empaths, on the other hand, are more interactive and verbal. Even though they're very sociable, they may be selective about their company. While they are open to outings, they often like to stick to the familiar and known territory. They also have unreliable energy levels. They may find it hard to decide whether they'd like to stay in or go out. Extroverted empaths are very open when it comes to their creativity. They even take pride in it.

Common Careers Adopted by Empaths

- Web developer
- Counselor
- Artist

- Veterinary technician
- Teacher
- Gardener
- Park ranger
- Graphic designer
- Librarian
- Editor
- Musician
- Social worker
- Professor
- Massage therapist
- Yoga instructor
- Therapist
- Dentist
- Business owner
- Nurse

Your heightened awareness, sensitivity, and empathy is a gift. It's not a curse or burden you need to conceal or switch off. Changing how you think about yourself can allow you to put your gifts to their best use. You will be able to use your empathy in ways that benefit you rather than drain you.

Chapter 3: Are You an Empath?

Envision this: You wake up, open your curtains, and let the sunshine through your window. "Today is a good day," you tell yourself and start getting ready for the day. You stop for coffee on your way to work and blast your favorite music in your ears. At this point, it feels like nothing can ruin your day. Everything is perfect until you run into a co-worker who's feeling under the weather, which of course, causes a huge shift in your emotions. Your good mood is long gone, and you feel just as blue as your friend. Does this sound familiar?

If you're an empath, you can feel the pain and experiences of others, just as if they were happening to you. This can make it challenging to provide your loved ones with the level of emotional support they need since you'll be trying to juggle the same emotions. As incredible as it's to be an empath, it comes with the inability to separate other people's feelings from your own.

We all have our own battles to fight that are both mentally and emotionally tiring; add to the mix being an empath, and it can feel like you're constantly fighting battles that aren't yours. Empaths get too caught up in the feelings and situations of others to the point of emotional exhaustion. This is also true for positive situations. While seemingly less burdensome than painful or sad events, extreme emotional stimulations can be a lot to handle, even if they're joyful and exciting. If you're an empath, you know you have a lifelong task of developing emotional management techniques and indulging in self-care. Otherwise, you'll be an anxious wreck.

If you're an extroverted empath, then the chances are that you're very familiar with the age-old question "should I go out or stay in?" Everyone feels torn between going out and taking the day off for themselves. However, for us empaths, it's different. We love connecting with others, but we fear that when our social battery runs out, we'll be quick to burn out. Being an empath means that you need some alone time to recharge, unwind, and process all your feelings and emotions. It's only fair after spending the day absorbing the pains, sadness, anger, excitement, worry, and fear of others. We know that if we are deprived of our fair share of alone time, we'll break down under pressure. Meanwhile, connecting with others can help us boost our mental health. It's a real struggle.

This brings us to our next point. If you're an empath, you're probably aware of the struggle that comes with people not understanding why alone time is a matter of life or death. Explaining why alone time is necessary is not always easy, especially when most people aren't informed as to what it means to be an empath – and how it is not the same as being a tad more compassionate, understanding, or sensitive than the average person to begin with. Besides, not all empaths are the same. Each individual uses this alone time for a unique purpose. For some, it's an opportunity to sift through the thoughts that revolve around in their heads. For others, it's when they work out which emotions belong to them and what they have absorbed from others. Some empaths simply use this time to reclaim their energy or strength, while others do it for all these reasons at once. Non-empaths don't need to spend as much time by themselves. Many of them also thrive in groups, which is why it can be hard to explain why an empath's alone time is that big of a deal.

Empaths need some time to adjust to the transition from low-stimulus to high-stimulus situations and environments and the other way around. This is perhaps why you may feel an odd sense of void after leaving large groups or parties or be extremely overwhelmed when making your way into a large crowd. Not everyone understands the need to take some time to process these staggering transitions and adjust to the strong waves of emotions that come with them.

Being an empath means so many things. It forgets to nourish yourself with the same amount of care, compassion, and understanding that you offer to others. It means that you find it hard not to go out of your way to help others, even if it compromises your own needs and well-being. It's also sensing negative emotions and instantly knowing that something is "off," even when no one else seems to notice. Being an empath can be extremely taxing, from being unable to withstand violence to being misunderstood and often taken advantage of. However, it's a gift that you wouldn't trade for the world if you took the time to understand.

It can be hard to determine whether you're an empath, especially when there's so much misconception about this "ability." The lack of education surrounding the topic, the frequent confusion between empaths and highly sensitive individuals, and the inaccurate labels and stereotypes can also leave you doubtful.

However, reading this chapter can help you determine whether you really are an empath.

Life as an Empath

When you're an empath, you learn that constantly protecting yourself is vital. It becomes second nature the more you start to understand yourself and become increasingly self-aware. You may have never really grasped your heightened sensitivity toward some TV and movie genres or your inability to tolerate harsh news and stories. You may have found it odd that you would rather know as little information as possible on some significant issues or events.

Now that you know you may be an empath, it probably all makes more sense. The world and its dynamics can feel a bit too heavy sometimes. We, the empaths of the world, have to carry the weight of being upset by all the horrible events happening on planet Earth, from natural disasters to the incomprehensible deeds that other people do. You might not have thought much of it at first, considering that adverse events would naturally sadden most people. However, it may have come across as a shock to realize that others don't feel things as deeply as you do. Growing up, many empaths don't realize that not everyone feels overwhelmed and wholly drained when others are hurting. Child empaths aren't aware that profoundly feeling the pain of others isn't considered an ordinary aspect of the human experience. You are very likely an empath if you relate to all of this.

You've probably tried to switch off your empathy at one point or another in your lifetime. The inability to get over feelings that aren't even yours, or the struggle to turn your thoughts off for just a few seconds, can ignite a deep sense of frustration within you. This is especially the case when someone close to you is involved. Empaths can't stomach the thought of having someone they deeply care about get hurt. Those close to you don't even need to express their sadness and sorrows aloud. Your heightened intuition and sensations will make you feel their emotions. Our empathetic imagination may keep you up all night, thinking about your loved ones who are in trouble.

As upsetting as it sounds, you may need to distance yourself from some people, regardless of how much you love and care about them, to maintain your mental, emotional, physical, and spiritual well-being. Some individuals are self-destructive. They don't care to take steps forward to improve their lives and their mental well-being. Unfortunately, their turmoil is yours. You can't sit back and help or support them from afar, as your empathy gets you deeply involved in their issues. Even though they probably don't mean it, these people can drain all your energy.

Some children who grow up to learn to be empaths sense familial issues. They may cry for months on end, for no apparent reason (or so their parents believe), due to a negative atmosphere in their family. Although parents try their best to keep these things hidden from their children to ensure that they're alright, empaths can feel this energy.

Although it comes with inescapable hardships, being an empath also has numerous upsides. Even if you've always disliked your hypersensitivity, you must admit that you admire your heightened consideration, understanding, and compassion toward those around you. As an empath, you hate the idea of others experiencing pain, and you surely never want to be the cause of it. Your peacemaking, great listening, and natural caretaking abilities may also lead to your friends warming up to you. The fact that you're very expressive also makes you likable.

Think about it. You are a better person because of your empathetic gifts. You are the one who determines whether your empathy is a sign of weakness or strength. If you're always going to feel these emotions and have empathetic tendencies, it only makes sense to let them be your source of empowerment. Let your love, loyalty, tolerance, and compassion be what sets you apart from the world and drives you forward. As an empath, you probably seldom hurt others yet spend so much of your time overthinking and analyzing how you treat those around you. Many empaths worry about unintentionally hurting others, even when they have no reason to. Empaths do their best to treat everyone the way they'd like to be treated, making them special.

Typically, the most significant challenge comes from the inability to find balance. This is why many empaths end up withdrawing - in an emotional sense – completely from challenging situations, hoping to avoid negative stimuli. While protecting your energy is a must, you can't just evade life altogether. Embracing your sensitivity and understanding that self-protection does not equate to avoidance can help. You are strong enough to endure all your emotions and heightened senses, which is why you are undoubtedly strong enough to face life with all its negative and positive aspects.

Quiz: Am I an Empath?

At this point, you should be able to tell if you're an empath. However, we put together a short quiz to help you confirm your opinion. If you check off most of these statements, then you're probably an empath.

- People are generally very easily drawn to me.

- I can tell how my friends feel before they even tell me.

- I am highly intuitive.

- People trust me enough to come to me with their problems.

- I cry easily when watching videos, cartoons, commercials, or movies.

- I often feel drained after social interactions.

- I have been told that I'm a good listener.

- Physical touch can sometimes feel uncomfortable or invasive.

- I've been told that I'm way too sensitive.

- The emotions of others easily influence my emotions.

- I often cry in public.

- My emotions drive me.

- Self-care is a priority.

- I can sense the energy around me.

- I'm very easily distracted.

- I indulge in spiritual practices.

- I need alone time or practice rituals to feel grounded and centered.

- Emotional music and lyrics can throw me off.

- I feel anxious and drained at large gatherings or parties.

- I don't feel comfortable meeting strangers.

- I'm very picky when it comes to touching people or things.

- I consider myself thoughtful, caring, and loyal.

- I usually feel it when things are "off."

- I feel different or misunderstood among others.

- I need time to recharge.

- I've always been great at caring for plants.

- I feel my best when surrounded by nature.

- I can somehow communicate or connect with babies or animals.

- Babies or animals naturally trust me.

- I burn out very easily.

- I sometimes cry to release my emotions.

- I feel physically heavy when I'm experiencing emotional pain.

- The weather influences my mood.

- I go out of my way to avoid witnessing disturbing images.

- I'm artistically gifted in some way.

What Type of Empath Am I?

As you already know, there are a total of 11 types of empaths in the world. This is why you may resonate with some traits more than others. As we explained in the previous chapter, you may identify with more than one type. However, the chances are that you'll have a dominant empathetic type that you strongly relate to.

As you may recall, you are a claircognizant empath if high levels of intuitiveness characterize you. While all empaths are intuitive, claircognizants can particularly sense how they should behave or act in certain situations or feel inclined to make certain decisions for no apparent reasons. Precognitive empaths also have heightened intuitiveness, as they can feel some situations or events before they happen. If you're a psychometric empath, you are affected by the energies of particular places, objects, or photographs.

If you're the kind of empath who's mainly into nature, you may be a flora empath. Perhaps you've always had the unique ability to sense the energy of plants. If you feel especially connected to the earth and are sensitive to natural disasters, on the other hand, you may be a geomantic empath. If you checked off the boxes that have to do with babies and children, then you're likely a fauna empath.

Can you tell how others are feeling before they even speak to you? In that case, you are more than likely a telepathic empath. You may also be an emotional empath if you can tune into other people's energies. If you can feel other people's physical pains, you are a physical empath. Medium empaths can communicate with spirits from the spiritual realm, and heyoka empaths can promote healing and mirror the emotions of others.

It's also important to remember that not all empaths are introverted. If you're an extroverted empath, you may have a higher tolerance when it comes to crowded settings and social gatherings. However, you would still need some time off to recharge. If you're an introverted empath, social gatherings can drain you really quickly.

Feelings of compassion can feel like a heavy weight to carry at times. However, empaths are used to being labeled names such as "drama queen," "overly emotional," or too much to handle." However, others don't realize that their lack of compassion is what we, empaths, find odd and even frightening. With that said, it would be nice to take a break from the never-ending feelings of compassion. Having no control over this constant sympathy, compassion, and empathy can leave you carrying the burdens of the world. It often leaves us suffering horribly, which is why we can't help but feel responsible for salvaging the situation. Though, we must admit that our empathy is a gift. It makes us better people every day.

Chapter 4: Empaths vs. Highly Sensitive People

We've established that empaths are people with deep feelings. They can instantly connect with others and the surrounding environment, often mirroring the feelings they pick up. So, generally speaking, doesn't that make them more sensitive than those around them? The answer is a definite yes, but that brings us to another point. If empaths are *highly sensitive* people, then what about highly sensitive people? Are highly sensitive people (HSP) and empaths the same? Not exactly.

Empaths and HSPs share many similarities, but there are differences. This chapter will delve deeper into the differences and similarities of both types of personalities.

What Is a Highly Sensitive Person (HSP)?

You can figure out that HSPs are more sensitive than ordinary people, if just from the name. However, people's sensitivity conveys their inner reaction to external stimuli rather than mirroring the feelings of those around them, as empaths do.

Scientifically speaking, highly sensitive people, or HSPs, have a heightened central nervous system sensitivity to the stimuli they absorb from their surroundings. These stimuli aren't limited to other people's emotions. Rather, their central nervous system responds strongly to all physical, emotional, environmental, and social stimuli. From a scientific perspective, it can be called sensory processing sensitivity or SPS.

Those around them usually describe HSPs as "being overly sensitive" or "reacting too strongly." Although they're often disparaged for their "oversensitivity," their sensitive nature gives them a lot of advantages.

HSPs have been studied meticulously by Dr. Elaine Aron and her colleagues. Their research found that HSPs make up about 20% of the population. They were able to summarize the characteristics of HSPs in four key aspects, expressed by the acronym DOES. DOES refers to the following traits:

- **Depth of Processing:** The ability to perceive and process information from their surroundings at a highly accurate speed. Despite that fact, they usually take a lot of time to make a decision since they need time to analyze information from every angle, study each course of action, and make a decision backed by reason.

- **Overstimulation:** Becoming overwhelmed by the amount of information they take in. Their sensory system perceives stimuli like sounds, smells, and touch to a much higher degree than non-HSPs, making them feel overwhelmed by everyday life.

- **Emotional Reactivity:** Reacting strongly to the stimuli they perceive and feel. "E" might also stand for empathy, which is the ability to feel others' emotions.

- **Sensing the Subtle:** Being able to notice and analyze subtle actions. Like a fine-tuned sensor, they're able to read another person's body language and understand their emotions from the way they talk or act.

How to Know If You're an HSP

There are a few ways to know if you're an empathetic person. Here, we've gathered a few questions to help you decide if you're indeed an HSP. Check out the statements that resonate with how you usually feel:

- You're easily overwhelmed by strong sensory stimuli – it can be a strong reaction to light, odor, touch, or any physical stimuli in general

- You always notice the subtle differences and details in your environment

- You're easily affected by how others feel

- You're very sensitive to pain and can't stand it

- You feel like you need to withdraw in crowded spaces or on busy days. You feel like you just need to go into a darkened room, jump into your bed, or enjoy some privacy to cool down the effects of being overly stimulated

- Drinking coffee or any other caffeinated beverage puts you on edge

- You have a rich and complex internal environment that you like to get lost in

- Loud noises make you uncomfortable

- You're deeply moved by art and music

- Sometimes, your nervous system is so overwhelmed that you need to withdraw and have some private time

- You are conscientious

- You get startled easily

- You get anxious when you have a lot of tasks to carry out in a short period of time

- You tend to notice when others are uncomfortable in their surroundings, and you know what to do to make them more physically comfortable

- You get annoyed when people ask you to do multiple things at once

- You try your best to avoid making mistakes or forgetting anything, even trivialities

- You can't stand watching violent movies or shows

- You become too stimulated and restless when there's a lot going on around you

- Whenever you feel hungry, you get strongly stimulated to the point that you become angry and lose focus

- You like routine, and any sudden changes rattle you up

- You notice the finer details and enjoy the delicacy of food, scents, sounds, or any form of art

- You do your best to create a comfortable atmosphere in which you can avoid getting upset or overly stimulated

- You're bothered by intense stimuli, such as crowded places, chaotic scenes, or loud noises

- You don't like it when others watch you while you're working. It makes you nervous, and you perform much worse than if you operate alone

- You were often told as a child that you are shy and sensitive

Your Score

If you've checked at least 14 or more of the statements above, then there are high chances you are a highly sensitive person. However, keep in mind that the results of any personality test only serve to help you better understand yourself. You should – by no means – base your life on it or use it as an excuse for a behavior you don't like.

Empaths vs. HSPs

Looking at the traits of an HSP, it's easy to confuse being an HSP with being an empath. Although there are a lot of similarities and overlaps, an HSP isn't necessarily an empath. Here are the similarities and differences between both personalities.

- **Similarities**

The truth is empaths are highly sensitive in nature. They share almost the same traits that HSPs have. Both types of personalities have a low threshold for stimulation; they need their alone time to recharge, are sensitive to physical stimuli in their surroundings, and have a limited threshold for enjoying their time in large groups. Both empaths and highly sensitive people love nature and enjoy quiet environments. They also like to help others and have a rich inner environment that they often get lost in.

• Differences

HSPs require more downtime to recover from the overstimulation of busy days and interacting with others when it comes to differences. Their ability to transition from a hectic atmosphere and connect with their quiet inner self takes more time than empaths. Most HSPs are introverted in nature, while empaths can be either introverted or extroverted.

Moreover, an empath experiences the sensitivity of an HSP on a much deeper level. Not only can they sense the subtle energy from their surrounding environment and people, but they also absorb it to the extent that they start mirroring what they've perceived. The ability to mirror their surroundings isn't something that HSPs have, and empaths unconsciously use this ability to enrich the experience they're feeling. As a result, they can feel what others feel so much that they may even exhibit the same physical symptoms. For instance, an empath can start blushing when they see someone embarrassed or get nauseous when another person has an upset stomach. The ability to mirror other people's physical reactions is known as somatic empathy, and that's something that only empaths can feel, unlike HSPs.

Moreover, empaths get lost in other people's emotions and thoughts to the extent that they may confuse them. They're often unable to discern their own experience from others, and you may notice that they start to act similar to the person they're with, and their behavior can change when they're with different people. Empaths are often highly intuitive and spiritual, while HSPs aren't necessarily so.

Generally speaking, an empath is probably an HSP, but not vice versa. If we consider empathy a spectrum, then empaths have the highest level of empathy, falling on the furthest right of the spectrum. HSPs lie right before them on the middle right, and ordinary people will have moderate levels of empathy in the middle of the spectrum. The further left you, you'll come across personalities with empath-deficient disorders, like narcissists,

Machiavellians, psychopaths, and other antisocial personality disorders.

According to the categorization mentioned earlier, the empathetic spectrum will look like the following:

Empath-deficient personalities → Normal people → HSPs → Empaths.

What about Introversion and Shyness?

There's a common misconception that empathy and high sensitivity are the same as introversion. Although around 70% of HSPs and more than half the empaths are introverts, they're all different descriptions for personality traits. It's also not uncommon for people to describe introverts, empaths, and HSPs as shy, which is why we should make a clear distinction between all of them.

For starters, an introvert is a person who recharges their inner energy by being alone. Being surrounded by people or interacting with others for too long drains their energy, and so they feel the need to find privacy and unwind after a long day of consuming their energy. On the contrary, an extrovert enjoys social encounters and feels rejuvenated after connecting with others. This doesn't mean that introverts don't have friends or hate social events. They still find communicating with others meaningful, and they enjoy it. They just have a limited social battery that runs out faster than that of extroverts. As such, introverts get exhausted much faster than extroverts, seeking solitude to deal with the repercussions of socializing. This phenomenon is often described as an "introvert's hangover."

Introverts aren't necessarily insecure or lacking in self-confidence. They aren't necessarily overly conscious of how others see them or how they act in front of others. Instead, these are traits of a shy person – they're people who are scared of social judgment. Shy people think multiple times about how they'll look to others if they act a certain way, usually ending up hesitating and not acting at all to avoid making "fools of themselves," as they internally think. They also get nervous and start panicking when they're put on the spot or if they think there are too many people watching them. Their fear of social judgment leaves them frozen in place, even if they desire to connect with others and be at the center of attention.

When Empathy, High Sensitivity, and Introversion Overlap

Empaths and HSPs can be introverted and shy, or extroverted and self-confident. The way they turn out has more to do with their social upbringing and experience than being an innate or genetic feature when it comes to shyness. For instance, an HSP who grew up being criticized by teachers and parents as being "too sensitive" can become shy and start withdrawing more into themselves, all for fear of being judged. Here, their fear of judgment has turned into insecurity based on the negative feedback they got as a result of showing their true selves.

Meanwhile, an empath who is also highly sensitive may have grown up in a loving environment, surrounded by people who appreciate their empathetic and deeply feeling nature. They realize that they have a gift and try their best to share it with others without fear of judgment, so they don't become shy.

An HSP or an empath can be introverted or extroverted in either case. This part has more to do with their genetics, and their social upbringing could influence their introversion or extroversion.

The Opposites of an Empath, HSP, and Introvert Are…?

Let's start with an easy answer. It's obvious how extroverts are the opposite of introverts. Thanks to their ever-running social battery, extroverts enjoy a great deal of satisfaction from dealing with people, unlike introverts whose batteries get drained the more they deal with people. It's also worth mentioning that the opposite of shyness is confidence and charisma.

That said, identifying the opposite of empathy and high sensitivity is not so simple. At first glance, you may be tempted to say that narcissism is their definite opposite, but there's more to the story. Narcissists indeed have zero empathy – they're just incapable of feeling others' emotions or connecting to their personal experiences, unlike empaths and HSPs. However, just because they lack empathy doesn't automatically make them the opposite of empaths and HSPs.

An empath is someone with high levels of empathy, while an HSP is highly sensitive to their surrounding stimuli. However, people with little empathy can also be HSPs, and those with little sensitivity can be empaths. While empathy and high sensitivity have their good and bad points, a person who lacks these traits can also live a healthy life with their own gifts. They aren't necessarily narcissistic, selfish, or trample on others to achieve their goals – they're just normal people who exist in the middle of the empathetic spectrum.

We don't need to associate a person with a personality disorder because they lack empathy or sensitivity. Every personality has strengths and weaknesses. When you learn to overcome your weaknesses, you start to use your strengths and become the best version of yourself. That's a life-long struggle, but it's worth the effort.

Are You an Empath or an HSP?

Although empathy and high sensitivity can overlap, you can determine which personality type you are by understanding their differences. If you're still unsure about your personality type, here are a few questions to help you figure it out.

1. How Do You Perceive Your Surroundings?

To put it simply, an HSP is a person who is hyper-aware of all the little details surrounding them – they're able to see and feel more of their surroundings. Meanwhile, an empath is closer to having high levels of clairsentience that enable them to feel what others feel.

2. How Does Seeing Others Upset Make You Feel?

Both empaths and HSPs feel upset when they see others upset, distressed, or in pain, although their reasons may differ. An HSP is empathetic by nature, so seeing others distressed makes them feel troubled. However, an empath will feel what another person feels – their feelings and emotions of distress are a result of mirroring another's. They don't originate their feelings; they're easily affected by others' feelings.

3. Do You Feel like It's Your Responsibility to Take Care of Others?

An HSP will feel troubled when they see someone else in distress, and they will try to help them. Since they're hyper-aware of their surroundings, they'll instantly notice when someone feels cold or hot and offer to turn the AC up or down. Meanwhile, an empath looks for meaningful emotional connections with everyone. They also have a strong need to please others and take care of them. When they find someone troubled, they make it their mission to listen to their story, offer a supporting shoulder, and cheer them up as they search for their own answers.

4. Do You Easily Get Overwhelmed, Emotionally, or Physically?

Both empaths and HSPs get easily overwhelmed by their surroundings. They can experience both emotional and physical burnout, although to different degrees. While a highly sensitive person will get more overwhelmed by the physical, sensory, and emotional stimuli, an empath will likely feel overwhelmed by the emotional overload of mirroring others' emotions.

5. Do You Find Narcissists Irresistibly Attractive?

There's an inexplicable attraction that almost all empaths feel towards narcissists. We'll get into this more in a later chapter, but if you feel attracted to toxic personalities, especially narcissists, there's a high chance you are an empath.

Common Challenges Empaths and HSPs Face

Since empaths and HSPs share many similarities, there are also a few common challenges that both types of personalities can face. Here are a few of the daily struggles of both empaths and HSPs:

1. They're Easily Overstimulated

Both empaths and HSPs are easily overstimulated by their surroundings. An HSP's nervous system will go into overdrive due to external stimuli, while an empath's psychological system will get overloaded by emotions.

2. They're Quick to Experience Emotional and Physical Burnout

As a result of feeling too many emotions and sensory information, empaths and HSPs frequently suffer from emotional and physical burnout. As a result, they undergo periods of withdrawals and lethargy during which they lack the motivation to do anything.

3. They Tend to Become Isolated and Lonely

Dealing with others may be draining, but what really gets to both empaths and HSPs is realizing that they experience life differently than others. For people who thrive on making meaningful connections with like-minded individuals, finding that no one around relates to their experience is one of the worst things ever.

4. They Easily Absorb Others' Negativity

Empaths and HSPs are highly tuned to others' emotions and subtleties. As a result, they get affected by others' moods without even noticing. They might suddenly get moody, angry, or sad without any reason, although it's just because they failed to realize others' negativity has infected them.

5. They May Develop Anxiety

Being under too much stress for too long can result in only one thing: psychological fatigue. Once that settles in, it's common for both empaths and HSPs to start developing anxiety or other mental disorders.

At first glance, empaths and highly sensitive people may sound identical, but they aren't. While an empath's superpower is their ability to mirror other people's emotions, a highly sensitive person's superpower is their hyper-awareness of their surroundings and sharp processing ability. That said, HSPs have levels of empathy, although not to the extent to that of the empaths, and while not all HSPs are empaths, most empaths are HSPs.

Chapter 5: The Empath and the Self: Addictions

There's a social stigma surrounding addiction, as well as a common misconception that addicts are usually homeless street people or victims of domestic abuse or upheaval. People who become addicts are often victims of their own thoughts and emotions. Their disease may result from failing to deal with a traumatic situation or feeling so hopeless that the person seeks any kind of instant comfort and numbing agent – and what better than a drug to help them escape their misery? When you look at it from this perspective, you start to understand how empathetic people can be even more prone to addiction than others.

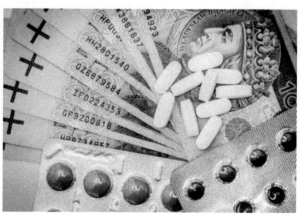

What Is Addiction?

Let's start with understanding addiction. A healthy human's brain is wired to react to pleasurable sensations by secreting dopamine - a chemical neurotransmitter that makes a person feel good. This neurotransmitter is often secreted when a person achieves something, feels proud, or experiences pleasurable sensations like having sex, winning money, or even eating a satisfying meal. To the brain, these experiences all "feel" the same, and so it secretes dopamine and makes its owner feel good.

The thing is, taking psychoactive drugs or engaging in addictive behavior, which we'll get into in a bit, triggers the same part of the brain that's responsible for pleasure. So, after getting a taste of this "high," the person starts craving it more. It doesn't help that repeated exposure to the addictive substance or behavior changes how the nerve cells in the prefrontal cortex - the part of the brain responsible for planning and executing tasks - works. These nerve cells become programmed to mistake liking the addictive substance or behavior to wanting it, hence the creation of the craving.

At this point, the dopamine secreted from using the addictive substance takes over the brain's reward system, and it makes the user feel there's nothing else that makes them feel as good as the substance of their addiction does. You'll realize how true that's when you learn that the brain becomes unable to secrete dopamine on its own, even if the user engages in an activity that previously felt rewarding, all because it's now relying on an external source to get triggered into secreting dopamine.

Types of Addiction

Until now, you may have thought that addiction is only limited to using hard drugs or abusing alcohol, but that's simply not the whole story. Addiction can take various forms, starting from using substances that can include more than drugs and alcohol to developing behavioral addiction. Here are a few types of addiction to help you get the full picture.

1. Substance Use Disorders

Addiction resulting from using drugs is medically referred to as substance use disorder or, more simply, addiction. It's divided into 10 categories according to the substance of use, although all 10 categories share the same symptoms of addiction. The abuser's brain depends on a substance to stimulate the reward and reinforcement system. The user develops compulsive behavior that forces them to keep using the drug at the expense of their normal ability to function. Most of these substances cause withdrawal symptoms when the user tries to quit, although to varying degrees.

Here's a quick overview of these categories:

2. Alcohol Use Disorder (Alcoholic)

Alcohol abuse is pretty common. After all, alcohol is available and legal to use. It's more commonly found in adult men, although the number of women abusing alcohol is rising. People can abuse alcohol due to its depressive effects on the brain, making them feel relaxed and forget their sorrows.

3. Caffeine Intoxication (Coffee Addict)

It may be weird to find out that caffeine can cause addiction as well, although it's true. Caffeine intoxication can cause insomnia, nervousness, restlessness, stomach disturbances, muscle spasms or twitching, irregular heartbeats, increased agitation, and fatigue.

4. Tobacco Use Disorder (Nicotine Addict)

Tobacco is a central nervous system stimulant. Smoking cigarettes or using any tobacco products, in general, can also cause addiction. According to research, 68% of adult smokers want to quit while 50% actually try to. Unfortunately, even if they do, they suffer from periods of intense cravings, mood disturbances, and lack of productivity, so most of them relapse.

5. Cannabis Use Disorder (Drug Addict)

Cannabis use disorder is more common among young people aged 18 to 29, unlike the previous disorders more prevalent in adults. Curiously, the prevalence of this disorder decreased with age.

6. Opioid Use Disorder (Heroin Addict)

Opioid use disorder refers to using hard drugs, like heroin, and prescription pain medications, like morphine. This addiction is most prevalent in those who have received opioid medication, after which they started using on their own. It's also sad to note that overdosing from opioid use is the most common cause of death in those younger than 50 years in the US.

7. Other Substance Use Disorders

We've only touched briefly upon the most common substance use disorders, but the list is much longer. Substance addiction can take many more forms, including using hallucinogens like phencyclidine, inhalants, sedative and hypnotics, stimulants, and other substances that alter the central nervous system and result in compulsive use.

8. Behavioral Addiction

Most people think that addiction is limited to using substances, but it can also result from engaging too much in addictive behavior. Here are some of the most common behavioral addictions.

9. Gambling

Gambling is one perfect example of how an activity can turn into an addiction. If you think about it rationally, you shouldn't engage in an activity in which you keep losing money, but that's just not how the mind of an addict works. Gambling provides an opportunity for an instant reward, namely money. This keeps the person fixated on trying to get this reward, often forgetting all about the negative consequences of the act. Those who fall victim to gambling can lose large sums of money, get bankrupted, and even lose important relationships, yet still crave the sense of reward that they never get. Gambling is now a recognized mental health disorder that also includes Gaming Disorder – or excessive video and digital gaming.

10. Food Eating Disorders

Even something as harmless as eating can develop into an addiction. Overeating and obesity have more to them than meets the eye – it's not merely the acts of someone who enjoys food too much. Most food eating disorders result from an underlying mental health cause, making them more of a symptom rather than a cause. Binge-eating is one of the most common eating disorders that cause obesity, but more types of eating disorders cause health hazards. Some of these disorders are anorexia nervosa, periods of self-starvation, bulimia, which is eating and purging, pure starvation, and other eating disorders that include eating substances that aren't food.

11. Other Behavioral Addictions

It turns out addiction can result from overusing almost anything. Take excessive video gaming, for instance, which has been added to gambling use disorders. Other behavioral addictions can also result from the excessive use of things that trigger the brain reward system, such as overusing social media, watching pornography, going on shopping sprees, and other excessive behavioral patterns.

Why Are Empaths More Susceptible to Addiction?

Empaths almost always give off the vibes of warm and loving creatures. They'll always be the first to listen to others' problems and lend a supporting shoulder. They're the ones who try their hardest to make the surrounding environment warmer, be it their workplace, home, or social circles. They're too focused on making other people's lives better that they never show their own suffering, and that's why most people fail to realize that empaths are also struggling. In most cases, empaths are struggling even more than everyone else.

Being an empath means being an emotional sponge that gets dyed with other people's emotional colors. They become happy when others are happy, but they also absorb negative vibes at high speed, such as sadness, anger, and depression. That's all thanks to their hypersensitive central nervous system. When you review what we discussed about addiction, this is a scary recipe for disaster.

An empath becomes emotionally overwhelmed much easier than others. They also experience pleasure from their reward system to a terrifyingly heightened extent. When you couple the extreme lows with the extreme highs they go through, you can start to understand why they're more prone to addiction than others. An empath can engage in addictive behavior to escape from the overwhelming pain and suffering they feel as a result of absorbing others' negativity. Once they feel the euphoria of using substances or the pleasure from engaging in rewarding activities, they become much more easily hooked than others.

Keep in mind that being an empath is not a mental health disorder. We're only referring to the over-sensitivity of the empaths' brains that makes them more susceptible to becoming victims of addiction. For an empath, the initial phase of addictions starts with their need to dull their constant overstimulation. In their search for relief, they can turn to sex, food, shopping, gambling, alcohol, or drug abuse to escape from their pain.

Addiction is more common in naive empaths who are unaware of the negative consequences of their empathy. However, more self-aware empaths may still willingly start using substances or engaging in addictive behavior to numb the overstimulation. Unfortunately, both kinds of empaths soon realize how addiction is a costly price to pay for enjoying a brief escape.

The best thing an addiction can do is provide instant relief from overstimulation, but even that soon dulls as the substance of use or behavior stops working as it did in the beginning. When an empath gets back from their "high," they feel the effects of overstimulation far worse than they initially did. This can force them to increase the dose – which soon will stop working – and starts the vicious cycle. Meanwhile, their oversensitivity and inability to numb the pain can lead to depression, anxiety, fatigue, and more mental and physical issues.

Symptoms of Addiction

In order to diagnose someone with addiction, they need to display two of the following symptoms at least:

> • They're using the substance or engaging in the activity for a longer period than they initially intended

- They tried to cut down, or have the desire to so, but failed

- They spend a lot of time trying to get the substance or engage in the behavior, and they need a lot of downtime following the activity to get back to normal

- They have a constant craving to use the substance or engage in the behavior when they're doing so

- Their use or behavior interferes with their ability to carry out their responsibilities

- They keep using the substance or engaging in the activity, even if that disrupts their social, professional, or personal relationships

- They stop participating in work, school, or social gatherings

- They may engage in the activity in risky places

- Despite realizing that the substance or behavior is causing psychological and physical problems, they continue using it

- They start increasing the amount of time spent on the activity since the same level doesn't work out for them anymore

- When they try to stop using, they start experiencing withdrawal effects – which can either be on a physical or psychological level

- They feel restless and paranoid when they're not using the substance or engaging in the behavior

- They always seek the substance or behavior to run away from their emotional distress

- They start to struggle with their financial situation, leading them to borrow money from others or even steal it.

Although checking only two symptoms can mean the person is struggling with addiction, the severity of the addiction is measured by the number of checked symptoms. Generally, checking 2 or 3 symptoms indicates mild addiction, while checking four to five indicates moderate addiction. If six or more symptoms are checked, this indicates severe addiction.

Self-Assessment

Not all addictions result from empathy, but empaths are more prone to addiction. Unfortunately, not all empaths are self-aware enough to realize the relation between their high sensitivity or overstimulation and their addictive patterns. If you're unsure about whether or not your overstimulation is feeding your addictive behavior, ask yourself the following questions:

- Do you constantly think to yourself that life would be so much better if you didn't use the substance/drink/overeat/engage in addictive behavior?

- Do you often feel the desire to quit?

- Have you tried quitting often but only lasted a short period and relapsed, perhaps stronger than before?

- Do you often engage in addictive behavior when you're overwhelmed by emotions, even if they're not your own?

- Do you often engage in addictive behavior when:

- You're feeling pain, anxious, depressed, or angry

- You're feeling hurt

- You're feeling uncomfortable

- You're unable to sleep

  o You feel insecure, criticized, rejected, or blamed

  o You feel emotionally threatened

o You feel social anxiety

o You're isolating yourself at home to avoid dealing with others

o You're feeling drained, physically, mentally, or psychologically

o You want to escape from the outside world

If you've checked one or more items in the previous list, that means you sometimes seek the comfort of addiction to cope with your hypersensitive nature. Checking four to five items means you may be suffering from moderate addiction, while checking more than six items can indicate that you're mainly turning to addiction to cope with your empathy.

How to Cope with Addiction

You shouldn't try to cope with the repercussions of your empathy through self-medication, which can so easily develop into an addiction. It's better to look for healthier ways to deal with your overstimulation while keeping your mind and body intact. Whether you're struggling with addiction or on the verge of falling over, here are a few helpful tips to get you started:

1. Be Honest with Yourself

The first thing you should know is that you're your own savior. There's no shame in admitting that you're struggling with a problem. It's the first step to getting your life back and living a healthier way, and no one will judge you. You don't have to admit it to others; merely becoming self-aware of your issues is a great first step to recovery and getting better.

2. Identify Your Addiction

Once you open the road to self-awareness, you'll start recognizing many behavioral patterns you may have overlooked before. Taking the previous self-assessment is a great way to identify your addictive tendencies and recognize your addiction.

You may be struggling with one or more kinds of addiction, so be honest enough with yourself to identify any behavioral or substance use addictions.

3. Differentiate between an Addiction and a True Need

Sometimes, it can be hard to differentiate between craving something and needing it. There will also be times when you struggle with thoughts like "just doing it for five minutes won't harm." However, distinguishing between a need and an addiction, or a healthy behavior and an excessively addictive one, is crucial in your recovery. For instance, eating balanced and nutritious meals is healthy and essential, but overeating and binge-eating, even if you don't feel hungry, is not.

4. Accept That There Are No Shortcuts to Happiness

The truth is that there is no shortcut to happiness. Using a substance or engaging in addictive behavior won't make your troubles disappear; it only puts them on hold. It's even worse when you sober up and feel the weight of overstimulation crashing in. Instead of feeling everything all over again, isn't it better to take baby steps in solving one problem at a time?

5. Be Aware of Your Triggers

Did you know that even those who have successfully overcome their addiction can relapse in a moment of weakness? They don't even need to seek the substance on their own, but merely passing by a place or hanging out with old friends can be enough of a trigger for them to use it again. The same holds for you – if you keep constantly triggered by what makes you seek addictive behavior, you'll find it much harder to hold back or quit.

6. Limit and Vent Out Stress

It's important to understand how absorbing others' negativity affects you on every level. Although you're naturally programmed to absorb the negativity, you can rewire your brain to react differently. When others feel down, recognize how that will affect you and learn to differentiate their feelings from yours. One of the best ways to limit other people's effect on you is to set healthy boundaries and limits. It's best to limit the encounter with stressful situations if you can, but if not, then find healthy ways to vent out the stress you've absorbed.

7. Pick Up Healthy Habits

There's a long list of healthy habits that can help you destress. You should definitely start with working out, which will have the added benefit of giving you a healthier body and mind. Try your best to maintain a healthy relationship with food, and do not overindulge in smoking, alcohol, or other harmful habits.

8. Practice Self-Care

Remember to take care of yourself just like you're doing your best at taking care of others. Take a long hot bath, go to a spa, practice meditation, pick up a hobby that fills you with joy, travel somewhere nice. Treat yourself - you've certainly earned it!

9. Seek Support

Lastly, be honest and brave enough to know when you need help. Don't feel ashamed or guilty - there are countless therapists and support groups who will welcome you and help you get back on the right track.

For an empath, addiction is often the result of an underlying problem and not the main issue. It usually stems from the need to numb the effects of being overstimulated after becoming psychologically drained from giving to others. An empath is quick to feel and mirror others, making them an emotional sponge for negativity. In an effort to escape this overwhelming sensation, an empath may seek to self-medicate with drugs or engage in behaviors that turn into an addiction.

If any part of this chapter resonated with you, there's no shame in that, but you need to help yourself. While you're doing your best to avoid addictive behavior, take the time to dive into the main reasons why you need to escape. It's hard and can be very triggering, but you won't go anywhere unless you solve the root problem.

Chapter 6: The Working Empath

While empaths may face more challenges in the workplace than others, they bring many positive qualities to the work environment. It's important to learn how to deal with your colleagues and bosses as an empath or a highly sensitive person to avoid being emotionally drained all the time. If you think of your empathy as a source of strength, you will be able to channel it in a healthy way when faced with stressful situations at work. It's also important to find out the best careers that work for you as an empath and which ones to avoid. This chapter will discuss how empaths interact at the workplace, how they can cope with demanding bosses and tough situations at work, and what they should consider before taking a job.

How Empaths Interact in the Workplace

As an empath, you can sense people's underlying feelings in the workplace by a simple conversation or merely looking at their faces. You can understand and perceive their emotions, which allows you to make a huge impact in the workplace. If you meet a new person at work, you'll probably get a true sense of who they really are after only a short encounter. Your intuition guides you to understand how they can handle stressful situations at work, which allows you to get through to them.

You pick up on subtle signals seen in the way they dress, body language, and tone of speech, among other signs, and automatically process this information to get a sense of what they are like even beyond the working environment. You are not doing that to judge your colleagues, but it's just a tool that you have that helps you interact with others. This information tells you what they truly feel about their job and what interests them. You can tell how they might react in different situations at work or in their personal life. It's not that you assume certain things about them, but you have this inner compass of the underlying qualities of people.

Sometimes, you may have a bad feeling about someone or feel a certain vibe. Empaths are usually affected by other people's energies, and they can even manifest as a physical sensation. You may have experienced a tingling or numbing sensation when someone tells you a story about a chronic pain they have been feeling or an accident they had. You know how people say, "I get you" or "I feel your pain"? For you, that's completely true! You are actually able to feel other people's pain. Some people may give you such a strong vibe that you interpret as a warning signal to steer away from them. You can't explain what this feeling is, but you have learned to trust it over the years because often, you turn out to be right.

You can pick up on the vibes of any room you step into. You can spot who is excited or feeling down that day. You immediately pick up on everyone's emotions, and you use this information to make decisions at work or learn how to deal with a certain situation. Your presence in the workplace positively influences the people around you. Any business depends on its workforce, and when you are a person who anticipates the needs of each employee, your abilities can be a great asset. You can spot the weakest links in your company and produce solutions to fix these issues.

Many businesses are becoming more and more aware of the importance of showing empathy in the workplace. This is because they can see the difference between understanding people's behavior at work and merely giving them orders without assessing their needs. When people feel their managers truly care about them and their needs, they become more willing to do their jobs. This is why more companies are hiring empathetic people for managerial positions.

Empaths can recognize people's thoughts and feelings about their jobs. They can sense when somebody is not challenged enough or if they are overwhelmed. While there are some pointers like an employee's performance review, an empath knows that there is more to it than just numbers on a screen. An empath treats an employee as a human being. While it may seem obvious, not all people recognize the importance of people's feelings about their jobs. However, being an empathetic leader is tricky because you'll need to differentiate between someone who is truly going through a rough time and another who is faking it. Since an empath is unusually intuitive, they'll be able to spot that difference quite easily. These qualities make you a great choice for a team leader, a trainer, or a mentor.

Your intuition also helps you create strategies because you can anticipate what the company needs and know how to use people's skills to fill those needs. In addition, you understand the market and know how to think like the customer because you can put yourself in their shoes. For instance, you use this information to make informed decisions when planning a marketing campaign. Your ability to sense people's feelings and needs allows you to create strong bonds at work, not just between you and your coworkers but between them and each other as well. You can also anticipate problems that may happen in the future and take steps to prevent them from happening.

As an empathetic team leader or manager, you are often successful at promoting the emotional well-being of your employees. This is because you truly listen to people and not just implement changes you think are needed in the workplace. *You get your information from the employees themselves.* You may know how to anticipate their needs, but you don't just use this information to create a change without having a conversation with them. This process creates a sense of loyalty within your team and allows people to work with a passion and treat the workplace as their second home and not just a source of income. You know how to lead by example because you treat everyone with respect and trust.

Another great quality you possess is the ability to resolve a conflict. Your understanding of each person allows you to see through the disagreements between people. Being an empath does not merely mean you can understand the feelings of others, but it also means you can invoke empathy in them. You help them see the other perspective and not just focus on their own needs. You know that by doing this, everybody comes out a winner. This is how you create a harmonious work environment by making people more empathetic toward each other.

The success of any business depends majorly on people's problems and conflicts. They may need to resolve conflicts to collaborate on certain projects. You may need to approach customers to convince them to buy a certain product, or your business needs to pique consumers' interest to raise brand awareness. All of these are people-dependent processes, which makes empathy key to understanding what people really need. As an empath, you can create a strategy, manage a team, or lead a marketing campaign because you can easily tune in to people's innermost desires.

How to Cope with Demanding Bosses and Tough Work Situations

You could face tough situations in the workplace, like having a controlling or demanding boss. Your manager may constantly make you feel that you are not performing well. They may not support your professional growth or are taking the "tough love" approach because they think it yields better results. They could be gaslighting you by overlooking all of your accomplishments or undermining them. This is a problem that many empaths face, working with manipulative bosses who take credit for their work and make them feel unworthy.

Many companies go through several changes in their lifetime. You may have a supportive boss one day, and the next, you may be working with a toxic one. While this may make your work life a living hell, a few benefits come out of this situation. When you realize you deserve more than this bad treatment, you'll learn how to stand up for yourself. As an empath, you may try to avoid confrontations, especially when you know the other person won't understand or respect your feelings. It's important to look at this situation as a learning experience. You'll find out that being exposed to a toxic person destroys your self-esteem and can have a major impact on your mental and emotional wellbeing.

First, let's look at why some bosses are cruel or intolerant of their employees. Some people only feel validated when they make people feel powerless. They derive their power from stepping over people's feelings. When your boss is yelling at you to get a certain task done, it's not just that they are result-oriented. They need to feel that they have a higher status over you. They may have dealt with many toxic bosses before they reached their position, and now it's their time to order people around. They may think this is the only way to behave, or they may be under a lot of pressure from their bosses. In any case, they don't care about what other people feel. As an empath, you put people's feelings at the forefront because you only know how to lead with compassion. You know how to break the cycle of toxic bosses, and when you lead with love and compassion, you pass on these values to future bosses.

You should know that a controlling boss usually derives their attitude from underlying feelings of insecurity. They feel powerless and victimized by their previous bosses, which is why they feel insecure in the workplace. If they were self-confident or emotionally secure, they would trust themselves to have an effect on people and urge them to fulfill their job's responsibilities without undermining their abilities. They wouldn't need to bully people to get results. Bear in mind that they won't be aware of this issue. They may even genuinely think that this is a good way to manage a team.

When facing a controlling boss, you can become emotionally drained very quickly because you need a working space where you can breathe. You are already affected by everything around you and need your boss to be flexible and allow you to take intermittent breaks and not smother you with orders. When you take these breaks, your mind can process the tremendous amount of information you receive daily and create an appropriate response to each situation. This is how you perform your best work. If you are controlled and ordered all the time, you cannot work as efficiently. This is because you don't feel safe enough to explore your creativity in the workplace.

So, what if you are working under a demanding boss right now? What can you do to handle tough situations at work? Whenever you are in a toxic relationship of any kind, you need to set some healthy boundaries. Take a break from the surrounding negative energy to protect yourself and your emotions. You may be thinking, "How can I set boundaries with my boss whom I interact with every day?" Well, the first step is not to let their words affect you. While this may sound very difficult right now, it starts with a simple mantra: "I am not going to let his negativity affect me" or "These are not my feelings, but his feelings."

Whenever you have a bad experience with your boss, first take a deep breath. You can take a quick break to practice a breathing exercise and let go of any negative emotions. You can perform this exercise for just a minute while at your work desk. It may seem like a simple exercise, but it goes a long way to helping you move on from this encounter. Concentrate on your breathing patterns and then tell yourself, "I am in control of this moment. I am safe within my own skin. I will not allow his words to affect me."

Write down this experience in your journal. Try to identify your feelings and write them down. Mention how you wanted to react or wish they would have handled the situation. Create another narrative to that experience to allow yourself to heal from that encounter. It's important to keep this information to yourself. Be mindful of who you trust with your innermost desires and life goals.

You have to be very careful with whom you share your thoughts because you are prone to be influenced by other people's energies. Even if they were not empaths, many successful people don't share their goals with people who could be jealous of these ambitions. They may upset some people because they are not sharing these secrets. However, when you keep your feelings and desires a secret, you are more likely to achieve your life goals and not have the ideas stolen.

It's important to know how to know your value in the workplace. Chances are, if you are feeling unsatisfied or unfulfilled at work, your boss or your company does not understand your value. If your boss is controlling or keeps undermining your accomplishments, maybe it's time to look for another job where people will value you. In the meantime, don't let their feelings and emotions affect you.

You must know that a boss who is overly critical of your performance is probably their own worst critic. They do not value themselves, which is why they feel the need to undermine other people's achievements, especially their subordinates who can't do anything about it. Remember that when you were hired, your value was recognized. Even if your current boss doesn't give you enough credit, understand it's not about you. Your real challenge is to know your worth. Then you can decide between staying or leaving this toxic workplace.

What to Consider before Taking a Job

When it comes to picking a career, there isn't one rule that works for every type of empath. You could thrive in several careers depending on your passion. However, consider a few things before taking a job. The odds are that you will already be attracted to a job opportunity that allows you to interact with people and provide a meaningful service to them. Most empaths feel emotionally satisfied when they serve others. However, these jobs have a downside because you can become emotionally overwhelmed, which you need to watch out for. But, in any case, an empath is usually susceptible to being emotionally influenced when interacting with people. Some industries require an empath like nurses and teachers as they need to be sensitive and intuitive to connect with others.

If you consider working in the medical field, you must understand that it could be an emotionally taxing job. It may give you great satisfaction to take care of others, but you have to be well aware of its emotional consequences. This is why it's important to practice self-care daily to protect yourself. You can test a career by volunteering in a certain field or working as an intern to see if it fits you.

You'll need to find out if the work environment is a positive and safe space. You want to find a place where you can genuinely connect with people. When considering a job, look for the company culture and the job description to see if you will be able to communicate with others. Empaths thrive on having human connections regularly. You may be more suited for a job that involves collaborations than a job that only requires individual work. Take the time to research the company's values by reading its mission and value statements on its website. Some former employees will write their reviews about working in that company. All this information will give you a good idea of whether or not this company is a good fit.

Some jobs suitable for empathetic people are social workers, nurses, teachers, life or career coaches, writers, marketing managers, and UX researchers. Some jobs entail direct communication with people. Others, like writers, might involve working individually, but you'll need to dig deep into a topic and examine characters and stories from all angles. You will also need to think about your readers to communicate your ideas to them. In a way, you communicate with others through your words, whether you are writing ad content, web copy, or movie reviews.

While there is no limit to what job an empath can take, some roles may not be favorable. These include executive or managerial positions that entail making tough decisions that impact many employees, demanding sales positions, and anything related to politics, which can be incredibly stressful to any person, let alone an empath.

This chapter discussed the most prominent qualities in the working empath and how they deal in the workplace. We mentioned how to handle a controlling or demanding boss and the reasons behind their behavior. We mentioned a few things to keep in mind when choosing a job and company to work with. It's important to keep this in mind to ensure that you work in a place that values your abilities as an empath.

Chapter 7: Empaths in Love

While empaths thrive on emotional connection and relationships, at the same time, many of them struggle in these interactions. This is what makes self-care crucial to empaths. You need to learn how to recognize a toxic relationship because you might find yourself going into one totally naively. This chapter will discuss the various relationships in an empath's life and how to deal with the issues that come up in those relationships.

Why Do You Struggle in Relationships?

We can all send and receive energy to and from each other. Each person can interpret these energies and signals in their own unique way. As an empath, you are more sensitive to these energies than most people. This is because you can't help but absorb these energies and be affected by them. You can easily pick up other people's vibes and get emotionally immersed in their troubles. This makes any type of relationship hard on an empath, whether it's romantic, familial, friendly, or even professional.

You are highly sensitive to people's feelings and vibes and animals, nature, and even objects. You have a sense of a person's character from only a basic interaction. You can determine their emotional state by just being around them because you pick up their body language and the tone of their voice. This is the case with anyone you meet, even for a brief encounter. When it comes to getting close to someone, you open your heart to that person and receive their energy. Your own energy becomes attainable to the other person, which is what makes you so vulnerable. It's how you connect with others and merge with their energies.

When you are overly exposed to another person's energy field and emotions, especially in a romantic relationship, you are bound to be overwhelmed. This is called empath fatigue, where you absorb too many emotions and cannot process them all. They end up affecting you immensely, and sometimes you may confuse them for your own emotions. When you are emotionally overwhelmed, you are forced to take a step back from these relationships because you can't handle being near that person any longer. This is why most empaths find it difficult to stay in intimate relationships for a long time. As an empath, you need to have your own space to process your emotions and rejuvenate. On the other hand, some empaths can't distance themselves from emotionally draining relationships. They become so invested in people's emotions and love to experience that connection.

Since empaths usually experience emotional fatigue and burnout in relationships, this can cause them to isolate themselves from people. This is a self-defense mechanism that they turn to when they feel emotionally depleted. As an empath, you may have distanced yourself from your family or friends because you can't handle the drama. You may have also broken up with a romantic partner because you could not have a moment for yourself. These behaviors may seem selfish to these people because they can't understand where you're coming from.

While empaths are intuitive about people's intentions and emotions, sometimes this intuition is clouded. This happens when they are intensely attracted to someone's energy or deeply invested in a person's emotions. In both these cases, empaths may still get an inner feeling that tells them to steer away from the person, but they choose not to listen to that feeling. This results in getting involved with toxic people like narcissists or manipulators.

These people are dangerous for an empath. They may be incredibly charming at first, but when they start to drain you emotionally, you are already too invested in the relationship to distance yourself from it. It becomes hard to listen to your inner voice because these manipulative partners know how to convince you of their perspective. You end up questioning yourself and believing what they are telling you. However, when you start to feel that your partner does not love you, you will start to withdraw or at least stick around until you have enough evidence against them. You may still want to believe that your relationship can be fixed, but once the trust is broken, you will start to listen to your instinct again.

As an empath, you often forgive people's mistakes and understand the reasons behind them. This can be extremely dangerous when you are dealing with toxic people. Whether it's a toxic partner, friend, family member, or boss, you may be subjected to emotional abuse over and over again if they take advantage of your compassion. You may even find that you attract people with emotional baggage or trauma because you are so well acquainted with emotional healing. You may be making excuses for people's mistakes and even share responsibility for what went wrong in these relationships. This is why many empaths experience anxiety and lack of self-confidence because people keep exploiting your emotions. You must remember that it's not your fault and learn how to spot these people and trust your instincts.

When you build any type of relationship on an unstable foundation, you will find yourself contributing to the relationship far more than the other person – this constant act of giving drains you. When you absorb your partner's negative emotions, the relationship starts to take on the characteristics of a codependent relationship. Suppose your partner constantly turns to you for approval or emotional validation. In that case, you may also depend on the satisfaction you feel when you are healing or fixing your partner's emotional wounds. This can make the relationship extremely complex, and it may bring you down emotionally to match your partner's energy.

You may be invested in a relationship by focusing only on your partner's needs at the expense of your own needs. You will go to great lengths to help them survive and overcome their problems, even if it takes a toll on your emotional wellbeing. This is another unhealthy relationship that empaths face. Your own compassion and empathy with other people's problems can be a double-edged sword. Your needs must be a priority because if you are emotionally drained, you can't give anything to people anyway.

As we know, empaths absorb other people's feelings. When you are in close contact with a person who is experiencing mood swings or anxiety, for instance, you will most likely experience those feelings. No matter how much you practice self-care or have become aware of this behavior, you can't help but soak up these emotions. This scenario is going to be particularly difficult to deal with, especially when it's coming from a close person. You may not absorb all their feelings, but you will definitely be affected by them.

Empaths usually absorb negative energies and transform them into positive ones because they know how to practice natural healing. However, if you are constantly exposed to this negativity, it becomes emotionally debilitating. When you feel loving emotions, you feel them so intensely that you think your heart cannot take them anymore. When you feel angry or down, this could affect your mood for days, and you may experience a general lack of motivation to do anything.

Empaths get emotionally invested in relationships very quickly and very intensely, so much so that you may lose these emotions as soon as you leave that person's energy field. Many people may accuse you of being selfish or heartless, but you may not even be aware of this. This is why part of practicing self-care is to be aware of how much influence you have on people's feelings as well.

How to Deal with Problems in Relationships

Now that we have discussed why you may struggle with relationships as an empath, it's time to talk about how you can deal with the most common problems. The first challenge is to work out whose feelings are in question and set boundaries. Many empaths battle to set healthy boundaries with people. Sometimes, you cannot differentiate whether your emotions are yours or belong to your partner. So, you should get yourself alone and work out what's going on. Take time to connect with your friends or participate in a hobby or activity that you enjoy. Then you can use this time to write about your emotions in your journal or practice mindful meditation. Distancing yourself from the intensity you are used to during the day can help you rebalance your energy and connect with yourself.

You have to find a balance between spending time alone and spending time with others. Sometimes, it could upset your partner when you favor your personal space and time too much. They may see you as distant or selfish because you don't want to spend time with them. It's important to communicate your feelings with your partner and listen to them as well. If your partner is not an empath, they may not understand why you need to spend so much time alone. This conversation can also be crucial to let them know that they can also enjoy their personal space to practice their favorite things. It's important to reach a middle ground where both of you can get what you need.

Another common relationship problem is that empaths don't know how to accept help from their partner. As an empath, you are used to being there for your partner, so it may feel uncomfortable when they are there for you. Bear in mind that it's normal to let your partner help you if you have experienced a problem at work, had a fight with a friend – or anything you face in life. When you are in a relationship with a loving and supportive person, allow them to be there for you.

As an empath, you can't help but be affected by other people's feelings. When it comes to your romantic relationships, this constant awareness of your partner's emotions can be emotionally draining to you and your partner. Your partner may have had a tough day at work and doesn't want to talk about it or is unwilling to take some personal time off to let go of some steam. You may not be aware that you are affected by your partner's mood shift. A good tip is to remind yourself to give your partner some space without being influenced by their mood shift. Take a mental step back from the situation and trust that they can deal with their emotions if they say so. When you practice this process several times, you will be able to let things be and trust your partner's ability to deal with their issues.

Sometimes, you may prioritize your partner's feelings and needs over your own. In an unbalanced relationship, you may find yourself always giving or trying to please your partner. In the process, you want them to be happy, but you find you can't talk about your own issues and emotions. This could lead you to try to keep the peace by any means, and you end up keeping quiet and not questioning your partner's decisions.

When your partner starts to exploit this dynamic, this behavior may lead to an unhealthy balance in the relationship. They become so used to being the center of attention in the relationship and neglect that you have needs too. This doesn't necessarily mean that your partner is abusive. It may mean that you need to assert yourself more and not be afraid to talk about your needs. In a healthy relationship, both your and your partner's feelings should be validated and respected. It's not a matter of picking a fight with your partner but about practicing speaking up about your emotions.

Start by having a conversation with your partner, as it helps to bring the issue to the forefront first. Try to discuss when both of you feel most overwhelmed so that you can understand what the other person is thinking. This conversation is often neglected after a heated fight. It helps to revisit the issue after both of you have calmed down. Suggest stopping an argument when a conversation gets too heated. Try to clarify what you mean and encourage your partner to do the same. Avoid interrupting each other when you talk so that you can listen to each other's feelings to the end. If you want, you can keep notes as your partner speaks so that you can respond to what they are saying when it's your turn. This encourages a mature conversation that can make your relationship a lot easier.

You will often feel that your partner doesn't understand where you're coming from, no matter how many conversations you have. You may have an understanding and supportive partner, but sometimes they just can't get why you are worked up about something. Let's say your partner made dinner plans to spend time with you. You could get worked up because you want to spend some time alone and may resent your partner because they didn't check with you first. Here, your partner intended to surprise you with their plans, but their timing was not right. Your partner may not understand because they don't ever feel the need to isolate themselves when they're having a bad day. They may want to get out of the house or do something fun. Both of your dynamics and responses to these situations are different, which is why they can't understand you at this moment.

When you feel that you can't communicate your emotions with your partner, it's best to create some space and revisit the issue later. This way, you will be giving yourself the space to process your feelings before talking about why you need to have some personal space. It's important to let your partner know that it's not about isolating yourself but taking some time off to recharge. When things get heated, you have to take a step back because you don't need to exhaust yourself even more. Just remember that your partner is allowed a slip-up every once in a while. They are trying their best to be there for you, and it's your job to make them understand your emotions. This only works in a healthy relationship, but if your partner is not willing to listen to you, it's a sign that they may not be right for you.

How to Stop Absorbing Emotions

By now, you have learned how empaths act as an emotional sponge, whether to their partner or other people in their lives. The empath in the relationship needs to learn how to stop absorbing emotions from others. First, you need to recognize whether the things you are feeling are your own. You may be unaware of the emotions you are carrying because of the story you listened to at work or a sad video you saw online. Many empaths find it therapeutic to keep a journal of their emotions, which they refer to whenever they feel overwhelmed.

In your journal, you can trace your steps for the day back to find out what it was that you saw or heard that set you off. When you write your feelings down on paper, they start to lose their intensity. What's more, you will be able to put a name to those feelings. When you name your feelings, you start to learn how to manage them. It's like a plan you have in writing to manage and control your emotions. It's also a way to know what caused you to be angry when you have been having a good day so far. Was it an angry coworker who has been having a rough day or a frustrated mother with her kids whom you saw on the street? If you can't find a reason for your anger, it's probably not yours but something you picked during the day.

Sometimes, you can sense picking up intense feelings from others. When you feel yourself becoming immersed, take a step back to the current moment and keep calm. Try to distance yourself physically from this intense situation. You can practice a breathing exercise in a separate room and remind yourself that these feelings are not yours. With enough time and practice, you will be able to observe intense situations as a bystander without being emotionally invested.

As we mentioned earlier, it's important to practice self-awareness and spend some time by yourself. Take this time to unwind and put all your feelings out in the open. This helps you become aware of your emotional triggers, making you better equipped to deal with them next time. One great tool to distance yourself from other people's emotions is to visualize a glass wall between them and you. You can see the other person's feelings without affecting you.

You can still distance yourself from other people's emotions and still be there for them. Since you pick up on people's vibes, you can listen to them and ask questions about how they are feeling. You will understand where their feelings are coming from while keeping your own feelings separate. This way, that person can share their emotions with you, which they will appreciate, and at the same time, you won't be affected by their turmoil.

In this chapter, we discussed why, as an empath, you struggle in different relationships and how you can deal with problems in a relationship. It's important to learn how to acknowledge your feelings and be there for others without being emotionally overwhelmed. Try to practice the tips mentioned in this chapter to maintain your mental and emotional wellbeing and find a good balance in your relationships.

Chapter 8: Parenting and Raising Empath Children

When you become a parent, you enter a new phase of life, unlike any other experience. Even if you have had pets, siblings, or you have seen children growing up in your household from infancy, having your own child is a completely different ball game. Even all your experience with babysitting your cousins is not going to help. Many people don't realize that hypersensitive persons – and those who can be classified as empaths – actually make extremely good parents. Because they are so hyper-aware of what is going on around them in their environment and other people, they have the key skills necessary to be good parents.

More importantly, they are extremely observant, which means they learn extremely quickly. As parents, they can observe their child, observe the child's reaction to certain stimuli, and learn what they need to do in different situations to calm the child t and create happiness, and it follows that the child will be much easier to deal with. Children, especially babies, don't enjoy crying, it's just the only way for the baby to communicate, and they are either saying they are hungry, uncomfortable, or that they want to go to sleep. The empathetic parent picks up on these things very well and can manage things smoothly.

The real problem is when you have a child that's an empathic baby, and you have a parent who isn't, or even worse, has a very poor sensitivity level and is on the other extreme of the spectrum. If the parents are on the insensitive side of the spectrum, it can be a recipe for disaster for both the baby and the parents. What is worse is that this problem is likely to only grow bigger as the child grows up, and the differences in the understanding of the parent and child increase.

Empathy is an emotion, a trait, a personality quirk, not a problem. This emotional predisposition should not be seen as a deficiency or a problem; rather, it's a gift and a unique ability that your child is blessed with. It's something that you should o develop and nurture. Don't turn it into a negative by blaming your child for it or suppressing it. Trying to suppress it or somehow extinguish it from their personality is an endeavor that will only backfire and have negative repercussions.

Signs of an Empathic Child

The first step towards creating a good environment at home and preparing the right circumstances for the child's upbringing is recognizing their unique traits and emotional and mental needs. Each child is different. Even two children categorized as empathic will have different needs, and this part of their personality will surface in different ways. These are some of the main things to look out for if you have an empathic child.

Different Social Needs

Generally, children enjoy being with children of a similar age, they enjoy spending endless hours playing and having fun, and they usually exhibit extreme forms of emotion. This is mainly because they are not aware of what is and is not socially acceptable. They are not yet disciplined to manage their time, behave impulsively, and haven't quite developed the habit of thinking before acting. They are spontaneous little people with a passion for everything. On the other hand, Empathic children tend to be more thoughtful.

For this reason, they don't always share the traits and passions of children their age. If your child is not comfortable with being with a large group of children, if they resist meeting new people, they just enjoy being at home and don't want to go out to play, don't look at this as a problem. They are empathic children, and they have very different social needs. This is partly because of their nature and partly because they are quite different at a physiological level. This difference is also exhibited in other ways.

Sensitivity

Children with a higher sense of empathy than average have different physiology to other children of the same age. Their sensitivity is part and parcel of their physiological makeup. Their senses, cognition, and emotions are all more sensitive than average. You might notice that your child is extremely responsive to certain sounds, they are quite picky about what they want to wear, they are uncomfortable in certain places, or they have a lot of favorites when it comes to clothes, food, spaces, and even people. This is because the things they classify as favorites offer their senses and minds the best kind of stimulation or the most comfort. They are easily disturbed by sudden sounds, smells, or even changes of plan.

They can't help being extremely sensitive to these things; it's just part of who they are.

Interactions Have an Impact

Due to this sensitive nature, everything can have a lasting impact, especially interactions. As an adult, you might have come across people in your life who can recall nearly all the bad interactions they have had in life and the good ones, people who hold grudges for a very long time, and people who are extremely slow to forgive. These are also the same people who have very deep bonds, and they can be quite hard to access since they have a tough exterior. However, once you are in that circle of theirs, they are extremely colorful and uplifting personalities. These are empathic and sensitive people, and what you see in your child is the early stage of that behavior. This is why it's extremely important to help them understand how they should process emotions and manage their interactions.

Butterfingers with Emotions

Everything from physical stimuli to thoughts to emotions can deeply impact the empathic child. When something happens, i.e., they get startled, wear something that bugs them, or they just aren't comfortable in a certain space, their reaction can be quite extreme. Parents often interpret this as bad manners or think the child is spoiled, but in reality, that problem is bugging them so intensely that their reactions seem extreme to people who don't understand empathy. For the empathic child, the issue that someone else would brush off as minor is, in fact, a major concern and really upsets an empath. It's not that their emotions are out of place; it's that we think they should behave a certain way, and we can't understand why everything is such a big deal. Try and understand that what you think is an overreaction is just an appropriate response for them in their minds.

Compassion

Empathy is what these children are known for, but in reality, it's a general sense of extremely potent compassion that they feel. Whether that's someone else's happiness, anxiety, sadness, or victory, they can feel it like their own. They are so absorbed in the people they are in that they just can't help but feel the same way. An empathic child is the kind of person who will burst into tears if they see a random kid in their class crying. It's just how they are. These children will even love inanimate objects like their toys or just a door they really like in the house.

Intuitive

Not only are they intelligent, but they are also extremely intuitive. Few things take this child by surprise because somehow, they can forecast everything that comes their way. This can be a problem in some cases, especially when it's a negative event or something you just don't want them to know.

How to Give Their Empathic Nature Direction

One of the most important things you can do for your child is to help them manage their emotions. Children make decisions based on what they feel, not based on what they should do or what the right thing to do is, and this is even more important to empathic children who feel everything very intensely. As a parent, you are their role model, and these are some techniques you can use to put them on the right path and show them how they can tackle their own challenges in the right way.

Communicate

Children might be young, but that doesn't mean they can't understand things and get their head around what you think are complex problems for them. There are countless examples of children not yet ten years old and doing things many adults fail to do. Be open with them about the realities of life. Don't try to oversimplify things for them or mask the reality of the situation with a talk that completely changes what is really happening. In doing so, you will show them that it's ok to communicate clearly and truthfully. This will make your job as a parent much easier, and your children will also feel comfortable talking to you honestly as you do with them.

Guide Them through the Emotional Battles

Realize your child is going to face problems with their emotions. There will be times when they feel overwhelmed with emotions and start to act unusually, out of frustration, and times when it's going to test your nerves, but you need to be there for them. Using good communication and patience, you can work through these problems. These critical times are when they need you the most, and these are the moments where they will learn how they can handle problems. The way you deal with them will be the blueprint they use to deal with the issues in their heads on their own when they face a similar situation later on.

Role Model

Problems are a part of life; they are bound to happen sooner or later. Don't hide this from your children, rather present this as a case study for them. Let them be a part of your life and be a spectator to the events you are going through as an individual. This way, they can get a hands-on experience of how "adults" handle things, and they can learn more effective ways of handling matters in their own lives.

Manage Your Behavior

All of these things put a lot of pressure on you as a parent and many responsibilities on your shoulders. You need to look at how you act, deal with your own challenges, and how good a role model you really are. If you are struggling with personal problems such as addictions, anger problems, or just challenges with your spouse, you want to set a good example for your children and show them how they should deal with these situations. This is going to not only show them how they can handle those particular problems, but they will get an understanding of how they can tackle these intense and complex emotions.

Tips for Parenting

The main thing with being a role model for your children is to identify your child's needs and find a suitable solution. Each child is different, and when dealing with an empathic child, their needs are more sensitive. You need to pick up on what they need and address this as soon as possible and as efficiently as possible to help them develop properly. These are a few different things you should do with your child, and you can use each strategy with more or less volume depending on what your child needs.

Give Them Time

Empathic children are very connected to their surroundings, the people in their life, and just day-to-day activities. They are completely absorbed in whatever is going on, and this is one of the reasons why they prefer not to do too much because even a little bit of stimulation is a lot for them to process. You don't want to rush your child through anything, whether at school or play. Give them enough time to process things at their own speed. This can seem like they are taking forever, but they realize that they internalize things very differently and need enough time to take things at their own pace. Rushing them through things will only make it harder for them and harder for you since you have to deal with them after each episode.

Talk to Them about Their Nature

There is nothing to hide or be ashamed about regarding empathic kids. If anything, it's a big blessing for the child and the parent, and as a parent, you should be proud of it. It can be tough, but it's still a great trait to have in your kids. Let them know about it, let them know why they are the way they are, and discuss the idea with them. This will not only cut you some slack because they will understand why you behave the way you do, but it will also give them a fresh perspective on their life. Being the intuitive people they are, combined with their intense observation, they already know that they are not like most other children in their age group. Discussing the nature of the empathic person with them will help them put things into perspective.

Teach Them the Right Jargon

Teaching your child how to communicate more effectively is really important, especially with younger children. The basis of communication is the language, and the more you can help them develop their language, the better they will be able to voice their thoughts and ideas. Teach them words that help them describe how they feel, the thoughts they are experiencing, and how they can better communicate this information. This will make it a lot easier for them and simplify your life as you will better understand what is going on. When paired with an open communication environment, this is a fantastic place for both the child and the parent.

Give Them Space to Express Themselves

Sometimes it's ok to be wrong, be silly, and just make the good old mistakes that children make. As a parent, we all want our children to never get hurt, never have a bad day, and be the best they possibly can be, but they are human at the end of the day. If there is something that you don't particularly like – but your child really enjoys – let them do it and be free to express themselves. If they want to dress a certain way or explore something new, give them enough room to know that they can express themselves and be who they really are.

Manage Their Media Exposure

Empathic children, and children in general, are very impressionable. We are all influenced by the media, whether child or adult. This can be a real problem when you or your child spend several hours a day with the media. Whether this is in the form of a video game, movies, cartoons, or just internet browsing, there needs to be a limit to how much they can consume. Media is designed to keep you distracted and to keep you addicted for as long as possible. This can be extremely overwhelming for the empathic child, and even though they want to disconnect themselves from it, they can't. This is where you need to step in and try to make some changes that will help them regulate their media consumption.

Understand the Impact of Your Behavior

The significant people in a child's life are their siblings, parents, guardians, teachers, and any other person with whom they can develop a bond and interact frequently. The behavior of these people plays a big role in how the child internalizes different things and the worldview they form. While you can't do much about changing other people, you can definitely improve yourself and make sure that you project the best image of yourself in front of your child. Try to be the person you would like your child to be when they grow up.

No child care routine is complete without some measures to enforce discipline. The great thing about empathic children is that they are very receptive to your energy and emotions. If you are upset with them about something, you don't have to do a lot to let them know. They will probably already know something is wrong when you walk into the room. They are very good at sensing their environment and what's even better is that they actually understand you. You don't have to be excessively loud or harsh, just talking to them about the problem will get your message across.

Ideally, you want to start with something that will develop some rapport and some good energy before you move on to discussing the actual problem. This way, you can get them to actually hear you out rather than just block out whatever you say because they don't feel the right kind of energy coming from you. Also, try not to beat about the bush too much. Get straight to the point but do it respectfully. Try to build a conversation rather than just going on about what the kid did wrong and how bad it's. You want it to be a two-way thing rather than just a lecture they have to endure. Also, to make things less problematic, *set clear boundaries.* In every aspect of their life, they should know what they can and can't do, and when they cross that boundary, make sure you let them know and make no exceptions. Just one exception will teach them that there is a way out and that they can be spared. It's difficult, but sometimes you just have to put your foot down and get things straight.

With these tips and tricks, you will hopefully set them up for success in the long run and give them all the knowledge and tools they need to live happy and productive lives. Remember, all of this won't happen in a day; it's a lifelong process, so don't be in a hurry to get anywhere because it's the journey that counts.

Chapter 9: Empaths vs. Narcissists

We've touched briefly on narcissism before in chapter four, discussing how it lies on the far left of the empathetic spectrum. Briefly put, an empath has levels of empathy while a narcissist lacks any at all. However, that's not the end of the story. There's so much more to being an empath and a narcissist. Moreover, there's almost always an instant attraction between the two personalities whenever they meet, be it in a romantic relationship, work, or social gatherings. They say that opposites attract, but what happens when these two kinds of opposites attract each other? It becomes fatally toxic for the empath.

Let's take a couple of steps back and start from the beginning. What, exactly, defines a narcissist?

Who Are Narcissists?

Whenever there's a guy taking mirror selfies or a girl who posts six pictures on Instagram a day, and you get the impression that they like themselves a tad too much, chances are you could be witnessing a narcissist.

While it's true that all narcissists have an inflated sense of self-importance, there are more defining traits that diagnose a narcissist. Most of us have narcissistic tendencies that show now and then, but a true narcissist thinks of themselves as superior to others. All they care about is themselves, and they'll set out to achieve their goals and make themselves feel good, often at the expense of others. While they trample on others' feelings, intentionally or not, they feel no remorse whatsoever for those around them. More often than not, they don't even understand how they affect others negatively, so blaming others for feeling wronged by their actions is justified in their minds.

Narcissism is a personality trait. This means that not everyone who has narcissistic tendencies is a true narcissist. True narcissists are medically diagnosed with having a Narcissistic Personality Disorder, or NDP. People with low levels of narcissism will fall on the lower end of the spectrum, while those with pathological narcissism will rank the highest on the narcissistic spectrum.

Narcissistic Personality Disorder is recognized as an official personality disorder in the Diagnostic and Statistical Manual of Mental Disorders (DSM-5). According to the DSM-5, to diagnose a person with a Narcissistic Personality Disorder, they have to check at least five of the following nine official criteria for NDP:

1. They have a grandiose sense of self-importance.

2. They are preoccupied with fantasies about themselves, often dreaming about their brilliance, power, success, beauty, or perfect love.

3. They believe they're superior, unique, and special. They would only rather associate with others they perceive as special or high-ranking and get disgusted by those they perceive as inferior beings.

4. They have an insatiable need for admiration and appreciation.

5. They display a strong sense of self-entitlement.

6. They lack any kind of empathy.

7. They often exploit others to their advantage.

8. They may envy others or feel like others are always envious of them.

9. They're arrogant, and they don't hide it.

That said, a person can be a narcissist without making it too obvious. You may be dealing with a narcissist yet fail to spot them, making it often difficult to diagnose a person with narcissism without the help of a qualified expert.

Traits of a Narcissist

Let's discuss the traits of a narcissist in further depth. A narcissist will often display the following traits:

1. They Change Colors

At first encounter, you'll find a charming and charismatic person who may even inspire you. However, one of the hallmarks of narcissism is that they draw people in by their superficial charm. They won't show their toxicity right away, especially if they try to woo someone romantically.

2. They Have a Strong Sense of Entitlement

Narcissists believe they're superior to others, full-stop. As such, they expect others to treat them in a special way deserving of their self-image. They believe they deserve all that's good and are entitled to the best – rules just don't apply to them.

3. They Display Manipulative Behavior

Narcissists like to get what they want, and they often get it by manipulating others. At first, they'll use soft tactics to get you to their side and give them what they want, but they may change tactics if that doesn't work. However nice they may seem to you, they always prioritize their needs.

4. They're Thirsty for Admiration

Narcissists love praise and admiration. They already have an inflated sense of ego, but they can never get enough of being validated by others for what they take pride in. You'll often find them bragging about themselves and exaggerating their achievements, all while waiting for you to affirm their superiority.

5. They Lack Empathy

Narcissists don't know how others feel, and they don't care either. They don't have a drop of empathy, so they often disregard others' feelings, thoughts, and needs as trivial or non-existent. They may harm others by their indifferent behavior and blame them for feeling hurt or being too sensitive.

6. They're Arrogant

There's no one more arrogant than a narcissist. Not only do they think of themselves as superior, but they make sure you know it as well. That's why it's common for narcissists to be described as rude or even abusive when dealing with others. This shows especially when they deal with people they deem inferior, people who the narcissist will get nothing from by being good to them.

7. They're Selfish

At the core of every narcissistic behavior, you'll find pure selfishness. Whatever they do, it's always for themselves, regardless of any effect it might have on anyone else.

Types of Narcissism

Although many do, not all narcissists allow their personalities to be so obvious. That's because there are different types of narcissistic personalities, which have everything to do with how they were bought up, genetics, and personality traits. Here's a quick overview of four different kinds of narcissism.

o Grandiose vs. Vulnerable Narcissism

Both grandiose and vulnerable narcissists share a lot of similar traits, but the difference between both lies in their *childhood experiences.*

A grandiose narcissist is someone who grew up getting everything they desired. They have been treated as superior for as long as they can remember, and the expectation from society to keep treating them as such grew with them as they walked into adulthood. They're often aggressive, dominant, flamboyant, super confident, and exaggerate their importance.

Meanwhile, a vulnerable narcissist is someone who grew up suffering from childhood abuse or neglect. As a result, they have an internal conflict between their inflated sense of grandiosity and how they've been treated, making them much more sensitive than grandiose narcissists. Their narcissism serves as a shield that protects them from their feelings of inferiority or inadequacy. They're easily offended and often feel anxious about how others see them, especially if they don't receive special treatment.

o Overt vs. Covert Narcissism

Narcissists can also be overt or covert. The best way to describe both kinds is being extroverted and introverted. An overt narcissist likes to be at the center of attention wherever they go. You'll find them to be the loudest and most arrogant and insensitive people in a group. They go around fishing for compliments and thrive on attention.

Meanwhile, a covert narcissist is more on the quieter side. They still have the same sense of grandiose self-importance as overt narcissists, fantasizing about success and power. However, they're not as "loud" as the overt narcissists in getting what they want or seeking attention. That's why it's much more difficult to spot covert narcissism, especially when it comes to relationships.

The Fatal Attraction of an Empath and a Narcissist

Does it feel like narcissists are the exact opposite of empaths? In a sense, they are. That makes it even more curious to find empaths instantly attracted to them. It makes sense for a narcissist to be attracted to an empath. After all, there's nothing like an empath's loving and caring nature to feed their ego and boost their sense of self-importance. An empath is a perfect person to listen, appreciate, support, adore, and selflessly give their all to a narcissist, so of course, narcissists will love having an empath around. But how about empaths? Why would they be attracted to someone as selfish, unloving, demanding, self-entitled, arrogant, and insensitive as a narcissist?

This has to do with the empath's feeling of responsibility for taking care of others. Despite their endless giving and the narcissist's unchangeable character, they believe that if they love their partner enough, they're bound to change and reciprocate their feelings someday. It certainly doesn't help that a narcissist appears full of charm and charisma at the first encounter – they shower the empath with superficial love and care to the extent that an empath feels like they've instantly fallen in love. However, empaths aren't only attracted to narcissists in a romantic sense or vice versa. The fatal attraction between both can take on many forms, whether it's a romantic relationship, friendship, or even professional acquaintanceship.

How to Tell if Your Partner Is a Narcissist

Regardless of the setting, dealing with a narcissist is energy-consuming. You may struggle to put your finger on the exact cause of feeling drained all the time, but once you realize you're dealing with a narcissist, your feelings are bound to become clearer. Whether you're dealing with a narcissist in the workplace, relationship, friendship, or at home, here are a few signs that the person you're giving your all to is narcissistically toxic to you.

1. They Were Super Charming in the Beginning

The first thing you'll notice about a narcissist is how charming they are. If you're in a relationship with one, then there are high chances that your love story started as a fairy tale. They were constantly bombarding you with texts, they showered you with love during the dates, and they confessed their undying love to you so quickly. A narcissist in the workplace or in social settings is highly charismatic and goes around showering people with superficial praise. They maintain a good relationship with everyone without letting anyone get close to them. It's only after dealing with them for an extended period that their masks start to crack, showing their true narcissistic selves.

It's easier to spot a narcissist at home since they usually don't have to keep the facade with their family members. They expect their relatives to worship them unconditionally, and their arrogance shows in whatever they do.

2. They Always Talk about How Great They Are

Narcissists will always steer the conversation to themselves. If you're telling them about achievement, they'll be sure to tale the various battles they've fought and won. If you're complaining about an issue or looking for support, they'll whine about how their own life is difficult, yet how they're coping perfectly well with the challenges. They'll make you feel like you're less than them no matter what you say, always going into a comparison about how much better they're doing than you.

3. They're Always Fishing for Compliments from You

Despite their constant efforts to belittle you and what you're going through, they'll still wait for you to compliment them on everything they say and do. Although they appear super self-confident, they actually feed off the compliments to validate their self-importance. If you fail to meet their expectations, they'll somehow turn on you and start attacking your weaknesses.

4. They Don't Show Any Empathy

There's nothing worse than the feeling you feel when you seek support from a friend or a partner, only to find yourself talking to an ice-cold wall with no emotions. This is the feeling you'll always get whenever you seek support from the narcissist in your life. They're simply unable to feel your pain and emotions. Whenever you complain, they'll either talk about their worries or belittle your pain - often, they'll do both at once.

5. They Don't Have A Lot - *if Any* - Long-Term Friends

Despite their need for admiration, or perhaps because of it, narcissists only maintain superficial relationships. They don't let others get too close to them for fear of being found out. As a result, they'll feel envious of your close friends and get moody when you try to hang out with them. They'll lash out at you or throw underhanded comments about your friends to make you doubt them. This will either make you feel guilty for hanging out with your friends instead of the narcissist or affect your relationships with the rest of your close people.

6. They Constantly Pick on You

They'll start by teasing you, but after a while, you'll feel like their jokes are becoming too cruel, real, and malicious. After a while, you'll feel they're constantly attacking every little thing you do – from the way you eat to the way you dress, talk, laugh, or even sleep. They'll always brush it aside as a joke if you confront them and turn the tables on you for being "too sensitive."

7. They Often Gaslight You

Gaslighting is one of the hallmarks of narcissism. It's a form of emotional abuse that makes you doubt yourself and deepens your insecurities. Narcissists are champions at gaslighting – they'll insert a few lies among a truth, accuse others of false things, manipulate the facts ever so slightly to the extent that you start doubting your reality. A person who's fallen victim to gaslighting will start doubting their reality and their perception of facts, become less confident and insecure, start wondering if they really are too sensitive, feel they can do nothing right and that everything is their fault, and feel there's something wrong without being able to identify what it's. As a result, they'll start to apologize often, make excuses for the narcissist's behavior, and question their responses many times before giving them.

8. They Always Think They're Right, and Rarely Ever Apologize

There's one rule that all narcissists hold true: they're always right. If you contradict them or point out their mistakes, they'll come up with a thousand justifications for their behavior. If they don't have any, they'll beat around the bush and tell you you're being too mean. Meanwhile, they'll make sure to punish you for questioning them, either by ignoring, gaslighting, or being mean to you.

9. They're Hesitant to Define a Clear Relationship

You don't have to define every relationship, as long as it's mutually agreed upon. However, if your partner is already exhibiting symptoms of narcissism, you should consider it a red flag if they keep dancing around defining the relationship.

10. They Refuse to Accept a Breakup

If you get into a relationship with a narcissist, they'll expect to hold the reigns of the relationship. They'll never let you go as long as they still have a use for you. They'll be the ones to break it off when they get bored, and they'll never accept you breaking up with them. That's a decision for them to make, and you don't have the right to break up with such "perfect" beings as them. If you try to walk away, they'll lash out at you, blackmail you, and use every underhanded method they know to make you feel guilty and manipulate you into getting back with them.

How to Deal with a Narcissist

Dealing with a narcissist drains your mental and emotional energy, maybe even your physical health. If you realize you're dealing with a narcissist, you must take the necessary measures to protect yourself. Here are a few ways through which you can do that.

1. Realize What's Happening

The first step to protecting yourself from a narcissist is to realize the emotional abuse you're being subjected to in your relationship. Although it will be difficult for you as an empath to blame others, you really need to stand up for yourself and consider that whatever is happening might not be your fault.

2. Ask Others for Their Opinion

If you've been dealing with the narcissist for so long that you're starting to doubt yourself, you definitely need to get an outsider's perspective. Look for someone you can trust and ask for their opinion of different situations. This will help you build a clearer image of what's really going on.

3. Set Clear Boundaries in Your Relationship

Once you start realizing that you're stuck in a toxic relationship, it's time to take some protective measures. Setting boundaries against the narcissist in your life will take different forms depending on the kind of relationship. With parents, siblings, and partners, you'll be stuck face-to-face, for the most part, so defining clear boundaries to help you co-exist together is crucial for your well-being.

4. Remember Their True Nature

A narcissist will never change, no matter how much love and appreciation you give them. If you ever feel sorry for setting boundaries or trying to walk away, keep this in mind. They'll never love you or treat you the way you love and treat them.

5. Know When to Walk Away

If setting boundaries doesn't work and they refuse to change the way they treat you, it's time you put yourself first and walk away. It's going to be super challenging. They'll use their charm to pull you in once again, apologize and tell you they'll change, and go the extra mile to win you over. However, know that's all a game for them – once they get you back, they'll treat you worse than before as a punishment. So, walk away and don't look back; it's time you start focusing on your well-being, dreams, and future.

The story of the attraction between empaths and narcissists is as old as the hills. Narcissists thrive on the admiration they can receive from an empath, while an empath feels the need to take care of narcissists and fulfill their emptiness. The story goes on to show how every single relationship between a narcissist and an empath results in the same fatal fate: the narcissist thrives while the empath withers away.

Chapter 10: Understanding Your Feelings

Having empathy is a great gift that can help you build relationships in your personal and professional life. However, emotions can sometimes be overwhelming. Many people can be overwhelmed when they are extremely sad, stressed, or going through a traumatic experience. Now, imagine feeling your emotions *AND* everyone else's around you; how overwhelming will this be? This is what it feels like to be an empath. They are always feeling their and everyone else's emotions which can be extremely overwhelming and take a toll on their mental health.

Being an empath isn't always easy. No one wants to feel other people's emotions. Whether you are taking on someone's sadness or happiness, it can be overwhelming either way. An empath may not always be aware that their emotions aren't theirs, which is why they may not understand the sudden change in their temperament. Empaths don't feel their emotions like most people because their feelings are much greater and deeper. For this reason, they need to recognize when they are feeling overwhelmed, which will allow them to understand their own feelings and separate them from others.

Signs That an Empath Is Overwhelmed

Empaths are often guided by their intuition and are also very sensitive individuals. It's their sensitive nature that allows them to take on and absorb other people's emotions, couple this with a strong intuition and high sensitivity, and you have the greatest friends and partners. However, this gift comes at a price to the empath, who gets overwhelmed, drained, and confused about which feelings belong to them and which belong to the people around them.

You have probably felt the symptoms of being emotionally overwhelmed a few times in your life, but you can't understand why you are feeling this way. Being aware of these symptoms will help you step back from the person or situation that makes you overstressed, establish healthy boundaries, and practice self-care to protect your mental health.

o **Mood Swings**

If you suddenly feel sad, lazy, or disinterested and haven't noticed anything that could have triggered these emotions, you are most likely overwhelmed by absorbing other people's energies. You can be happy and excited, and all of a sudden, you feel sad and anxious, or you can be calm and relaxed, and suddenly you feel angry and agitated.

These sudden changes in your mood are a sign of being emotionally overwhelmed. As mentioned, empaths mirror people's emotions, which helps them understand what those close to them are going through. However, you will need to step back when it starts affecting your mental health, and you start to suffer from severe mood swings.

o **Panic Disorder**

A panic disorder or a panic attack is an unfortunate side effect of being a sensitive empath. Feeling different emotions all at once can be simply too much, leading to anxiety and panic attacks.

o **Feeling Exhausted**

Constantly taking on other people's emotions and energies can make you feel drained and exhausted. When you feel someone's anger, grief, anxiety, fear, or suffering, you will start feeling tired. These emotions can stress your body and overtire your nervous system, and you won't even be aware of it. You will feel tired and exhausted all the time to the extent that you won't be able to keep your eyes open. Therefore, if you find yourself constantly fatigued for no apparent reason, then you have probably internalized other people's energies and emotions, and your body can't take it anymore.

o **Skin Problems**

It isn't just your body that suffers; all of these emotions will take a toll on your skin as well. Usually, various emotions can show on our skin; when exhausted, we get dark circles under our eyes, and stress can trigger acne. This has always been the case with skin and emotions; what is inside always appears outside. When you harbor so many emotions inside of you, especially negative ones, your body and mind will become overwhelmed and overstressed, and symptoms will manifest on your skin. You will start to suffer from hives, rashes, and breakouts. This is your skin telling you that something is wrong, and you need to pause and examine what is going on inside of you.

o **Mental Issues**

As you know, negative emotions can also seriously impact your mental health. We all go through hard times that can take a toll on our well-being. As an empath, you don't only feel your negative emotions, but you are absorbing and internalizing everyone else's too. So, mirroring emotions like fear, anger, or grief can cause you mental issues like anxiety or depression. In this case, an empath will want to find an easy way to numb the emotional pain they have been feeling to opt for unhealthy coping mechanisms like binge eating, heavy drinking, or substance abuse. They will go for anything that can ease their emotional pain and suffering. Most empaths aren't aware of why they feel that way; they just know that something isn't right and want to go back to their old selves.

Opting for unhealthy coping mechanisms can have severe consequences and can cause serious problems. Alcohol or drugs are merely a temporary escape, not a solution. Empathy isn't a disease that requires a cure. You simply need to find healthy coping mechanisms to protect you from feeling overwhelmed all of the time. Once you learn how to cope with being an empath, you will be able to use your gift to help yourself and others.

Healthy Coping Mechanisms

Absorbing other people's emotions is something that you can't control. Naturally, you don't want to spend your whole life feeling crushed by emotions that aren't even yours. For every problem, there is a solution. Having healthy coping mechanisms will help you deal with your emotional overwhelm.

o **Working Out**

Working out is a great way to help you deal with emotional overwhelm since it will help take your mind off anything you feel or think of. Emotional overwhelm can make an empath feel stressed and anxious. As you probably know, working out isn't only beneficial to your physical health but also your mental health, as it can reduce your anxiety stress and improve your overall mood. There are various types of exercises that you can try, but the Autoregulation exercises will help reduce the panic and anxiety that can result from feeling emotionally overwhelmed. These exercises can also help calm your mind and body. They usually include meditation, breathing exercises, and muscle relaxation. Don't wait until you are stressed or anxious to practice these exercises but incorporate them into your daily routine to help prevent emotional overwhelm.

If you don't have the time to go to the gym or work out every day, you can opt for short exercises that will make a huge difference. You can try exercises like jumping the rope for one minute, making 20 burpees, or 100 meters sprint.

○ Confront Your Emotions

One of the biggest mistakes empaths make bottles their emotions up and refuse to acknowledge or talk about them. It isn't healthy to bury your feelings, and it can be so much worse when they are other people's emotions. Pushing down other people's negative energies and issues can have severe and serious consequences. Feelings can never be hidden or shoved down because they will always find a way to rise to the surface, and when they do, they will be strong and agonizing. Famous psychologist Sigmund Freud has done many studies about repressing thoughts and emotions and how they can affect your mental and physical health. Repressing your emotions can lead to high blood pressure, stress, and many other diseases. To protect your body and mind, you need to stop repressing the feelings you absorb from other people.

The easiest way to do that's to confront all of the negative emotions you have been absorbing. We understand this will not be easy, and you may be anxious or afraid of uncovering these feelings. However, working on getting strong mentally will help you face and deal with these feelings and emotions. Confronting them will allow you to learn so much about the people in your life: their fears, struggles, anxiety, and pain. You may come to learn a few disturbing things, too, when tackling these emotions. However, it's part of being a human; the good, the bad, and the very ugly.

We have discussed in a previous chapter how an empath needs to spend some time alone to recharge after having their energy drained from being around people and absorbing their energies. Spend some time alone or in meditation so you can process and comprehend all feelings, thoughts, and energies to which you've been subjected. When you fully understand all of these negative emotions and energies, you will be able to release and get rid of them easily.

o **Meditate**

If you want to be mentally strong to explore your emotions, you need to work on boosting your mental strength. Meditation has always been one of the best methods to improve your mental discipline, which is probably why it has been practiced for centuries, and its popularity hasn't died down. As an empath, making meditation a part of your lifestyle can have a positive impact. Meditation will give you the chance to focus on the present moment and help you clear your mind and be alone with your thoughts. Practicing meditation every day will also help you get rid of all the emotions you have been absorbing all day.

Meditation is easy, and if you are new to it, you will find many guided sessions online. However, the premise is pretty much the same. You need to sit comfortably in a quiet spot with no distractions, try to be present and focused on the here and now, don't think about the past or worry about the future or things that aren't real or may never happen. Be focused on this moment; it's all you have. That said, some thoughts or worries may creep in while meditating. Don't try to fight them or let them interfere with your meditation. Just imagine that they are clouds, and you are watching them passing by. Don't give them any attention.

In addition to meditation, spending some time alone can also help you manage emotional overwhelm. As mentioned, being around people can drain an empath and cause emotional overwhelm. Therefore, if you spend a couple of hours every day alone in a quiet room, you will be able to manage your feelings and energy. Additionally, you should also try breathing exercises to calm yourself down. It's very easy, and you can do them anywhere. Just take a deep breath through your nose and release it through your mouth. Like meditation, you also need to focus on this very moment. Forget the world around you and only focus on your breathing.

o Express Yourself Through Art

Art has always been a great outlet for people to express themselves and get rid of their negative emotions. If an empath wants to cope with emotional overwhelm, they need to tap into their creative side. There are various types of art that you can try, like painting, writing, singing, acting, and many more. Find something that you enjoy or are good at, and go for it; whatever form of art that you choose will help you release all of the negative emotions that have been consuming you for so long.

Art is very relaxing and can help reduce stress for anyone, not just empaths. Just like exercise and meditation, art can help you clear your mind. This is because art will help you stay focused on the task you are working on, so you will not be concerned with anything else. For instance, if you are writing or painting, you will only be focused on the project at hand and feel a sense of calmness and relaxation because you are creating something.

This coping mechanism can help you understand your emotions. For example, when you put what you are feeling on paper, you will give yourself the chance to understand these emotions better as they will be clear to you, and you won't have to wonder about your feelings. Additionally, art can help you express yourself. Maybe one day you can be a famous artist or writer. Sensitive souls like you can excel in these careers.

Many studies have shown the positive impact of art on people who have suffered trauma in their lives. Understandably, empaths aren't traumatized individuals, but they exhibit similar symptoms. These studies have shown that art can reduce depression in traumatized adults, proving that it can help empaths cope and manage emotional overwhelm.

○ **You Can't Help Everyone**

Although empaths are gifted individuals, they aren't superheroes. They may seem like it, though, since they can understand exactly what someone is thinking and feel the emotions of the people around them. It's a unique ability indeed, but what exactly do empaths do with this ability? Empaths are always aware of the pain and struggle the people around them are going through. Your compassionate and sensitive nature will make you feel responsible for them and that you need to act fast to help them out. Additionally, you probably believe deep down that if you help these people, they will feel better, and, in turn, you will also feel better and get rid of all of the negative emotions that have taken over your heart and mind. In other words, if you make a miserable person feel happy, an angry person feels calm, or make someone scared feel safe, then there will be no negative emotions for you to absorb, and you will feel better as well.

However, you aren't a superhero, and you can't save everyone or fix their problems. You can't just walk down the street, feel someone's pain, and offer to help. Although it's a sweet thought, it's unrealistic. Just as you need to separate your emotions from other people's, you need to accept that other people's problems aren't your responsibility to solve or your burden to carry. This can damage your mental health. If you allow yourself to be concerned with everyone else's problems and try to produce solutions, then you will not have any time or energy for your problems or well-being. You will neglect yourself and your needs for the sake of others, and eventually, you will burn yourself out and won't be able to help anyone, including yourself. The key here is to find balance. Help others only when you can, and you shouldn't let it interfere with your well-being. There are also times when you will have to put yourself first, which is ok. There is nothing selfish about that, even if some people try to take advantage of your sensitive nature to convince you otherwise.

For instance, if a friend is asking you to drive them to the airport and you have an important meeting, you can't just drop everything for them. As mentioned in previous chapters, you need to say no without feeling guilty and set boundaries. Your friend can simply ask someone else or call an Uber, but they shouldn't expect you to ignore an important meeting when they can easily find other options. Another thing that you need to understand is that you can't save everyone. An empath may feel disappointed if they fail to help someone. For instance, if you have a friend who is an addict and you are trying to help them get into rehab and get clean, but they refuse, you can't feel bad or guilty about it. Normally, you don't want to see your friend suffer and want to save them. However, you need to understand that you can't help someone who doesn't want or accept your help, and you can't save people from themselves. You need to stop carrying the world's burdens on your shoulders. You aren't Superman.

You have a gift, and if you learn how to use it, it can change your life for the better. However, to take advantage of your abilities, you first need to understand your feelings and know when overwhelmed. Once you recognize the symptoms of being emotionally overwhelmed, you can try any coping mechanisms mentioned here to help you manage these feelings. Incorporate these mechanisms in your lifestyle and daily routine to help prevent feeling overwhelmed before it happens.

Chapter 11: Setting Boundaries

Relationships with friends, family, coworkers, and even just strangers you come across in life need to be managed in a way that benefits you both. We often interact without paying attention to how this interaction impacts the other person or us. We go by routine, by intuition, and we follow a form of communication and interaction that we have developed, without much thought over why we have developed it that way or what functional purpose it serves. This is especially true for people with a higher sensitivity since all of these interactions have a much deeper impact on empaths.

Interactions as an Empath

We all feel emotions, we all feel things like empathy and compassion, but these feelings are far more intense when it comes to the empath. An empath will feel like even the smallest interaction has had a profound impact. Just a small problem with a friend, a little scrap with a coworker will send the empath down a thought rabbit hole, where they start analyzing things at a much deeper level than necessary. There is no need to look into things in so much detail, but the empath cannot help him or herself. Similarly, if they feel a good emotion from some interaction, they will often take it out of proportion again, which can lead to thinking too much, leading to all kinds of challenges down the road.

For instance, if they have a good conversation with someone, an empath will expand on this interaction thinking about how great that person was, how they must be wonderful in all aspects of their life and will think it will be a good idea to get to know them a bit more. In reality, this could be very far from the truth. Just one interaction, or even a few interactions, doesn't mean a person is completely good or completely bad.

All these interactions impact the mental and emotional health of the empath. Continuing to think about things in such an unnecessarily deep manner is both a cumbersome process and one that doesn't always lead to good results. This is why having boundaries in relationships is very important. Even if personal relationships are between siblings, parents, or your significant other, having some boundary line is always beneficial.

It's important to set boundaries and detect boundaries that others have placed and respect the space they want to have. As empaths feel everything so intensely, it's very difficult for them to stop themselves and resist the urge to become emotionally attached to someone. In reality, the person might not be comfortable with this, which could lead to all kinds of uncomfortable situations.

Types of Boundaries

The right kinds of boundaries help us manage our relationships better, and for empaths, this means it also helps to regulate their emotions and the way they think. Without a good boundary setup, it can be very easy to waste energy and emotions on things that really don't need it and not provide enough to things that do need more energy and emotional input. Here are the main kinds of boundaries that are used in social life.

  o **Physical**

This is the one you might have felt most in your life and even found problematic. As humans, we want to have our "personal space." This is not about having your own home or your own room but literally just having enough space around you when you are in an interaction. Even before social distancing was a thing, it was generally considered bad manners to stand too close to a person if you were waiting in line with them or being too close to someone when you are sitting at the dinner table.

This relates to the physical space that we have around us. Generally, when it's someone that you are comfortable with, you won't mind them being really close to you; you might not even mind them having their arm around your neck. With people you don't know that well, you will want more space, ideally at least two or three feet away. With people who are complete strangers, you will want at least four or more feet of space from them.

  o **Sexual**

Related to physical boundaries, one that's more about the personal relationships that we have are the sexual boundaries that we like to have. For instance, for some people having a kiss in public or just having any kind of public display of affection is a serious problem. It makes them extremely uncomfortable and can really upset them.

For others, holding hands and other displays of affection don't affect them at all. In fact, not having public displays of affection from their partner can even make them angry. Similarly, different people want their relationships to advance at different speeds. Everyone has their own unique ways of dealing with intimacy, so it's best to give people as much space as you can in this regard.

o **Mental**

Mental boundaries can also be classified as intellectual boundaries generally. When you don't "get along" with someone, you want to have a bit more space between you and that person. When you meet someone who thinks like you, or at least you feel like you have a mental connection, you don't mind them being that close to you. Similarly, when you have that connection with someone, it's not just about physical proximity, but that person is close to you in your mind; they naturally just have a higher ranking in your mind when you think about them. This is also about how open you are about expressing yourself and the extent to which you actually share your real thoughts and ideas with people. When you feel mentally connected to them, you also tend to have a level of trust, which really changes the relationship's dynamic.

o **Emotional**

Emotional boundaries have to do with how we process things that we go through in life and specifically the interactions we experience. Emotional boundaries are tied to all the other kinds of boundaries we have painstakingly put in place. Generally, when a physical, mental, or other boundary is crossed, this also impacts how we feel. Similarly, different people also have a natural disposition as to how open or closed they are emotional. This influences how emotionally attached they are in certain situations. Empaths tend to have very open emotional boundaries, and this is the unique trait of empaths which can be good or bad, depending on the situation.

What Boundaries Are

When we think of setting up boundaries, it helps to know what exactly these boundaries are for, the kind of benefits we are looking to achieve from having these boundaries, and how they can benefit other people in our life. For empaths, on the plus side is that they help to restore self-respect. Empaths often get dragged into so many different relationships and roles so easily that they forget that they are unique individuals. They start to feel like a doormat that exists only to fulfill the social needs of others and should not have any personal requirements from the relationships they are in. Every relationship is a two-way street. As an empath, you have just as much right to expect something from that relationship as the other person who expects you to always be there.

Boundaries are a way for us to define what we are and what we aren't. For empaths, especially, it can get really overwhelming and confusing to be in so many different roles simultaneously. As you develop your ability to set boundaries and create limits on interactions, you are essentially working on yourself and improving the quality of the relationship. Rather than wasting yourself on every person you come across, you should focus on a few interactions and make them as high quality as possible.

This will give you more control over how you lead your life and give you more freedom to live as you desire rather than under the pressure of the relationships you foster. Also, look at boundaries as a way of respecting the people around you. You are not just being present there for the sake of it, but rather you are there to give them the very best of you.

What Boundaries Are Not

At the same time, you should also know how to effectively use boundaries and not use this as an excuse to save yourself from certain people or interactions. Having boundaries around you doesn't mean that you are isolating yourself from life or ignoring people in your life. It's simply that you are optimizing your social life, which will benefit everyone. However, if you feel like you just don't want to be around someone where you don't feel comfortable, there is no harm in drawing a line there creating some space. Similarly, you should impose these boundaries in such a way that it doesn't offend people, nor do they feel like you are trying to push them away. After all, they are still a part of your life, but you just want things to be a bit more streamlined.

Having boundaries doesn't mean you are selfish; it means you know what is right for you and what your priorities are, and you are focusing on your life. As an empath, it's in your nature to be overly concerned about people, and if you realize this isn't the best way to deal with things, then boundaries will help you. Again, this doesn't mean you suddenly don't care, but you are certainly not concerned with things that are none of your business. It's all about giving yourself direction in your interactions and improving the quality of life by focusing your energy on a specific direction.

How to Set Boundaries

At this point, you have already spent several years living as an empath. The people around you perceive you a certain way, and you are probably accustomed to living in a certain way. The way you behave in social settings the way you interact with people are all things that are going to go through a slight change when you start to change the way you set boundaries for yourself. While it might seem like a difficult task, it can be done and will be beneficial in the long run. Here are a few techniques you can adopt.

○ **Understand Your Requirements**

The first exercise is to self-evaluate and understand your requirements, what makes you happy and what doesn't. You can start off with a pen and paper and note down what really makes you uncomfortable in your current social relationships. In this exercise, you can cover all your relationships and even think of hypothetical examples. As you know how you would react in any given situation, you can hypothesize how you would behave in a given situation if it were to come up, such as meeting a new boss, having an interview, or meeting someone new through a friend.

In this way, you'll develop a list of all the things you want, the things you like, and a list of things you prefer in your social interactions. From here, you can start to examine what you need to change and how you can go about it. You might find that you are fine with how you interact with new people and those that are not very close to you, but you aren't happy with how you deal with your very private relationships. This will be the blueprint for changing your interactions and what areas you want to focus on. From here, you can implement the following techniques to achieve the desired results.

○ **Learn to Say No**

If there is one word an empath doesn't have in their dictionary, it's "no," and yet this is the most powerful word to use to build boundaries and good relationships. One of the biggest challenges for the empath is they get dragged into situations, or they push themselves into situations they don't want to be a part of in the first place. And so, the starts the process of living in uncomfortable situations, difficult to get out of, once you're in it. On the other side of the coin, when the empath cannot say no to themselves and cannot push themselves into the direction that they really want to go in, they are left regretting making the wrong decisions. Just by saying no, either to themselves or to other people, the empath can build the boundary that they need to safeguard their interests and the interests of others. Saying no will be difficult by trying to do it with the small things and build up the capacity to say no to the big things too.

○ **Stand Up for Yourself**

Realize what it's that really makes you happy, what you prefer, and where you really want to go with your life. As an empath, you are constantly swayed by emotions that don't belong to you, and it's easy to lose track of what you really want to do. The ability to stand up for yourself goes hand in hand with the ability to say no to the things that you don't want and to say yes to the things that you do want as the empath is so preoccupied with other activities and other commitments, they often unwillingly have to forgo the things they really want. Creating boundaries will help you create the time and energy you need to stand up for yourself and pursue your own dreams rather than living a life where you are a victim of your own nature.

o **Communicate Clearly**

Thinking through all of these things, deciding what you want to do, and even planning how you will do it's no good if you aren't voicing these ideas and communicating what you want. Use all kinds of communication at your disposal to voice your concerns and show people what you really want for yourself and what you expect from them. Empaths are fantastic listeners, and they have a knack for understanding what is going on around them, but when it comes to speaking and pushing information out, they can have trouble. Start with the circle that you are most comfortable in and start expressing yourself more freely to build this into your character and improve.

o **Take a Moment before Deciding**

People who are empaths act based on their emotions and impulse a lot more simply because they feel things so intensely. In some cases, they can't stop themselves, and it's a reflex reaction rather than a calculated decision. Whether you are saying no to a situation or agreeing to something, the important thing is not to do it in haste. Take a moment before you make a decision, step back, look at things from a different angle and then plan a course of action. This momentary pause can help you look at things from a neutral perspective, whereas in the heat of the moment, we are often driven by emotion and have a limited outlook on the matter.

The transition phase from being the person you have always been into being someone who actively implements boundaries in their life and abides by the social guidelines that they have laid is not a fast or easy transition. You should be prepared to face resistance and even be ready to lose some people. There will undoubtedly be people who will not agree with this new version of you, but that's ok. If someone is not willing to accept you for a person who stands up for themselves and has a way of doing things, they are most likely in your life for the benefit you provide them and do not want to provide you with any benefit. Over time you will grow thicker skin, making the transition phase easier to deal with. The most important thing is to stay at it in the initial phase, which is the most difficult time of the transition.

Chapter 12: How to Control Your Emotions

Managing emotions can be extremely challenging for an empath because of their natural manner of dealing with emotions, as we've discussed in previous chapters. Along with the positive, we've seen the dark side too, where an empath can go down the rabbit hole of self-destruction if they don't properly manage their emotions. They are also quite impulsive and have difficulty seeing the big picture. Even when it's an experience that doesn't have anything to do with them directly, they feel it intensely.

This impacts the way they personally feel, how they interact with other people, and how they act in their own life, and it can leave a lasting impact on their minds.

When it comes to properly managing emotions for anyone – specifically empaths – a few different stages of emotional processing can be broken down as follows: The first stage is where they are actually exposed to the stimuli, and they internalize emotions. The second stage is when they have received the message and are processing it in their minds. The last stage involves how they react to this stimulation and how they internalize the entire experience. For an empath, every stage needs to be managed. Let's look at each stage and what can be done to make the impact less potent and more manageable.

Absorbing Emotions

The first thing to address is how an empath internalizes different things going on around them. Even though it can seem relatively easy for other people to maintain a calm state when something goes wrong or are incredibly excited about something, things are very different for the empath. The empath doesn't willingly absorb things at a deep level; the problem is that they are extremely sensitive and automatically absorb things deeply and intensely, and fast. When an average person is still thinking about what they have heard, the empath is already bursting into tears, thinking of other extreme situations that will arise from this bad news. Here are a few strategies to help make the process of internalizing information a little more manageable and the impact a little less severe.

Understand the Emotion

Empaths are not only very sensitive to the emotions of others, but they are also extremely sensitive to the energy that other people bring. This is usually characterized by a situation where an empath is feeling completely normal or even slightly positive, then they either get a phone call or someone joins them, or they talk to someone, and there is a sudden and a drastic change in their emotional state. They are suddenly angry or sad, or they look like they are stressed out, and all these emotions and feelings seem to be exaggerated. As the empath, your first response to this scenario should be to work out exactly what it's you are feeling and try to identify it for yourself.

We often mix up our own feelings in the heat of the moment. When we feel excited and happy about something, we are on the brink of extreme emotion, and even something small could trigger a person to go in the opposite direction. Naming the feeling will give you more control over what is going on in your mind and give you a sense of direction. At the same time, it can help to think of the source of the emotion. Sometimes you will realize that you are angry because you just spoke to someone, telling you how frustrated they feel. Just because you feel an emotion doesn't mean that it's yours to feel. Empaths have an uncanny ability to internalize emotions that aren't theirs.

o **Ground Yourself**

There is a reason why counting sheep helps children go to sleep. This is a process known as grounding, and the aim is to get one thing that the mind can focus on so that it can stop processing the hundreds of other things going on. When you focus on one object, that object fully occupies the attention to the exclusion of anything else. It helps you let go of emotions operating in the background not related to the present moment. A great strategy is to look for something around you and focus on that or start counting from 1000 backward or mentally repeat some affirmations you remember. Anything you can do to shift your attention will help.

o **Be Self-Aware**

Check in with your feelings often and try to be as self-aware as possible, living in the present. If you have suddenly felt a change of emotion, try going back to a moment you remember just before the emotional change. When you are more self-aware, it's easier for you to bring that last good moment back and then work through what happened that brought about the change. This way, you can develop more control over how you feel even after you have gone through a major emotional change. Also, being self-aware will help you understand what it was in your surroundings that triggered the change. This way, you can better understand your triggers and why you feel these sudden changes in certain situations.

o **Visualize**

Visualization can be used in various ways to manage emotions and even manage your mind. When it comes to developing immunity against other people's emotions, it's a good idea to use some form of defensive visualization. Thinking of a thick, bulletproof glass often helps. You visualize that you are surrounded by a thick glass through which you can hear the people around you, but you cannot feel their energy. It's a kind of insulation protecting you from their energy and is giving you a small space that you can fill up with your own energy. As soon as you feel that your emotions have been changed, bring the glass into the mind, and visualize their energy on the outside and your own energy, or the emotion that you prefer at that moment, surrounding you.

o **Dig Deeper**

Sometimes we talk to someone, and we think that we understand what they mean or how they feel, whereas, in reality, they feel quite different. With your glass wall around you, take a second to ask the person to elaborate on how they feel and what is going on in their mind. This can bring you around to a perspective that you might not have previously considered, and it can help you stop feeling extreme emotion. The chances are that the person might not feel like the way they described it when they said something, or they might have meant it differently. Rather than responding based on a hunch, get down to the bottom of it and then decide how you should feel and react.

o **Reinforce Boundaries**

You have to realize that some people might just be using you for your empathic nature. They know that you will offer ears and a heart and a mind where you will feel their problem deeply. They might come to you just for this one trait alone and leave you feeling much better while making you feel horrible. This is where you need to understand your relationships and have the right kinds of boundaries in place to stop people from using you for the wrong things and stop making yourself available for the wrong things.

o **Let Go**

Sometimes, when we've spoken to the person and gotten down to the basic problem, we've highlighted our problem, but we still feel horrible. It happens; sometimes, things are just as bad as they sound, and you are right to feel the way you do. The problem is when you have absorbed the matter so deeply that you aren't willing to move on and let it go. There is a time and a place for every emotion, and once you have felt it, learned from it, and decided to move on, it's time to let that emotion go. Again, you can use visualization to help you through this process.

○ **Emotional Balance**

Balancing your emotions is something that you will have to put a lot of effort into if you want to live a mentally bearable life. Many empaths don't realize that they are putting themselves through a tough time because they have grown accustomed to feeling uncomfortable. This can result in health problems, chronic mental problems, and real physical consequences of the emotional turmoil they are constantly exposed to in extreme situations.

○ **Processing Your Emotions**

The first thing is to sit down with yourself and understand how you feel. Regardless of what is going on around you, what others are saying, and how you feel about others, the focus is on how you feel deep down inside. There is a chance that you are quite happy about things or that there is nothing personally troubling you, but under the burden of other people's feelings, you can't help but feel the way you do. Also, because empaths are so preoccupied with the emotions of others, they often forget to process their thoughts and feelings and never make time for themselves. Ideally, you should be processing your feelings daily, either independently or with another person.

The process is easy and can be done in a few minutes. For instance, when you have your coffee every morning or go running in the evening, you can take that time to go through your feelings from that day. If you like to talk to someone else, discuss it with your spouse when you are in bed before going to sleep. Talk to a friend once a week when you meet up. Do anything that makes you feel comfortable, but do it regularly and do it thoroughly.

o **Putting Yourself First**

Prioritizing your feelings is really difficult for empaths as it goes against how they are designed. Even when you sit down with a spouse to talk or talk to yourself about how you feel, you can't seem to bring those emotions to the forefront. That's where you need to start focusing on your own needs and caring less about people who are not that important. The only way you can be a strong pillar for others to rely on is if you are in the right state of mind.

You can start by taking care of your body. Eating the right food, getting enough exercise, seeing the doctor regularly, all these things will help you make yourself your number one priority. Take some time for yourself daily and have some time each week to focus on doing things that you love. The positivity you'll generate will also help you better process other things in your life. Learn to celebrate your victories, not just the joys of others.

o **Moving On**

When you celebrate with a friend, it feels amazing to be in that company and feel that happiness. This is something that can bring a smile to our face even ten years later when we remember that moment. However, the negative things that we feel are also just as potent, and a bad memory can ruin your day even a decade later. The skill here is to let go of things that aren't serving you and focus on the things you truly cherish and memories that positively impact your life. This is where it really helps to have good strong boundaries that you really stick to and also have boundaries in your mind that will tell you what is yours to own and what isn't. When you start caring for yourself, celebrating the good things, and talking about your feelings regularly, it becomes easier to deal with the negative things. Otherwise, they seem to like this massive demon that you don't even want to think about, let alone tackle.

○ **Managing Emotions**

The most challenging part of processing emotion as an empath is managing how these emotions manifest themselves. Being blessed with an intense ability to feel all kinds of stimuli, the way an empath expresses their feelings is unlike anyone else's. Here are a few tips to help you cope with expressing the emotional energy you feel.

○ **Understand the Impact**

It's not the inherently bad emotions but rather the impact they have on our lives that's the culprit. It's good if you can feel things very intensely. It makes the experience of life that much more enjoyable and potent and makes you the unique person you are. The problem arises when you start seeing that the emotional stress you are going through impacts your relationships or negatively influences your friendship with someone. Warning bells must start ringing when it gets to a point where you feel numb to emotions, or you can feel nothing else but an overwhelming amount of that emotion.

Similarly, it's a serious problem if it's getting to the point where you can't concentrate at school or work. In many cases, people start resorting to drug abuse to somehow balance out the emotional turmoil they are going through.

All these are examples of situations where the problem is getting out of hand. This is why it's important that you realize the impact of your emotions and be careful that it doesn't impact your life.

o **Regulate Rather Than Suppress**

Some people think that simply ignoring how they feel or somehow just not addressing what is going on inside them will help to solve the issue. This is not the case; in fact, it will only backfire. When people come up with problems such as depression, suicidal thoughts, anxiety, and even physical ailments like chronic muscle pain or other diseases, there is a high possibility that this is the extra emotional pressure trying to find a way out. The mind and the body are one, and you can regulate your mind through things like meditations and therapy, and you can also regulate your body through exercise and a better diet. There is no need to feel bad about how you feel, just accept what it's and try to work through the issue.

o **Journaling**

Journaling is a very powerful tool because it not only helps you record what is happening but it gives you the time to really think about what is going on. More importantly, you must journal by hand, where you are actually writing with pen and paper rather than typing. The process of writing is also very therapeutic, and the way it impacts our brains is very different from just typing in front of a computer. Whether you journal daily or just journal when you feel like it, the ability to write helps you clarify problems in your mind and will often bring you to an idea that you had not encountered earlier when you were just brainstorming.

o **Breathing**

A lot of meditation exercises are based on breathing alone. Some people like to do chants or sing or have music playing, but simply sitting down in a quiet room in a comfortable position with your eyes closed, just focusing on your breathing, is more therapeutic than you can imagine. Not only is this an exercise in itself, but consider focusing on your breathing whenever you are going through a situation with extreme emotion. Whether you are happy or sad, just take a big deep breath, and it will recenter your thoughts. It brings more oxygen into the brain at a physical level that helps you think more clearly and drives other harmful toxins out of the brain. Take a slow deep breath, hold it for a couple of seconds, and gradually exhale. Repeat as many times as you feel necessary.

Nearly all of these management techniques will take time to master, and you will be required to be in a mindful state when you practice these exercises. In the heat of the moment, the last thing you'll remember is to give yourself space and breathe, but if you can keep this in mind and try to do it as often as you can, it will eventually become a routine and a natural response to the situation. In a way, think of this as teaching yourself how to feel again. You are re-engineering how you respond and even how your body reacts to certain stimuli.

Chapter 13: Empath Wellness

Now that we have covered the basics to let you explore your abilities, help you understand relationships, and touch on emotional management, we will be unfolding the connection between empathy and wellness in this chapter. As empaths are highly sensitive people, the surrounding energy can drastically affect emotional and physical energy. Your ability to feel the energies surrounding you and absorb them adds up to your fatigue. Furthermore, the exhaustion levels are boosted when you find it hard to escape negative energies. For other individuals, listening to music or taking a nap can be relieving, whereas an empath struggles to escape these energies, ultimately affecting wellness. Repeatedly absorbing these emotions makes you energetically exhausted. Before we go further, It's important to understand wellness. Many believe that wellness is all about improving physical well-being.

Nevertheless, that's not true at all. Think of wellness as an umbrella term, a collective of physical, mental, and spiritual well-being that keeps the body energetic, the mind relaxed, and the spirit enlightened. We'll discuss the negative effects of empathy on physical well-being, the circumstances under which an empath experiences a drain of physical energy, and ways you can practice regaining energy levels.

Empathy and Physical Well-Being

Before we explore the physical effects of negative empathy, let's be clear that we are not healthcare professionals providing advice but are only sharing this information with you after extensive research from reliable sources to help improve physical wellness. If you ever feel concerned about your health, never hesitate to contact your doctor or visit a healthcare facility near you for adequate management.

As mentioned earlier, you are greatly affected by the surrounding energies that affect your physical wellness – the combined effect of emotional and physical distress results in empath fatigue. In most cases, this burnout is not triggered suddenly. There has usually been a chain of stressful events or experiences leading up to this empath fatigue. Mental, physical, and spiritual well-being are all affected, and repeated exposure to traumatic events can lead to a person experiencing emotional and physical effects.

Physical Effects

- Sudden and frequent headaches occur anytime throughout the day or night.

- Being unproductive while performing everyday tasks.

• Infrequent sleep and increased symptoms of sleeplessness.

• Experiencing the feeling of nausea and vomiting most of the time. This feeling of fullness decreases your food intake drastically, leading to malnutrition.

• Feeling exhausted, having low energy levels, and an unwillingness to perform daily activities.

• Triggers poor changes in the appetite.

• Can lead to drug abuse or self-medication in search of finding a remedy for the physical effects.

• Avoiding activities related to the workplace and not getting involved in interacting with people due to low physical energy.

Emotional Effects

Empath fatigue is an accumulation of emotional and physical effects. Let's read about the emotional effects mentioned below.

• Limiting your social circle and not being willing to meet anyone.

• Experiencing an elevated sense of numbness.

• Feeling a lack of energy and avoiding interaction with people.

• Not being able to connect with others.

• Feeling angry, depressed, hopeless, and powerless while doing the simplest of tasks.

• Increased thoughts about the suffering that other people go through.

• Losing the sense of time and space at times.

• Blaming oneself for the problems.

The physical and emotional effects pile up day after day, resulting in empathy fatigue. This constant stress due to traumatic events and feeling the pain of others further aggravates depression and anxiety, and that decreases physical wellness. Let's quickly review your body's physical response to anxiety and depression.

The Body's Response to Anxiety and Depression

Anxiety and depression occur due to constant emotional triggers that ultimately lead to physical responses. As empathy fatigue adds up to depression and anxiety, you could experience physical effects like stomach pain, lightheadedness, and even result in cardiovascular diseases. Obesity and chronic pain are some other manifestations that can occur due to depression and anxiety. Furthermore, serotonin levels decrease significantly, resulting in poor sleep, digestion, and metabolism. Serotonin is a key hormone produced by the brain that stabilizes the mood, makes us feel happy content, and aids in improving communication functions of the brain.

Working out an exercise routine can also be beneficial in improving your physical wellness and helping lower anxiety and depression levels that build up in an empath. Studies suggest that following a physical exercise routine is as effective as taking anti-depressant medications. Besides improving the blood flow to vital organs, promoting growth, and boosting the immune system, exercise releases endorphins in your body that can revitalize your body, elevate your mood, and start experiencing events in a positive light over time.

Furthermore, exercise helps stretch the muscles that relieve tension in the body, making you feel relaxed. As the mind and body are closely linked, improved physical wellness gives you the power to ward off negative energies, save your physical energy from getting depleted, and help you revitalize within no time.

Not only that, but exercise is also a great lifestyle modification you can focus on to help you get over the trauma or the negative energies affecting your well-being. Adding up the benefits of exercise, you should have improved memory, higher self-esteem, and resilience when faced with mental and emotional challenges. Before you start an exercise routine, it's best to consult the related healthcare professionals and get yourself evaluated or get recommendations for the safest exercises for you to do.

Diet and Empathy

As mentioned previously, empathy is a powerful gift that can reap tons of benefits when you can completely practice self-care. Focusing on what you eat in your diet is a crucial aspect of self-care that we empaths have to learn to get the best possible outcome in terms of wellness. As empaths, negative emotions and mood swings can disrupt digestion, leading to symptoms like bloating and abdominal discomfort. When an empathetic person is already overwhelmed with emotions, many foods can further disrupt the digestive system.

Instead of listening to others for diet recommendations, trusting your body is the best way to know the foods that keep your digestive system healthy and make you feel comfortable. Here are some diet recommendations you can try to support your physical wellness better.

- Staying conscious of your body's response to consumption of certain foods and noting information to create a diet that works for you.

- Go for warm water instead of cold water and replace beverages with herbal teas.

- Eat foods that are cooked well can help digest. However, it does not mean that you should skip eating raw fruits and vegetables. Try understanding your body's response and select the adequate foods for the best results.

- Avoid excess chilies and use spices like cinnamon, ginger, or turmeric to help improve digestion.

- Make a schedule of meal times and stick to it, which will maintain consistent bowel movements.

- Chewing your food and eating slowly also helps greatly with digestion.

Most people follow diet plans to control certain diseases. For example, people with inflammatory bowel syndrome avoid eating dairy products as it can aggravate the disease. Similarly, food influences the traits of empaths. For example, most processed foods contain chemicals that make you crave these foods, ultimately making the urge unbearable. Consuming these poorly nutritious foods affects the body physically and leads to endocrine and hormonal changes that further deteriorate physical wellness.

Undoubtedly, negative emotions take a toll on physical wellness, but the chemicals found in our food can also negatively affect the body, making you feel low on energy. By following an appropriate self-care routine and focusing on improving diet, you can improve energy levels. Besides feeling energized, your ability to perform tasks increases, and your goals become clearer.

Why Empaths Feel Drained

Whatever type of energy is in the immediate environment, empaths quickly assimilate and register it and get affected without understanding the consequences or how it even happened. The suffering and emotions surrounding you will trigger responses to help others while not knowing how to protect your energy. Let's explore the causes that drain up your energy, leaving you with a feeling of physical exhaustion.

- **Hyper-Perceptive to Emotions**

We all have friends that never get tired or feel drained, but for an empath, you need to take care of your personal space to conserve energy because of the consequences you will suffer. Interacting with a lot of energies at once results in physical exhaustion that can further manifest symptoms that affect your body. It takes a lot more time to reset energy levels when you are overwhelmed by the emotions and energies you encounter throughout the day.

- **A Sensitive Body**

Most empaths feel emotional sensitivity up to a level that starts negatively interacting with their physical bodies. Each empath is unique and responds differently to physical stimuli. The threshold of physical stimuli for empaths varies and changes over time. However, life and circumstances can help empaths deal with the physical pressure and develop tolerance. For example, if you are working at a hospital, you might feel an emotional and physical overload at first, but after a few weeks, you will naturally develop resistance towards these emotions as you start managing your sensitivity levels. You are naturally wired to feel the energies around you and perceive the emotions of others like your own. Using this ability to profoundly connect with others instead of becoming overstimulated by the energy is a technique that empaths need to practice maintaining their energy levels.

- **Physical Spaces**

You are picky about the physical spaces you interact with. Most empaths prefer a soft and ambient environment that helps them recharge and enjoy their time. Visiting physical places that emit negative vibes constantly drains your energy levels, leaving you physically overburdened and exhausted. We all have a finite amount of energy that fuels our body to perform everyday tasks.

- **Experiencing Collective Energy**

Planetary shifts like changes in weather, temperature, earthquakes, and related geological changes influence the energy levels of empaths. Conserving your energy by practicing grounding routines will do you a lot of good.

- **Poor Self-Awareness**

Caregivers put the needs of others ahead of their own and bother less about themselves. This constant caregiving routine for an empath can quickly deplete energy levels, making it hard to continue the same routine. Neglecting your needs like not resting enough, eating a bad diet, and overexercising will all take a toll on physical wellness.

Only a tender heart can feel someone else's pain and suffering. There are times when empaths start absorbing too much like an energy sponge that greatly affects their physical well-being. This overload of emotional and physical stress makes you less compassionate. The key to being compassionate to others is to practice self-compassion first. By doing this, you reserve energy and stamina to be compassionate and help heal your own empathy fatigue.

- **Protecting Your Energy**

As we've said in previous chapters, being an empath can be likened to having a superpower that gives you the ability to interpret and feel various forms of energy around you. This beautiful gift of feeling others' energies can become a nuisance if you don't know how to manage your energy reserves to avoid getting physically drained. Here are some tips and lifestyle modifications you can practice in your daily life to be in control of your energy.

- **Setting up Boundaries**

One of the most important things for an empath to do is to set up clear boundaries in relationships, social life, and at work. It might be one of the hardest things to do for you, but setting up boundaries that define your physical space is crucial. Explore your boundaries, set rules, and try not to let your guard down. Remember that these interventions protect your energy and wellness, not deny others the help or genuine emotional support that they might require from you. Empaths might consider setting up boundaries with being selfish for oneself. However, that's not the case, as these boundaries will define you as a person with clear priorities. Staying honest about your willingness to help others and saying being clear on what you want or not can help you better take care of your energy.

- **Daily Meditation**

Besides incorporating an exercise routine and changing your dietary habits, practicing a daily meditation routine will most likely relax your mind, boost up your energy, and improve your physical well-being.

- **Be Aware**

Figuring out the type of interactions and people who deplete your energy is a great way to understand how you feel. After an interaction, you might feel either energized and uplifted or drained of all your energy. As a highly sensitive person, it's essential to be selective of the company you spend time with and recognize the interactions that make you feel good or drained. In addition to recognizing your comfort levels, note down what choices you are making, because as empaths, the energies you absorb from your surroundings have a physiological impact on your well-being. Getting familiar with your baseline energy levels and differentiating your emotions from others can help you manage your physical energy and stop it from depleting.

Throughout the day, take note of the moments that help you get energized and practice avoiding the moments that ultimately put you in a chronic state of exhaustion. As you start improving your energy levels, appreciate your progress, no matter how small, to keep you motivated to achieve better results. Cherishing these moments uplifts your spirits, makes you feel revitalized and leads you to a direction that eases out fatigue.

- **Acting Responsibly**

You always take on or try to share the trauma and suffering of others that only drains your physical energy without resulting in any fruitful outcomes. Taking responsibility for the energy you are emitting and knowing that you are not responsible for someone else's emotions or that you don't have to lend a helping hand every time they ask for it.

- **Spend Time Alone**

A drain of physical energy renders you unable to carry out daily activities effectively. Giving your body time to relax, recharge, and replenish the energy is essential. With as little interaction with people as possible, spend your time in nature. Relax at home, or book a vacation but be sure that you spend enough time in nature to absorb the positive energy.

- **Maintaining Balance**

Striking a balance between things is an essential aspect that should be worked upon. For example, balancing your work and personal life is a crucial aspect that almost every individual tries to improve. Likewise, maintaining a balance between the self-care routine and the pain and suffering you feel for others is an essential task to do. When you're feeling stressed out, relax and work on ways you can balance your everyday routine and get the best possible results.

- **Asking for Help**

Whether it's family, friends, relationships, or support groups, never hesitate to reach out for help if you are in a constant caregiving position and share the responsibilities to get that much-needed rest.

- **Adequate Sleep**

Following an adequate sleep routine is essential for an empath to revitalize and restore their depleted energy levels. Overstimulation of senses throughout the day is naturally calmed during deep sleep of the sleep cycle. Our sleep is divided into different stages, out of which deep sleep or slow-wave sleep is the third one. Sleep hygiene is essential to follow a better sleep routine. You find the refuge of your bed satisfying when it's comfortable, placed somewhere quiet, and is surrounded by a peaceful environment.

The feeling of being physically and emotionally overwhelmed makes it hard to sleep adequately. You can consider practicing meditation or practice yoga to help regulate your sleep cycle. Listening to natural sounds of rainfall, water, and nature can help rejuvenate your senses while you drift away into a deep sleep. Some people also get so stuck in a traumatic life event that it affects their daily sleep patterns.

- **Establishing Connections**

Human connections are an important aspect that can easily affect when experiencing an energy drain. Establishing new connections with people becomes difficult as you don't feel like you have adequate physical and emotional energy. Understanding why you need to connect and rediscovering your purpose can fuel up your energy levels.

- **Spending Time**

Laughter and enjoyment are two emotions to cherish with friends and your loved ones. During a burnout, it might be hard to plan on your own. You can consider spending time with friends and family who genuinely feel your burden and who will help you out through stressful times.

Empaths are energetic beings who can feel the surrounding energy affecting their emotions, physical energy, and well-being. Each interaction with the outside world is an energy exchange that empaths can feel within themselves. This unprecedented ability to feel gives empaths the ultimate power to heal others and connect with them emotionally. However, being unwilling to look into yourself and neglecting self-care is what takes a toll on physical energy and wellness.

Chapter 14: Mastering Your Mental Energy

Humans are naturally hardwired to feel other people's pain and empathize with them. This empathy influences us to help, volunteer, and even go for careers related to the service industry. We are more than connected in this technological age, especially through digital and social media platforms. However, this increased connectivity leaves a debilitating impact on the emotions of an empath. When highly sensitive people like empaths practice altruism and empathy without incorporating self-care in their lives, it leads to an emotionally compromised state followed by depression and anxiety. Controlling your emotional responses during these times is necessary because the build-up of negative energies will ultimately drain your mental energy if it goes too far. This chapter will discuss how your mental energy gets affected and share with you steps to help you regain focus and clarity of mind.

Virtually every metabolic process occurring within our body requires energy. Similarly, when being empathetic, energy is used that can deplete your mental resources. Many jobs and workplaces like prisons, hospitals, day-care facilities leave a person in these emotionally charged industries open to becoming seriously exhausted if they are not mindful of keeping their mental resources protected. Every person has a threshold for how much empathy they can offer. After that, the emotional overload starts taking a mental, physical, and spiritual toll.

Situations That Affect Mental Energy

Several situations can be mentally exhausting for an empath and result in an energy drain, leaving the mind clouded, decreasing the ability to concentrate, and slowing down cognitive functioning. Below are some situations empaths find mentally challenging.

- Trying to be recognized among peers and get accepted

- When guilt rises due to repeated self-blame after experiencing negative energy

- Forcing yourself to act upon everything and perceive responding as an obligation

- When interacting with people who are not true to you or are holding back and not opening up to you

- After experiencing a situation where you have been taken advantage of

- Constant emotional fatigue leads to mental distress

- Violence or horror deeply upsets you.

- Carrying on with relationships that lack a true and sincere bonding

- Interacting with people or meeting up with overly dramatic people

- Facing abuse from peers

- When feeling insecure, unwelcome, or don't feel like you are at the right place

Besides the situations mentioned above, evaluate your routine when at work, around people, and at home to recognize the situations' effect on you. Furthermore, pay attention to each situation you encounter and ask whether facing these situations would be fruitful or not.

Utilizing Your Mental Energy

Here are some steps you can incorporate into your daily life to gain control of your mental energy and redirect it into a skill that improves your mental well-being rather than depletes it. You might be compelled to take every responsibility that comes up, but it will only make you unable to manage your mental energy.

- **Set Boundaries**

As mentioned in the previous chapter, it's essential to recognize yourself, your priorities, goals, and the path you want to carry on in your life. After getting a complete understanding of what you want, set up boundaries according to your preferences. As you are softhearted, most people might just want your company or take advantage of your caring nature. Therefore, it's up to you to decide what to take on and the things you need to let go of, as only you can be the one responsible for your own physical and mental well-being. Setting up boundaries does not mean that you have to stop being a caring person. The point is that you only have to help when it's required and after ensuring that there will be no negative effects that could disturb your mental energy.

- **Develop a Strong Personality**

Developing a strong and well-defined personality at social gatherings or work is essential. Empathizing with people and experiencing emotions on different levels slightly changes the identity of empaths. This fluctuation in the personality can drastically affect your relationships as the personality changes can result in mistrust. This mistrust triggers an emotional surge that affects physical and mental wellness. Instead of modifying your habits and faking emotions to please others, act naturally and let them recognize your true self. Allowing others to tell you how to act is never an option as it can lead to you being manipulated and abused.

- **Building up Self-Confidence**

Mentally draining situations are not a problem when you have enough self-confidence. When working in teams, empaths feel guilty about not being accepted and can develop insecurities if they are faced with people emitting negative vibes. It's easy to recognize what others are thinking about you as an empath. Boosting your self-esteem is essential if you are encountering such an issue. Tell yourself that no one in this world is perfect and try to accept the situation as it's without feeling bad or becoming overwhelmed by thinking about others' opinions of you.

- Company Matters

The people surrounding you define the levels of mental energy you will be carrying through the day. By following an objective approach, refine your social circle and surround yourself with people that support you. If someone is being abusive, ignore them. You might lose a lot of friends in the process, but the ones left will be those who truly cherish and enjoy your company.

- Handling Distress

Being compassionate is a form of emotional empathy that we all practice at different levels. Taking on others' problems and making them our own might win us great appreciation in society, but the risks to our mental heal can be disastrous. Instead, redirect your mental energy into practicing compassion, a mild form of empathy that provides a way to use your mental energy and empathy in adequate proportions. Whenever you are experiencing mental or physical pain after being exposed to trauma or suffering, remind yourself that the situation you are experiencing is not happening to you.

- Filter Your Consumption

Your body and mind react to what you take in, especially in the form of news. Take social media as an example. When working at your office, imagine taking a quick peek at your news feed, and you are bombarded with information and news that triggers a shift of energy that clouds the mind, slows down cognitive abilities, and lowers your mental energy. If you feel stressed out after a few minutes of social media usage, try giving it a break for a day or two. Don't worry that you'll miss out on anything important as you will always hear about a major event or news from friends and family around you. The point of limiting social media usage is to prevent exposure to events and the type of news that only makes you emotionally drained. By avoiding the things that make you upset, you will gradually control your emotional and cognitive abilities.

- Maintain an Objective Approach

Just like emotional management, try to figure out the feelings that make you energetic and the ones that drain you. Be in control and avoid getting exposed to emotional situations. After all, it's your thoughts and your decision to give priority to them. As empaths, you are always open to energy and feel almost every type of energy at a certain level. How the energy affects you depends on the intensity with which you perceive it. If you try to see a certain situation from a different perspective, its effect on your mental energy decreases. Furthermore, controlling your work environment is essential if you want a clear and productive mind. Working in workplaces with open floors and maximum interaction might not be conducive for an empath. Remote working is a better choice for empaths as it will help conserve our energy without depleting it.

- Practice Clarity

Whenever we see ourselves get ignored by our peers or the ideas we pitch in at the office get turned down, negativity starts to develop, weakening our cognitive abilities and lowering mental energy. If left unresolved, the negativity gets contagious and affects your mood, productivity, and work efficiency. As empaths are energy beings, visualizing a protective aura around you can help prevent you from picking up negative feelings that use up your mental energy.

- Relax Your Mind

Negative emotions affect you one way or another. When interacting in the office or socializing with peers, they can take hold of your mind, use up all your mental energy, and result in physical manifestations like increased muscle tension and an elevated heart rate. Calming your nerves can help lower the emotions triggered after encountering negative energies. During a stressful event like experiencing the pain of others, meditation or breathing exercises can significantly help release mental stress build-up. Be in control of your thoughts and stop pondering over any form of negative energy. Instead, shift your focus to relaxing thoughts. Shifting your thought process and aggravating constructive thoughts will help you attain peace of mind and clear foresight.

- Setting up Priorities

As an empath, you have to cope with things that come up every day. You might be able to resolve a few issues bothering you, but many issues in one day will drain you. Trying to control everything around you might not be possible, and you'll end up frustrated. The less you focus on irrelevant things, the more energy you have to tackle the important things. Therefore, prioritize what you want to focus on and avoid wasting your energy on useless experiences.

- **Managing Negative Energy**

There is a plethora of emotions like anger, disgust, fear, grief, insecurity, and internal conflict that interfere with your ability to analyze the situation you are putting yourself into, cloud your judgment, and deprive you of mental energy. Besides focusing on positive emotions and avoiding thinking about negative ones, you can try several different techniques like exercise, meditation, ignoring the cause of negative emotions, and reviewing emotions in a positive light to ward off the negative effects of emotions on your mental health well-being.

- **Detox**

Empaths can sense the energy with which they are interacting. Even the type of food we consume has vibrational energy to mitigate mental stress. Eating vegetables, fruits, herbal teas, and whole foods will help to strengthen your mind, whereas low vibrational foods like poultry and milk products can negatively affect mental well-being. In addition, exercise helps clear out any bad energy, helps in detoxification, and triggers the production of happy hormones, making your mind sharp and clear.

- **Self-Care**

Besides working on your mental energy, implementing a self-care routine is also an essential aspect to consider. Here are some quick tips on the type of self-care routines you can follow to help calm down your overstimulated nerves for better energy control.

1. Adding bath salts and essential oils to your bath will add up to the calming effect.

2. There are a lot of massage techniques used to regain mental focus – as a relaxed body will help the mind to work effectively.

3. Spending time with animals can help change your mood from negative to positive.

4. Choose activities like Reiki, music, and meditations.

5. Listening to positive affirmations can help you ward off negative energy build-up when you're mentally stressed out.

6. When feeling mentally exhausted, try doing activities that make you laugh. Watching your favorite comedian crack jokes is a good way to help soothe those overexcited nerve endings.

7. Using essential oils can also create an ambient environment around you, making it easy to relieve anxiety stress and strengthen your brain over time.

8. Meditation and journaling can help you recognize your thoughts and feelings if you find it hard to be clear.

Recognizing Empathy Skills

There are several downsides of being an empath, and some empath attributes can be turned into skills to boost productivity and efficiency. Practicing empathy while being extremely aware of your inner self creates a sense of happiness and wholeness. Your unique abilities and skills can even be used in several professions for the benefit of many. Let's read about the empathy gifts you possess that can be used as a skill at work, home, or when socializing.

- **Self-Awareness**

Empaths devote themselves to developing an understanding of their feelings and connecting to the energies around them. Use your experience to learn to improve your self-awareness by knowing your limits and the number of interactions you can easily handle. An empath with a strongly developed sense of self-awareness not only makes you happy but also helps others by letting you deliver effectively. To explore more on self-awareness, you need to be connected more to yourself. Asking yourself the questions will help develop better self-awareness that leads to better growth and allow you to regulate your mental energy as required.

- **Observation and Perception**

Being highly perceptive, having great observation skills, and registering the types of energies you interact with our natural skills that only empaths possess. As empaths can easily recognize surrounding energies, this gift can effectively empathize with people. Recognizing this ability to have a deeper perception of things can be used to help differentiate genuine feelings from fake ones. Using your energy recognition capabilities, the underlying issues of the other person can be understood and be guided to move forward with life.

- **A Simple Life**

Being an empath requires you to reset, revitalize, and ground your energies from time to time. Experiencing a surge of energy and emotions can make an empath exhausted. That's the reason most empaths are drawn to live in quiet, peaceful places where they can tune in with the surrounding energy vibrations.

- **Being Creative**

Due to their highly sensitive nature, empaths can express themselves extensively through their creative abilities. The way they communicate and connect deeply with the surrounding environment gives them the skill to express themselves fluently through impactful words or help others find energetic balance.

- **Healing Others**

Empaths can regulate energy and heal others. This gift to sense other people's plight and the trauma without exchanging words is what makes empaths unique. This skill can be used for the benefit of society. Empaths who recognize this opt for careers where they can put it to good use - like working in healthcare facilities and hospitals. As you learn to use your special healing skills, you will naturally be able to tell if your help is not required. The gifts of an empath allow them to see the possible paths of healing or help needed. However, it's up to the person seeking help to take your advice or leave it.

- **Quality of Life**

As you start looking at your traits as gifts and start mastering control over your mental energy, you will be able to get aligned with the energies of this world, explore your true self, and live life the way you want it to. Using these skills to your advantage helps improve the quality of life.

- **Socializing Skills**

When empaths keep mental distress to a minimum, they can suffer serious negative effects, especially when socializing. By understanding how you are affected by someone else's energy, you can decide on the best way to approach them. This skill can be used at the workplace, while communicating, and even in relationships.

It's pretty easy for an empath to get caught up in life as you will be experiencing different forms of seen or unseen energies along the way. However, effectively recognizing your abilities and using them adequately can help you stay healthy and let you have control over your physical and mental energy. Remember that you are here to enjoy life to its fullest. With time, you will experience joy, happiness, sadness, failure, success, triumph, and every other related physical or emotional trigger. Therefore, never hesitate and enjoy life in all its variety. As you explore your journey as an empath, it's best to join support groups or find like-minded people through digital platforms, as it will help create a support network to provide you with the relevant assistance and the ability to navigate this world. Recognizing what others feel is an asset that a few possess. With these abilities, it's easier for you to screen out genuine people from fake ones in any situation.

Chapter 15: Empath in a Cruel World

Imagine you're walking around the mall, just looking around the shops and taking a closer look at whatever catches your eye. You hear a couple arguing, a baby crying, and a frustrated mother, all a couple of steps away. These are everyday occurrences, right? These are all things that are bound to happen wherever there are people. But being an empath, you try to get away as quickly as possible. It's already too late, though. You feel a weird sensation in your stomach as anger and frustration start boiling up inside of you for no apparent reason. Only you know why you're absorbing what's going on around you, and you already know your day is going to be difficult to navigate.

When you touch something or someone you believe is weak, you feel an unsettling sensation. You may lean on a tree or touch an animal, and you can just tell that they're sad. You feel this odd sensation that only disappears when you take your hands off the subject. By now, you have realized that these are not your own emotions, but they feel like they are. Passing by a group of angry people, like rallies, can make you feel sick to your stomach. You feel the tension in the room when no one else notices, and you can almost tell what a person is like before you get to know them. You also just know if someone is a good person or if something doesn't sit right with them. Your first impressions are spot on.

It's even worse if you find yourself surrounded by a group of unhealthy individuals; it literally tears you down. Exposing yourself to several peoples' energies at once can be emotionally and physically draining. Even if your friends aren't necessarily unhealthy, everyone has their battles to fight and be an empath. This is why you can feel everything- the pain, the anger, the sadness, the cries for help, and the desperation. People say that they're fine even when they're wounded inside, which is why you can't just ask how someone is doing and move on with your life. Everyone lies about their feelings. We all know that everyone does it, but non-empaths don't think much of it. However, being an empath makes you wonder how and why we have all been trained to deny and lie about our feelings.

While it's undeniably difficult to live life knowing all about other people's predicaments, this ability is quite enriching. You get to be involved in the human experience more than any other human, which other people don't think is possible. Your encounters are always intricate and dynamic.

These things happen to you all the time. You can't just get rid of these experiences, or turn them off, no matter how hard you try. You explain to your friends repeatedly that you can't do anything about it, but they just don't understand. Being an empath makes you the peacemaker of all your social groups. It's a given since you feel upset whenever anyone else feels sad, which is why you always try to resolve conflicts before they even begin.

Being an empath in the world we live in today is a challenge. Sometimes it feels like the world is becoming more and more violent. Perhaps it's because technology and social media have made it possible for us to learn about gruesome global happenings in an instant. Maybe people are just becoming crueler by the day. The chances are that the pandemic has also made it harder for you. The soaring number of deaths, people in pain, and the rise in mental illness rates are enough to make you suffer.

If you think about it, being an empath is like being naturally academically gifted. During the first few stages of elementary school, you believe that everyone is like you. However, as you grow and make it to middle school then high school, you realize that you're gifted in a sense, which puts you at an advantage. You learned t you can understand, in a deeper sense, how and why you stand out. In your case, you understand that you can find out why you tap into what you sense in other people's emotions. Once you become masterful enough, you can even help others develop these abilities, regardless of whether they were naturally gifted with it. Most people can develop and enhance their empathetic abilities unless they have certain personality disorders that get in the way.

You may have always despised your abilities as an empath. However, if you think about it, would you really want to trade your brain for a normally functioning one? Sure, it gets tiring at times, but learning how to gain control of your reactions and separate your feelings from those around you will allow you to realize that you possess a wonderful gift.

This chapter will help you understand your fears about living in today's society, as well as how you can address them. You will find out how you can find your internal safe and peaceful place and manage the emotions elicited by the events that happen around you. You'll also find out how to keep societal issues and anxieties at bay.

Addressing Societal Fears

Being an empath comes with numerous societal and emotional triggers. Certain events or situations can trigger an overload, making you feel emotionally exhausted, anxious, and even depressed. The word "triggered" is something that we keep hearing more and more nowadays. People are throwing the word around carelessly, often in the incorrect context. So, what does it really mean to be triggered? A triggered individual is deeply impacted by overwhelming emotions that result from a traumatic event, situation, or memory. The minds of empaths tend to develop specific triggers after witnessing overly sensitive events. If severe enough, the individual could develop PTSD.

In most cases, an empath's mind will come up with a very chaotic loop of unending feelings, which would cause great distress. Empaths get triggered by the slightest incidents. They have no control over their undesirable emotions and sensory overload. This is why empaths are likely to develop fears that affect their ability to navigate the outside world.

We collected some emotional triggers that you may encounter in your society and how you can address them in a healthy way.

Feeling Misunderstood

Many people don't bother to take the time to understand others. If you're an empath, this is something that you may struggle to wrap your head around because you are naturally going to be able to understand people and be empathetic with them. So, you can't help but fear the apathy of those around you. The chances are that you've been used, made fun of, or called "dramatic," "weird," or other ignorant terms, at least a couple of times during your lifetime. This may be why you're probably very afraid of being misunderstood. Being understood is something you long for, which often leaves you doubting yourself. You start to wonder if you're really odd, unintelligent, or even crazy. You may wonder if something is wrong with you because no one seems to understand how your brain is wired.

If you want to address this issue, then the first thing to know is that there is nothing wrong with you. Your empathy doesn't make you odd, crazy, or unintelligent. Your gift makes you *very* emotionally intelligent. Your ability to dig deep into other people's feelings and emotions is incredible. You should remind yourself that no one needs to learn about how you think or how your brain works. As long as you're always working on understanding it and putting your abilities to their best use, then you're good to go. Find comfort, or rather power, in being misunderstood. Your abilities make you unique. Your ability to think in a way that's so foreign to others puts you at an advantage. So, the next time someone tries to make you feel inadequate, remember that they probably feel threatened by your extraordinary sensations and perceptions.

Feeling Unwanted

Our world is very cruel. People like to hurt and tear down what they don't understand, and as we explained above, many people don't understand you. They don't understand your ability to tap into the energies of others or your heightened intuitive senses. The fact that you can tell exactly how they're feeling can frighten them. Fear is at the bottom of so many things that make you unhappy because people simply don't understand you, and with that misunderstanding comes alienation. All the while, you are picking up on these emotions and trying to make sense of them. You may feel like an imposter and wonder why anyone would actually want you around. It helps to remind yourself that these are just intrusive thoughts. Having been abandoned once or encountering people who intentionally make you feel inadequate doesn't mean that intentionally making you feel inadequate doesn't mean you're not wanted. You are more than your empathy. While there are people out there that will love you for it, they will also love you for all the other traits that make you who you are. If someone doesn't love or want you wholly, know that they're toxic and that it would be time to reconsider your relationship or friendship with them.

Feeling Valueless

If you're an empath, you probably have difficulty saying no, even when saying yes compromises your general well-being. Aside from the compelling need to help those around you, part of the reason why you rush to cater to the needs of others may be because you want to feel valued. You probably already know that some people may use you for your kindness and compassion, which feeds into your fear of being worthless. As counterintuitive as it sounds, you become more and more obsessed with ensuring that all the needs of others are fulfilled. Reinforcing the idea that you may be perceived as "less than" can cause you to lose yourself in a spiral of unwanted harmful emotions. Once you find yourself stuck in that hole, it can feel impossible to make your way out.

If you're struggling with feelings of being unworthy, always remember that everyone on Earth has a certain purpose or value, particularly you. You were blessed with these unique abilities for a reason. If anything, they increase your value and not diminish it. You should take the time to think about what self-worth means to you. Do you think someone else would be unworthy just because they care a little bit more about others? Aim to destroy these false perceptions about yourself because your power to feel the emotions of others is extremely valuable. The world needs more people like you. Indulge in activities that can help boost your self-esteem and raise your vibrations. Take the time to practice self-care and recite positive affirmations.

Feeling Unloved

As an empath, you are characterized by your excessive compassion and tendency to nourish others. Other people may not express their feelings the same way that you do, making you feel unloved. Because you have so much love to give, there is a great fear inside you – you think your feelings are never reciprocated. This is why many empaths end up isolated in an effort to protect themselves from potential heartbreak. You may even have thought about shutting everyone in your life out to save yourself the hurt. The need to feel loved is natural. However, running away from social life is not a solution because the fact is that you've always been loved. From the moment you were born, there were always people who loved you and cared about you. This is why you shouldn't let the lack of reciprocation break you in any way.

Not Feeling Accepted

While growing up, there have been many times when you felt left out. There may have been things or activities that you've had to sit out because your empathy got in the way. These moments may have made you question whether you are actually accepted in your community. We tend to attach our self-worth to how much we're loved and accepted by others. This can be very damaging because everyone is worthy, regardless of how others perceive them. You can't be loved, accepted, and understood by everyone, even if these are things that you give to the world. You're an empath, but not everyone else is. So, it only makes sense that you focus on the relationships and friendships that already make you feel loved, valued, and potentially understood.

The Inability to Just "Get Over It"

How many times have you been told to just "get over it?" You've probably tried time and time again, believing that your reactions were over the top. Questions like "is there something wrong with me?" and "why am I too sensitive?" may have clouded your brain. You may have always feared the possibility of never being able to just get over it. However, remember people don't spend as much time thinking about the words that come out of their mouths as you do. You strongly feel for others and everything that you experience, so just getting over it, at least overnight, is not possible. In fact, you don't even need to get over your experiences. All you need to do is move forward and grow around them.

News and Society

As mentioned above, technological breakthroughs and social media have made learning about different events and news worldwide. Unfortunately, the world is not a nice place, which is why you may constantly inevitably hear about things that make you sick to the stomach. Some news may even make you horrified about leaving your home or interacting with others altogether. However, you should be avoiding the news and not people instead. To thrive as an empath, you need to be part of your society and not a product of it, which is why you should contribute positively through charity, volunteer work, environmental clean-ups, and more.

Self-Protection Methods

Practicing self-protection strategies and incorporating them into your life and routine can help you navigate life as well. These exercises can be extremely helpful whenever you're feeling stressed or absorbing too much of the negativity of others. There are numerous strategies to help you release your stress, worries, and unwanted emotions - experiment to find the ones that work best for you.

Symptom Separation

Whenever you're feeling upset or experiencing a sensory overload, take time to think about whether these emotions belong to you or to someone else. If there's no apparent reason behind the way you're feeling or experiencing a sudden change in a physical sensation or mood, then you're probably absorbing the symptoms of someone else. In this case, try to indulge in activities that calm you, such as practicing grounding techniques, deep breathing, or walking around in nature.

Get Away

Once you identify what's bothering or unsettling you, you need to get away from whatever is disturbing you. See if you're calmer and more relieved. You may worry about offending others. However, you need to start putting your well-being first. If you're in a park, a movie theater, or even a doctor's office, change seats to get away from the source. If you feel uncomfortable in a certain restaurant or cafe, always remember that you don't have to stay there. You can find your peace and enjoy being somewhere else. It's fine to say no and seek refuge from overwhelming locations and situations. You need time to recharge and recollect yourself.

Set Boundaries

If you're an empath, then you already know that nothing transfers energy faster than physical touch, and of course, the eyes. If someone makes you feel uncomfortable, limit physical touch and eye contact. Always remember that hugs and other physical interactions are a choice and that no one is entitled to overstep your boundaries.

Aside from physical interactions, you need to set general limits with people, especially those who drain your energy. You are in control of the time you spend listening to others and giving them advice. You don't need to be at the beck and call of others, go to all outings, or cater to their requests. It will take a lot of time to change how you communicate and interact with others. However, a change like this is necessary to ensure your physical, mental, and emotional well-being.

Practice Earthing

Empaths have a built-in inclination to spend time in nature. They love it and find peace there. Surrounding yourself with a green and clean environment can help rid you of negative energy and feelings. The Earth promotes inner healing. You can walk barefoot in the sand, grass, or soil and pay attention to how it feels. You can also lie down in the meadows or meditate outdoors.

Go Offline

Take regular breaks from social media and technology. These devices give us way too much information, which is the last thing that you need as an empath. Avoid using your phone for at least half an hour first thing in the morning and before you go to bed. The things you see online can set the tone for the rest of the day and hinder the quality of your sleep. You should also avoid going online often throughout the day. Make sure that you take sufficient breaks during the day and avoid visiting resources you know may trigger you.

If you're an empath, you are probably overwhelmed with social anxiety. You are always extremely conscious of people's emotions and, therefore, always hyper-aware of everything that comes out of your mouth. You've trained yourself to choose your words carefully, which is why it can always feel like you're walking on eggshells whenever you're in a group. You may have developed various fears throughout your upbringing due to your abilities. Fortunately, there are numerous ways to address them and navigate life in a healthier way.

Chapter 16: Embracing Your Spirit

In the last chapter of this book, we will focus on an empath's spiritual life. A highly sensitive person might feel out of place in a world that's not designed for them, but when they connect to their spirit and essence, they know they are one with "all." The purpose of this chapter is to equip you with methods on how to achieve this connection – particularly through meditation. You can also find some tips on setting up a daily spiritual routine and what you can do in this routine.

What Is Spirituality and Why Is It Important?

Spirituality is the experience of connecting with something greater than ourselves. It might be a sense of oneness with the universe or a feeling of deep peace and love. For an empath, it can be essential to connect with their Spirit to feel grounded and aligned.

When we connect with our spirit, we become more authentic and self-aware. Our spirit represents truth and authenticity, while we represent creativity and uniqueness. When these two meet, they bring forth the best of us – our essence or heart space.

Spirituality Could Mean Different Things for Different People

Spirituality doesn't have to mean anything specific. It could be praying, meditating, being in nature, or even just taking some time for yourself each day. The important thing is that it connects you with your innermost desires and brings forth a sense of peace and joy.

For example, some people like to meditate, while others enjoy yoga or walking in the park. As long as you are doing it for your own good and not anyone else's, then all is well!

Identifying What Works for You

The key to embracing your spirit's finding what works for you. There is no right or wrong way to do this, as long as it brings you closer to who you truly are. The best way to find out is to experiment and see what feels good. Some ideas to try are:

Meditating can be done by anyone regardless of your spiritual beliefs. This helps you quieten the mind and connect with "all." If this stresses out an empath or highly sensitive person, don't force it. Try walking in nature instead, with natural serenity to help ground you.

Writing in your journal or creating art is fun and insightful because both allow us to connect with our deeper selves and empower us. Another way to do this is by using Reiki energy healing, particularly if the empath has experience with it already. It brings out the compassionate side that just wants to help others.

Attend a yoga or meditation class, where you can learn more about different techniques and find one that resonates with you. There is no need to be religious to do this – many people who are atheists or agnostics enjoy these practices.

Spending time in nature offers a sense of peace and connection. This could be taking a walk in the park, sitting by a lake, or simply looking at trees and flowers. It's all about finding what makes you feel good.

Creating a Daily Spiritual Routine

Once you have found out what works for you, it's important to create a daily spiritual routine. This could involve a combination of the things you have discovered, or it could be something completely different. The important thing is that it brings you joy and helps connect you with your spirit.

Some ideas to get started are:

> • Prayer or meditation in the morning to set the tone for your day. This will help you stay centered and focused.

> • A walk in nature or a quick stop at the park before going to work. It may seem insignificant, but it makes a difference!

> • Sitting quietly for 20 minutes after dinner – or even right before bedtime. This is your time and no one else's, so block out any distractions from others as much as possible.

> • Take a yoga or meditation class if you still feel like you're missing something. It could be that it's all about the community and support for others, which is just as important.

- Spending time with pets or plants (if they don't die on you). This brings out your nurturing side while also making you feel good about yourself.

Reaching Out to Others from a Place of Peace and Love

Lastly, it's important not only for the empath but for anyone, in general, to reach out and help others unconditionally – from a place of peace and love instead of fear or anxiety. This can be accomplished through volunteering at shelters, food banks, or even just by writing a letter to your local politician about an issue that matters to you.

The key is to do something that feels good in your heart and helps connect you with others in a positive way. Doing this opens up the door for more compassion and understanding in the world, which is what we need now more than ever.

When we connect to our spirit and embrace who we truly are, the world becomes a better place. We no longer feel like outsiders; instead, we become empowered to make a difference in the world.

The Benefits of Connecting with Your Spirit

- Feeling more at peace and content in life.

- Having a stronger sense of self-awareness and understanding yourself better.

- Being more compassionate and understanding towards others.

- Feeling a stronger connection to nature and the universe/all That's.

- Experiencing less anxiety and fear in life.

- Having a greater sense of inner wisdom and intuition.

- Finding joy in the little things, no matter what is going on around you.

- Being able to unconditionally love yourself – and others – from a place that does not judge or criticize but only wants to help. This means learning how to take care of ourselves first before we can help or support others.

- Being more empathetic and compassionate towards those who are suffering because we now know what it feels like for someone to judge us, criticize us, and find fault with everything that we do. We no longer feel the need to defend ourselves against these attacks; instead, we see them as opportunities to help others unconditionally.

We are all in this together, so let's have each other's backs and support one another through our Universal journey.

Meditation Methods

There are several types of meditation, and each has a different process. Some techniques may be more effective than others depending on the individual's personality, emotions, and lifestyle.

- **Sitting Method**

Sit in a comfortable position where you can see your belly rise and fall with each breath. Close your eyes. Start to follow the sensations of breathing, the coolness, pressure, or slight tickle as air passes through the nose on inhalation, and the feeling of greater ease when exhaling out past tension-filled areas like the throat and mouth.

Some people like to focus on a particular word, sound, or phrase to keep the mind present and not drift away with thoughts.

Other methods include repeating affirmations aloud while breathing in and releasing tension by saying "ahh" as you exhale. By chanting specific syllables such as "om," you can also connect with the energy of the universe.

- **Guided Visualization**

This is a process where you allow your imagination to take control and guide you on a journey. It can help explore different aspects of yourself or gain insight into a problem or situation.

You may want to find an audio recording, possibly from a yoga teacher or a meditation guide, where you can follow along with the words.

- **Sensory Method**

This is a guided practice using different senses to help relax and refocus on your body's present moment surroundings. You could also incorporate music when emotional memories arise by saying "ahh" as you exhale; this allows tension to release.

You could also incorporate different scents such as lavender or peppermint to help stimulate certain emotions associated with them, for example, using a calming scent when feeling stressed out.

- **Mindfulness Meditation**

This type of meditation focuses on breathing and being aware of each moment, here and now. It also clears your mind from ruminating thoughts that are not true or helpful.

You may want to start with focusing on one particular sensation during this process, such as how it feels when you inhale through your nostrils or notice the belly rising and falling.

Over time, you can add in different objects of focus such as sounds, physical sensations, or thoughts. You simply label the experience without judgment and let it pass on by.

- **Focused Meditation**

This type of meditation uses to focus. Focus on one particular thing or idea to cultivate more clarity and insight. For example, it could be a question that needs addressing, such as "what do I need to own about this situation?"

You can then visualize what the answer would look like once acknowledged, for instance, seeing a mental image of a new home.

- **Self-Inquiry**

This type of meditation is about finding the answer to who you are and what makes you unique within yourself. You can ask questions such as "what am I experiencing right now?" or "how do I want to feel?"

You can then turn these into positive affirmations such as "I am at peace" or "I trust my intuition."

The process of self-inquiry is also an opportunity to reflect on how you have been showing up in life and what changes could be made when the time is right.

- **Transcendental Meditation**

This is a more traditional style of meditation that involves repeating a mantra, such as an *om* or *peace*. It focuses on the breath and can be done by sitting upright in the lotus pose with hands on your knees. Alternatively, you could sit in a half-lotus position (one leg over the other).

To begin this technique, breathe in and out deeply a few times to relax before silently repeating your mantra. You should continue for around 20 minutes, but you can simply bring your focus back to the mantra if thoughts or distractions arise.

When you find a meditation technique that works for you, make sure to stick with it. Consistency is key to training the mind and developing a spiritual practice. You might also want to set some time aside each day to devote to your routine.

- **Practicing Forgiveness**

This is an important step on the spiritual path as it allows for a release of anger, resentment, and bitterness, all of which can build up and cause. It can be difficult to forgive someone who has hurt us deeply, but it's a powerful act that sets us free.

There are many different ways to approach forgiveness, such as writing a letter (but not sending it), imagining the person in your mind, or even just saying "I forgive you" aloud.

This practice allows for a renewed sense of peace and lets us put any past grievances behind us to move forward with more open hearts.

You may want to offer some guidance on how others might achieve forgiveness from those they have hurt.

Spiritual practices such as these can be incredibly transformative for empaths and highly sensitive people, imparting a sense of peace and connection often missing in our fast-paced world. When we take the time to slow down and connect with our innermost selves, we can access a deep well of wisdom and love that's always available to us.

- **Recognizing Your Creator**

This personal practice can be very powerful for empaths and HSPs. It involves looking at the world around you and seeing the divine fingerprints of God or the universe in everything.

This could be something as simple as noticing the beauty of a sunset or feeling moved by a song. It's about opening your heart and mind to the possibility that a higher power is at work in our lives, even when we can't see anything.

When we begin to recognize the divine in all things, it can bring about a sense of awe and wonder that touches our hearts deeply. It can also help us feel more connected to others and remind us that we are all part of something bigger than ourselves.

When we take the time to slow down and connect with our innermost selves, we can access a deep well of wisdom and love.

Being mindful of the Divine is a powerful way to recognize you are not alone and can give us a sense of meaning when we feel disconnected from others.

Whether or not you feel that you have been hurt by religion or God, you still can find solace in this form of meditation as well. People tend to forget that even non-believers can have a sense of spirituality.

• **Become More Accepting of Your Spirituality**

It's important to let go of any guilt or shame surrounding your spirituality, as this can prevent you from embracing it fully.

People raised in religious households may feel conflicted about their beliefs because they were taught that some things should be kept private. However, if you believe that there is something greater than yourself out there, it's worth exploring.

Accepting your spirituality means that you are open to the idea of greater power and are willing to learn more about it. This can be a journey that takes time and patience, but it's well worth the effort.

When we connect with our spirituality, we tap into a deep source of compassion and love that's always available to us. Embrace this connection and allow it to guide you on your path in life.

• Practicing Spiritual Reflection

One of the best ways to connect with your spirituality is by practicing spiritual reflection. This involves taking some time each day to sit in silence and simply be with your thoughts.

You may want to focus on your breath or allow yourself to wander freely through your mind. The important thing is not judging or criticizing yourself but simply observing what comes up.

Practicing this form of reflection helps you to find peace and clarity amid chaos, providing a calm center to return to when your mind is overwhelmed by outside stimuli.

This could be difficult for empaths who are constantly bombarded by outside stimuli. It might be best to suggest that they try this practice in a quiet room or out in nature where there aren't as many distractions as possible.

Spiritual reflection can help us connect with our inner selves and heal any feelings of disconnection we have from other people, the universe,

It's also a great way for empaths and HSPs to cope with busy social lives or volatile emotions that might otherwise feel overwhelming.

When we take the time to slow down and connect with our innermost selves, we can access a deep well of wisdom and love that's always available to us.

• Accepting Your Faults

It's also important to accept your faults and work on making positive changes.

Nobody is perfect, and we all have things we need to work on. This includes empaths and HSPs.

It can be a powerful step towards change when you acknowledge your faults. It can also help you feel more connected to others and remind you that we all struggle with different things.

Being honest about our shortcomings will help us learn from past mistakes and avoid repeating them in the future. It also means being willing to ask for help when you need it.

This could be difficult, as many empaths pride themselves on their independence and do not want to appear weak. However, it's important to remember that we are all human, and no one can do everything on their own.

We become humbler and more compassionate towards ourselves and others when we accept our faults. This creates a foundation of self-love that can be built upon over time.

Embracing your spirituality is an important step on the path to self-discovery.

- **Recognizing the Goodness in Others**

Another important part of embracing your spirituality is recognizing the goodness in others.

When we seek out the best in people, we will connect with them on a deeper level. It also helps us build positive relationships and create a more peaceful world.

This can be difficult for the empath, who are often more sensitive to negative environments and difficult personalities.

However, don't assume the worst of somebody before you know their intentions. Everyone has a different way of thinking or acting that might seem strange from an outsider's perspective, but it only reflects who they really are on the inside.

You can help by avoiding gossip, judgmental thoughts, and negative comments. Try to see the good in others before you pass judgment on anything they do or say.

Being more open-minded can help you empathize with people who might seem different from you at first glance. It also helps foster a sense of unity that's critical for creating positive change in our world.

- **The Power of Writing a Journal**

One way to embrace your spirituality is by writing in a journal.

When we take the time to express our thoughts and feelings, it can be incredibly liberating. It also allows us to reflect on our lives and see how we've changed over time.

Journaling can also help us connect with our intuition and access information that might not otherwise be available to us.

This is a great spiritual tool that can help empaths in many different ways! It's also a wonderful way for children, teens, or highly sensitive people with disabilities to express themselves when they might not have the words to do so verbally.

In addition, journaling can help us see the good in others and notice how we've grown.

It can be difficult to find time to write every day, especially when you have other responsibilities like school or work that take up your energy. However, everyone needs to make time for self-reflection at least once a week – if not more often.

Journaling can also be a great way to find your spiritual center and connect with the world around you on a deeper level. Try it out for yourself, even if you feel like you're not ready yet! It's never too late to explore who you are as an individual.

• **Hobbies and Activities that Connect You with Your Spiritual Side**

Many different activities and hobbies can help you connect to your spiritual side.

Some people enjoy going for walks in nature, while others might prefer to meditate or read religious texts. There is no wrong way to do this!

The important thing is that the activity brings you joy and allows you to connect with your inner self.

This could be something as simple as coloring, crafting, or taking photos. It's up to you to find what works best for you!

Empaths often have a naturally strong connection to their spiritual side, which can manifest in different ways but is most commonly characterized by a deep sense of compassion and humility.

When we embrace our spirituality, we become more connected to the world around us. We also learn to love ourselves for who we are, warts and all. This creates a foundation of self-love that can be built upon over time.

Conclusion

People often struggle with ideas such as self-identity, self-awareness, self-image, and nearly everything that has to do with self-analysis is a challenge. This is largely because they either don't have the tools to self-evaluate, or they don't have the patience to go through the process and simply accept reality as is without any judgment. The reality is that we don't choose how we want to be. We are all born with gifts, tendencies, behaviors, and even a mindset. The great thing is that this doesn't have to be the rest of your life. You can make the changes you want to see, and even if you can't completely change the way you are as a person, you can still develop a lot of control over how you are and how you manage your strengths and weaknesses. Throughout this book, we have looked at some of the best ways for you to highlight your strengths and weaknesses, which will help you get a better understanding of what kind of an empath or a highly sensitive person you are.

The other main challenge most people have in life is dealing with different circumstances. Specifically, they don't know how they can steer themselves in such a way that they benefit from what is going on, and they leverage their innate abilities and strengths. Being a highly sensitive person or an empath is not bad, but the difference is in how you use this skill. If you approach it the right way, it can work in your favor and give you the competitive advantage you need. If you fail to recognize your abilities and you work in a way that you are going against the grain, it will only make it harder for you and possibly also make it harder for the people around you.

Using the tips and techniques that we have covered in this book, you can ensure that you excel in every aspect of life. More importantly, as a teacher, parent, worker, or friend, you can develop deeper and more meaningful relationships while also looking out for yourself. Empaths have an incredible set of talents and unique abilities that can make them excel in every area of life, however at the same time, they are also prone to a few problems, and they have some challenges that others won't understand. If you are careful about managing the highly sensitive person inside you, life can be made so much easier. This doesn't have to be a drastic change; slowly and gradually, you can work on yourself, start to build on your strengths, and try to guard against your weaknesses.

Living a happy and fulfilling life is more than just fulfilling your desires. Even if you can get everything that you always wanted, but you are still not comfortable in your own skin, those material objects will not give you the satisfaction or happiness you hoped for. To achieve real peace, you need to achieve peace within yourself and understand who you are rather than just following the herd. You are in control of your life, and it's the only one you get, so make the decision today to improve your conditions.

Here's another book by Silvia Hill that you might like

SILVIA HILL

MEDIUMSHIP

AN ESSENTIAL GUIDE TO
BEING A MEDIUM,
SPIRIT CHANNELING
AND SPIRITUAL
DEVELOPMENT

Free limited time bonus

Stop for a moment. I have a free bonus set up for you. The problem is that we forget 90% of everything that we read after 7 days. Crazy fact, right? Here's the solution: we've created a printable, 1-page pdf summary for this book that you're reading now. All you have to do to get your free pdf summary is to go to the following website: **https://livetolearn.lpages.co/silviahill/**
Once you do, it will be intuitive. Enjoy, and thank you!

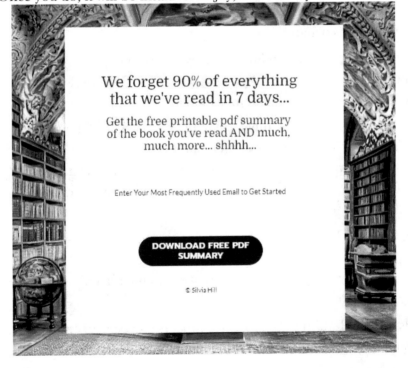

We forget 90% of everything that we've read in 7 days...

Get the free printable pdf summary of the book you've read AND much, much more... shhhh...

Enter Your Most Frequently Used Email to Get Started

DOWNLOAD FREE PDF SUMMARY

© Silvia Hill

References

Baker, J. (2021, August 10). The three kinds of empathy: Emotional, cognitive, and

compassionate. Sacred Structures by Jim Baker. https://sacredstructures.org/messages/the-three-kinds-of-empathy-emotional-cognitive-and-compassionate

Bariso, J. (2018, September 19). There are actually 3 types of empathy. Here's how they differ--and how you can develop them all. Inc. https://www.inc.com/justin-bariso/there-are-actually-3-types-of-empathy-heres-how-they-differ-and-how-you-can-develop-them-all.html

Campbell, L. (n.d.). What is an empath, and how do you know if you are one? Verywell Mind. Retrieved from https://www.verywellmind.com/what-is-an-empath-and-how-do-you-know-if-you-are-one-5119883

Firestone, L. (2017, March 28). Empaths: Is being an empath a superpower or a super-stressor?

PsychAlive.

https://www.psychalive.org/empaths

Parpworth-Reynolds, C. (2020, May 13). 10 famous empaths – some of these may surprise you.

Subconscious

Servant. https://subconsciousservant.com/famous-empaths

Raypole, C. (2019, November 25). What is an empath? 15 signs and traits. Healthline.

https://www.healthline.com/health/what-is-an-empath

Regan, S. (2021, August 16). Think you could be an empath? 12 signs to watch out for & what it

really means.

Mindbodygreen. https://www.mindbodygreen.com/articles/empath

Sólo, A. (2019, January 18). 13 signs that you're an empath. Highly Sensitive Refuge.

https://highlysensitiverefuge.com/empath-signs/

What is empathy? Learn about 3 types of empathy. (2020, June 24). TakeAltus.

https://takealtus.com/2020/06/empathy-1

Are you an introverted or extroverted empath? (2018, June 29). Retrieved from Judith Orloff MD

website:

https://drjudithorloff.com/ask-dr-orloff/are-all-empaths-introverts

Athar, K. (2020, November 29). 16 signs you're an introverted empath (and 5 tips to make life easier). Retrieved

from Nomadrs website: https://nomadrs.com/introverted-empath

LindstromExpert, B., & 02/06/, S. (2021, February 6). 11 Types Of Empaths – and how to

know which one you Are. Retrieved from YourTango website:

https://www.yourtango.com/experts/brittney-lindstrom/read-if-you-want-know-what-type-empath-you-are

Stamatinos, A. (2016, September 23). 10 Reasons Being An Empath Is A gift. Retrieved from The Minds Journal website: https://themindsjournal.com/being-an-empath-gift

Valko, L. (2019, November 29). 14 problems only empaths will understand. Retrieved from Highly Sensitive Refuge website: https://highlysensitiverefuge.com/14-problems-only-empaths-will-understand

Deadwiler, A. (2018, October 18). Life of an empath. Retrieved from Medium website:

https://acamea.medium.com/life-of-an-empath-cda7da43da10

Valko, L. (2019, November 29). 14 problems only empaths will understand. Retrieved from Highly Sensitive Refuge website: https://highlysensitiverefuge.com/14-problems-only-empaths-will-understand

Are you an HSP or Empath. What's the difference? (n.d.). Empathdiary.Com. Retrieved from

https://www.empathdiary.com/messages/are-you-an-empath

Are you highly sensitive? (n.d.). Hsperson.Com. Retrieved from

https://hsperson.com/test/highly-sensitive-test

Bell, E. (2018, April 26). What it means to be a Highly Sensitive Person or HSP. The Anxious Empath. https://emmaclairebell.com/highly-sensitive-person-hsp

Dodgson, L. (2019, January 7). The difference between empaths, highly sensitive people, and introverts. Insider. https://www.insider.com/difference-between-empaths-highly-sensitive-people-and-introverts-2018-6

Funniest Empath Quiz & More. (n.d.). Empathdiary.Com. Retrieved from

https://www.empathdiary.com/quiz

Granneman, J. (2015, July 8). Are you highly sensitive? {Take the Highly Sensitive Person Test}. IntrovertDear.Com. https://introvertdear.com/news/highly-sensitive-person-test-quiz

Granneman, J. (2019, December 13). 21 signs that you're a highly sensitive person (HSP). Highly Sensitive Refuge. https://highlysensitiverefuge.com/highly-sensitive-person-signs

Harrison, T. (2020, December 24). Are you A true empath or just sensitive? Take this quiz to find out. The Minds Journal. https://themindsjournal.com/empath-or-hsp-quiz

Hollywood, J. (2014, August 24). Empath: 8 signs you might be one (with quiz). Exemplore. https://exemplore.com/paranormal/Empath-Self-Assessment-8-Common-Traits-of-Empathic-People-with-Pictures

MelwaniExpert, K., & 08/27/, S. (2020, August 27). How to tell if you're A Highly Sensitive Person (HSP) or an empath. YourTango. https://www.yourtango.com/experts/kavita-melwani/are-you-highly-sensitive-person-hsp-empath-how-tell-difference

Sólo, A. (2020, June 17). The difference between introverts, empaths, and highly sensitive people. Highly Sensitive Refuge. https://highlysensitiverefuge.com/empaths-highly-sensitive-people-introverts

Ursano, I. (2019, February 4). Are you A highly sensitive person or an empath? Find out now. Amazing Me Movement. https://amazingmemovement.com/highly-sensitive-person-quiz

What type of details usually caught your attention? (2021, September 11). Quiz Expo. https://www.quizexpo.com/wpqquestionpnt/what-type-of-details-usually-caught-your-attention

Wright, S. (2020, November 20). Am I highly sensitive, an empath, or just shy? – Perspectives Holistic Therapy. https://www.perspectivesholistictherapy.com/blog-posts/2020/11/20/am-i-a-highly-sensitive-person-empath

Empaths and addiction: From alcohol to overeating. (n.d.). Psychology Today. Retrieved from https://www.psychologytoday.com/us/blog/the-empaths-survival-guide/201906/empaths-and-addiction-alcohol-overeating

How does being an empath have to do with addiction? (n.d.). Lastresortrecovery.Com. Retrieved from https://www.lastresortrecovery.com/addiction-blog/what-does-being-an-empath-have-to-do-with-addiction

deBara, D. (2021, July 9). 8 jobs that are great for empaths (and 3 that typically Aren't). The

Muse.

https://www.themuse.com/advice/jobs-careers-for-empaths

Empathintheoffice.Com. Retrieved from https://www.empathintheoffice.com/blog/how-to-work-for-a-controlling-boss

Brady, K. (2019, July 24). Being an empath: 7 ways to stop absorbing other people's emotions. Keir Brady

Counseling Services.

https://www.keirbradycounseling.com/empath-and-absorbing-other-peoples-emotions

Nasamran, A. (2021, March 1). Highly sensitive child parenting strategies. Atlas Psychology.

https://www.atlaspsychologycollective.com/blog/highly-sensitive-child-parenting-strategies

Clarke, J., MA, & LPC/MHSP. (n.d.). Covert narcissist: Signs, causes, and how to respond. Verywell Mind. Retrieved from https://www.verywellmind.com/understanding-the-covert-narcissist-4584587

Dodgson, L. (2018, January 23). Empaths and narcissists make a "toxic" partnership – here's why they're attracted to each other. Insider. https://www.businessinsider.com/why-empaths-and-narcissists-are-attracted-to-each-other-2018-1

Stone, J. (2018). Narcissistic personality disorder: An unbiased psychological study of Donald trump. Createspace Independent Publishing Platform.

Bock, H. (2018, January 30). 5 telltale signs an empath is overwhelmed. Linkedin.Com;

LinkedIn.

https://www.linkedin.com/pulse/5-telltale-signs-empath-overwhelmed-halley-bock

Michaela. (2020, August 19). 6 ways to cope with empath overwhelm. Introvert Spring.

https://introvertspring.com/6-ways-to-cope-with-empath-overwhelm

Anastasia. (2018, July 1). 7 boundary exercises for empaths and sensitive people. Kind Earth. https://www.kindearth.net/7-boundary-exercises-for-empaths-and-other-sensitive-people

Margarita Tartakovsky, M. S. (2018, December 9). How empathic people can set effective, loving boundaries. Psych Central. https://psychcentral.com/blog/how-empathic-people-can-set-effective-loving-boundaries

Brady, K. (2019, July 24). Being an empath: 7 ways to stop absorbing other people's emotions. Keir Brady Counseling Services. https://www.keirbradycounseling.com/empath-and-absorbing-other-peoples-emotions

Raypole, C. (2020, April 28). How to control your emotions: 11 strategies to try. Healthline. https://www.healthline.com/health/how-to-control-your-emotions

Anastasia. (2018, July 1). 7 boundary exercises for empaths and sensitive people. Kind Earth.

https://www.kindearth.net/7-boundary-exercises-for-empaths-and-other-sensitive-people

Are you a physical empath? (n.d.). Psychology Today. Retrieved from https://www.psychologytoday.com/us/blog/the-ecstasy-surrender/201402/are-you-physical-empath?amp

Cooks-Campbell, A. (2021, December 8). Why are empathy fatigue and compassion fatigue so common? Betterup.Com. https://www.betterup.com/blog/empathy-and-compassion-fatigue?hs_amp=true

Duan, H., Wang, Y.-J., & Lei, X. (2021). The effect of sleep deprivation on empathy for pain: An ERP study. Neuropsychologia, 163(108084), 108084. https://doi.org/10.1016/j.neuropsychologia.2021.108084

hollow. (2021, June 25). Empathy fatigue: How stress and trauma can take a toll on you. Cleveland Clinic. https://health.clevelandclinic.org/empathy-fatigue-how-stress-and-trauma-can-take-a-toll-on-you

The energy of empathy. (2019, November 30). The Eden Magazine. https://theedenmagazine.com/the-energy-of-empathy

Valko, L. (2019, November 29). 14 problems only empaths will understand. Highly Sensitive Refuge. https://highlysensitiverefuge.com/14-problems-only-empaths-will-understand

Alison, A. L. (2020). Empath Workbook: Discover 50 successful tips to boost your emotional,

physical, and spiritual energy. Alison L. Alverson.

Annesley, C. (2020). Empath: Beginner's guide to improve your empathy skills, increase self-esteem, protect yourself from energy vampires, and overcome fears (a guide to protecting yourself against energy vampires and narcissists). Harry Stewart.

Fairygodboss. (2019, September 20). 5 ways for empaths to manage tough work situations. Insider. https://www.businessinsider.com/5-ways-for-empaths-to-manage-tough-work-situations-2019-9

Hope, A. (2021). Empath healing: A short guide to finding your sense of self and understanding highly sensitive people's emotional abilities to feel empathy and deal with energy vampires. Creative Publishing Solution.

Levenson, R. W., & Ruef, A. M. (1992). Empathy: a physiological substrate. Journal of

Personality and Social Psychology, 63(2), 234–246.

https://doi.org/10.1037//0022-3514.63.2.234

Bailey, A. (2021, December 7). 10 surprising signs that you might be

psychic.bodyandsoul.com.au website: https://www.bodyandsoul.com.au/mind-body/10-surprising-signs-that-you-might-be-psychic/news-story/7220ada2fd93f329915bbaa529a78eb6

Deibe, I. (2021, June 17). Are YOU psychic? The 8 signs you have psychic intuition. Daily Express. https://www.express.co.uk/life-style/life/1449500/are-you-psychic-eight-signs-you-have-psychic-intuition-evg

Estrada, J. (2020, February 25). We're all a little psychic—here are 4 ways to develop that intuitive muscle. Well+Good website: https://www.wellandgood.com/how-to-develop-psychic-abilities

Kazek, K. (2017, October 30). The strange tale of Edgar Cayce, Alabama's Sleeping Prophet al website: https://www.al.com/living/2017/10/the_tale_of_edgar_cayce_alabam.html

Matson, M. (2019, March 20). 5 healing ways to balance your chakras (right now). Brett Larkin Yoga website: https://www.brettlarkin.com/chakra-balancing-healing-ways-balance-chakras

Sentinel. (2018, December 18). What's the difference between a medium and a psychic? Associated Press website:

https://apnews.com/article/archive-9390228c3292452da78fd0f67aba261b

Skope. (n.d.). Benefits of clairvoyance.Skopemag.com website: https://skopemag.com/2020/08/14/benefits-of-clairvoyance

Zapata, K. (2019, September 18). Mediums don't actually "talk" to the dead. Oprah.com website: https://www.oprah.com/inspiration/what-is-a-psychic-medium

Dunne, C. (2018, September 10). A factchecker goes to psychic school: can you predict what happens next? The Guardian. https://www.theguardian.com/lifeandstyle/2018/sep/10/psychic-school-montclair-what-happened

Garis, M. G. (2020, July 28). How to use each of the 4 'Clair' senses to receive information psychically. Well+Good. https://www.wellandgood.com/psychic-clair-senses

Richardson, T. C. (2021, December 17). A professional psychic on how to develop the 4 "clairs" of intuition. Mindbodygreen. https://www.mindbodygreen.com/articles/the-4-types-of-intuition-and-how-to-tap-into-each

Rosen, R. (2010, June 11). Developing your 5 Clair senses - Rebecca Rosen. Oprah.Com. https://www.oprah.com/spirit/developing-your-5-clair-senses-rebecca-rosen/all

Who is the best psychic of all time? (n.d.). Kake.Com.https://www.kake.com/story/41300988/who-is-the-best-psychic-of-all-time

Clairaudience for psychic beginners. (n.d.). Pinterest.https://www.pinterest.com/pin/391531761332884265

Listen to Clairaudience (Clear Hearing) Psychic Development with Cheri Michelle from show The Divine I AM - season - 1 on gaana. (n.d.). Gaana.Com.https://gaana.com/song/clairaudience-clear-hearing-psychic-development-with-cheri-michelle

Reader, C. (2021, February 22). How to tell if you have clairaudience: 8+ clairaudience signs, abilities, and more. Chicago Reader. https://chicagoreader.com/reader-partners/how-to-tell-if-you-have-clairaudience-8-clairaudience-signs-abilities-and-more

Richardson, T. C. (2021, December 17). A professional psychic on how to develop the 4 "clairs" of intuition. Mindbodygreen. https://www.mindbodygreen.com/articles/the-4-types-of-intuition-and-how-to-tap-into-each

Audible UK. (n.d.). Audible.Co.Uk. https://www.audible.com/pd/Clairvoyance-The-Ultimate-Psychic-Development-Guide-to-Extrasensory-Perception-and-Intuition-Audiobook/B08Z5MXP4R

Clairvoyance: The ultimate psychic development guide to extrasensory perception and intuition (hardcover). (n.d.). Rjjulia.Com. https://www.rjjulia.com/book/9781638180166

Kelly, A. (2018, July 2). Am I psychic? How to tap into your own psychic abilities. Allure. https://www.allure.com/story/am-i-psychic-how-to-tap-into-psychic-abilities

Psychic development: A comprehensive guide for beginners to develop psychic abilities, clairvoyance, and heal your body - 2 books in 1: Thir (paperback). (n.d.). Thereadingbug.Com.https://www.thereadingbug.com/book/9781802684117

(N.d.-a). Udemy.Com. https://www.udemy.com/course/clairvoyance-and-psychic-development

(N.d.-b). Barnesandnoble.Com. https://www.barnesandnoble.com/w/clairvoyance-and-psychic-development-peter-longley/1135554180

Are you clairsentient? The 12 signs plus 6 ways to grow clairsentience. (n.d.). Pinterest. https://www.pinterest.com/pin/414894184426343820

Kahn, N. (2021, August 3). The meaning of clairsentience, according to psychics & astrologers. Bustle. https://www.bustle.com/life/clairsentience-meaning-psychics-astrologers

Sprankles, J. (2020, August 17). Clairsentience: What it means to be clairsentient, and is it real? Scary Mommy. https://www.scarymommy.com/clairsentient

Nielsen, B. (2019, September 17). Different Modes of Sensing - part 1: Claircognizance. Core Potentials. https://www.corepotentials.ca/blog/2019/9/14/different-modes-of-sensing-part-1

Chandler, N. (2020, December 7). Astral projection: An intentional out-of-body experience. HowStuffWorks. https://science.howstuffworks.com/science-vs-myth/extrasensory-perceptions/astral-projection.htm

Kahn, N. (2020, October 14). How to experience astral projection, according to an astrologer & psychic. Bustle. https://www.bustle.com/life/how-to-experience-astral-projection-astrologer-psychic

Rindner, G. (2021, February 19). Yes, astral projection is real, but Behind Her Eyes doesn't paint the full picture. Oprah Daily. https://www.oprahdaily.com/life/a35550715/what-is-astral-projection

The amateur Astral travel guide. (2013, May 12). The New Indian Express. https://www.newindianexpress.com/lifestyle/spirituality/2013/may/12/The-amateur-Astral-travel-guide-476418.html

The dos and don'ts of Astral Projection. (2012, August 5). The New Indian Express.
https://www.newindianexpress.com/lifestyle/spirituality/2012/aug/05/the-dos-and-donts-of-astral-projection-393870.html

Walker, J. (2021, April 9). A Netflix-inspired journey to the astral plane. The Ringer.
https://www.theringer.com/tv/2021/4/9/22373149/behind-her-eyes-how-to-astral-project-netflix

Mudgal, V., Dhakad, R., Mathur, R., Sardesai, U., & Pal, V. (2021). Astral projection: A strange out-of-body experience in dissociative disorder. Cureus, 13(8), e17037.
https://doi.org/10.7759/cureus.17037

Raypole, C. (2019, July 30). Out-of-body experience: What's really happening. Healthline. https://www.healthline.com/health/out-of-body-experience

Rindner, G. (2021, February 19). Yes, astral projection is real, but Behind Her Eyes doesn't paint the full picture. Oprah Daily.
https://www.oprahdaily.com/life/a35550715/what-is-astral-projection

The parapsychological association. (1958). Nature, 181(4613), 884–884.
https://doi.org/10.1038/181884a0

Crosten, M. (2021). How to communicate with your spirit guides: The real story of connecting to spirit: Discover how to talk with spirits. Independently Published.

Estrada, J. (2019, June 5). How to find your spirit guide clique and call upon each specific one for guidance. Well+Good.
https://www.wellandgood.com/how-to-find-your-spirit-guide

Five steps to deepen your relationship with your spirit guide. (n.d.). Kripalu. Retrieved from https://kripalu.org/resources/five-steps-deepen-your-relationship-your-spirit-guide

Insighttimer.Com.

https://insighttimer.com/ahelpfulearth/guided-meditations/connect-to-your-spirit-guide-angels-and-higher-self

Richardson, T. C. (2021, March 17). 6 types of spirit guides & how to communicate with them. Mindbodygreen.

https://www.mindbodygreen.com/0-17129/how-to-effectively-communicate-with-your-spirit-guides.html

Do you think ghosts talk to mediums? (n.d.).Quizony website: https://www.quizony.com/am-i-a-medium/12.html

Lapidos, R. (2019, March 26). How to communicate with spirits, according to a

medium.Well+Good website: https://www.wellandgood.com/how-to-communicate-with-spirits

What is a medium? (n.d.).eomega.org website:

What is A psychic reading, and why you should try one. (n.d.).Where Y'at website: https://www.whereyat.com/what-is-a-psychic-reading-and-why-you-should-try-one2

Contacting The Spirit World: How to develop your psychic abilities and stay in touch with loved ones. (n.d.). Com.Au.

https://www.hachette.com.au/linda-williamson/contacting-the-spirit-world-how-to-develop-your-psychic-abilities-and-stay-in-touch-with-loved-ones

Lapidos, R. (2019, March 26). How to communicate with spirits, according to a medium. Well+Good. https://www.wellandgood.com/how-to-communicate-with-spirits

Plants, shamans, and the spirit world. (n.d.). Fed.Us.

https://www.fs.fed.us/wildflowers/ethnobotany/Mind_and_Spirit/shamans.shtml

Ray, S. (2015, July 27). 13 signs that show the spirit world is trying to make contact with you. India Times.

https://www.indiatimes.com/lifestyle/self/13-signs-that-show-the-spirit-world-is-trying-to-make-contact-with-you-238617.html

Richardson, T. C. (2021, March 17). 6 types of spirit guides & how to communicate with them. Mindbodygreen.

https://www.mindbodygreen.com/0-17129/how-to-effectively-communicate-with-your-spirit-guides.html

Frenzel, L. (2021, April 1). The ultimate personal communication method perfected. Microwaves & RF.

https://www.mwrf.com/technologies/systems/article/21158152/microwaves-rf-the-ultimate-personal-communication-method-perfected

Hogan, B. (2021, August 19). Want to connect better with others? Practice telepathy to deepen your relationships. HelloGiggles. https://hellogiggles.com/lifestyle/what-is-telepathy

Iozzio, C. (2014, October 2). Scientists prove that telepathic communication is within reach. Smithsonian Magazine. https://www.smithsonianmag.com/innovation/scientists-prove-that-telepathic-communication-is-within-reach-180952868

Prasad, R. (2014, September 8). Communicating through telepathy achieved. The Hindu.

https://www.thehindu.com/sci-tech/communication-through-telepathy-demonstrated/article6391358.ece

Siddhi, V. (2019). Iris publishers. Online Journal of Complementary & Alternative Medicine,

1(3), 1-4.

https://irispublishers.com/ojcam/fulltext/is-telepathy-allowed-or-is-controled.ID.000515.php

Telepathy is real. (n.d.). Insidescience.Org.

https://www.insidescience.org/video/telepathy-real

Christianity.com Editorial Staff. (2020, May 18). What is Divination? Meaning and Bible

Examples. Christianity.Com.

https://www.christianity.com/wiki/christian-terms/what-is-divination-meaning-and-bible-examples.html

creepyhollows, & » M. A. C. (2009, December 11). How-To Read Runes. Instructables.

https://www.instructables.com/How-To-Read-Runes

Kelly, A. (2018, July 16). A beginner's guide to numerology: How to find your Life Path Number. Allure.

https://www.allure.com/story/numerology-how-to-calculate-life-path-destiny-number

Norris, R. (n.d.). The beginner's guide to reading tea leaves.

Byrdie.https://www.byrdie.com/guide-to-reading-tea-leaves-5084385

Reading tea leaves beginners guide. (2020, October 6). Simple Loose Leaf Tea Company. https://simplelooseleaf.com/blog/life-with-tea/reading-tea-leaves

Regan, S. (2020, May 8). Read between the lines: A starter guide to reading palms at home. Mindbodygreen. https://www.mindbodygreen.com/articles/palm-reading-for-beginners

Wigington, P. (n.d.-a). Automatic Writing. Learn

Religions. https://www.learnreligions.com/automatic-writing-2561401

How to use A pendulum: The A-Z guide. (n.d.). Tiny Rituals.December 23, 2021, from

https://tinyrituals.co/blogs/tiny-rituals/how-to-use-a-pendulum

Lapidos, R. (2019, April 9). How to use a pendulum, the crystal that can help you make decisions. Well+Good. https://www.wellandgood.com/how-to-use-a-pendulum

Mael, M. (2018, August 16). Cleansing your crystals by smudging. Michal & Company. https://michalandcompany.com/cleansing-your-crystals-by-smudging

Shine, T. (2018, September 10). How to cleanse crystals: 10 ways, plus tips for charging, activating. Healthline. https://www.healthline.com/health/how-to-cleanse-crystals

Wigington, P. (n.d.). Learn to use a pendulum for divination. Learn Religions. from https://www.learnreligions.com/pendulum-divination-2561760

Chinggay. (2020, September 28). Tarot deck creation: 10 steps to creating your own tarot deck —. Practical Magic. https://www.practicalmagic.co/pm-blog/2020/9/28/tarot-deck-creation

Four Tarot suits: The minor Arcana. (2015, April 13). Learn Tarot in a Day.

http://learntarotinaday.com/tarot-suits-minor-arcana

Tarot.com Staff. (2018, December 4). The Major Arcana Tarot card meanings. Tarot.Com. https://www.tarot.com/tarot/cards/major-arcana

Timmons, J. (2021, October 7). How to do A basic tarot reading for yourself or A friend. Mindbodygreen. https://www.mindbodygreen.com/0-18172/how-to-do-a-basic-tarot-reading-for-yourself-or-a-friend.html

Pen, G. H. W. (2021, July 25). Psychic protection - the amethyst eye - medium. The Amethyst Eye. https://medium.com/the-amethyst-eye/psychic-protection-b7ebdcbf303c

The Practical Psychic Self-Defense Handbook - by Robert Bruce (Paperback). (n.d.). Target.Com. https://www.target.com/p/the-practical-psychic-self-defense-handbook-by-robert-bruce-paperback/-/A-77907797

THE WITCH'S SHIELD: Protection magick & psychic self-defense. (n.d.).

PublishersWeekly.Com.

https://www.publishersweekly.com/978-0-7387-0542-2

Garis, M. G. (2020, July 28). How to use each of the 4 'Clair' senses to receive information psychically. Well+Good website: https://www.wellandgood.com/psychic-clair-senses

Hurst, K. (2018, October 15). Twin flame love: Stages & signs finding your mirror soul partner. The Law Of Attraction website: https://www.thelawofattraction.com/twin-flames

Lindberg, S. (2020, August 24). What are chakras? Meaning, location, and how to unblock them. Healthline website: https://www.healthline.com/health/what-are-chakras

Rindner, G. (2021, February 19). Yes, astral projection is real, but Behind Her Eyes doesn't paint the full picture. Oprah Daily website: https://www.oprahdaily.com/life/a35550715/what-is-astral-projection

Scalisi, A. (2020, August 9). Life path calculator: The hidden meaning of birthdays. The Haven Shoppe website: https://thehavenshoppe.com/spiritual-meaning-of-numbers

What are binaural beats? (n.d.). WebMD website: https://www.webmd.com/balance/what-are-binaural-beats

What is a medium? (n.d.). eomega.org website: https://www.eomega.org/article/what-is-a-medium

Your core numbers. (n.d.). Retrieved from Numerology.com website: https://www.numerology.com/articles/your-numerology-chart/core-numbers-numerology

Zapata, K. (2019, September 27). Mediums don't actually "talk" to the dead. Oprah Daily website: https://www.oprahdaily.com/life/a29229839/what-is-a-medium

Psychics and mediums: 5 popular myths debunked. (2021, September 13). The Carousel website:

https://thecarousel.com/lifestyle/careers/psychics-and-mediums-5-popular-myths-debunked

Printed in the USA
CPSIA information can be obtained
at www.ICGtesting.com
LVHW021125050923
757273LV00006B/62